★HOW-TO
★STORYBOOK TAPES
AND MORE . . .

Will Disney's *Pinocchio* be too scary for your kids? Is there any educational value in a *Strawberry Shortcake* movie? *KIDVID* answers all your questions regarding hundreds of video cassettes in a comprehensive range of categories. Now, you can make responsible, informed decisions about the videotapes you rent or buy for your children. Give your child the best in entertainment and education—choose your videos with *KIDVID*!

Harold Schechter is a concerned parent and editorial advisor for *The Journal of Popular Culture* and *The Journal of American Culture*. He is a professor of English at Queens College, and has published books on film and culture, including *Patterns in Popular Culture* and the acclaimed *Film Tricks: Special Effects in the Movies*.

"Parents are often asking me about videos suitable for children. I had no answer until I read *KIDVID*. Millions of parents will now thank Harold Schechter."

—Dr. Sol Gordon
Director of the Institute for
Family Research and Education

KIDVID

A PARENTS' GUIDE TO CHILDREN'S VIDEOS

Harold Schechter, Ph. D.

PUBLISHED BY POCKET BOOKS NEW YORK

For my children
LIZZIE and LAURA

Another *Original* publication of POCKET BOOKS

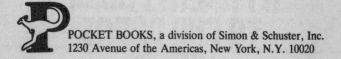

POCKET BOOKS, a division of Simon & Schuster, Inc.
1230 Avenue of the Americas, New York, N.Y. 10020

ISBN: 0-671-60412-0

First Pocket Books printing June, 1986

10 9 8 7 6 5 4 3 2 1

POCKET and colophon are registered trademarks
of Simon & Schuster, Inc.

Printed in the U.S.A.

Introduction

If you are a parent with a VCR, you've probably had an experience like this one. Your six-year-old son is housebound for the day because of bad weather or a rotten cold, so you head off to the neighborhood video store to pick up a good children's tape. When you arrive, however, you discover that the film you were hoping to get—Walt Disney's *Pinocchio*—has just been rented by someone else. Your son has already seen at least eleven volumes of *He-Man and the Masters of the Universe,* and the *Faerie Tale Theatre* tapes you've tried have seemed a bit too sophisticated for him. So you start poring over the shelves in the hope of finding a kiddie cassette that will be entertaining and, if possible, worthwhile.

You pick up one that looks interesting: an animated sequel to *The Wizard of Oz* with Liza Minnelli supplying the voice of young Dorothy Gale, the character made famous by Judy Garland (Minnelli's mom) in the original 1939 version. Is it any good? You ask your friendly videoshop manager, but he hasn't seen it either and doesn't know any more about it than you do. How about this cartoon retelling of classical Greek myths, narrated by Peter Ustinov? It sounds promising, but there's an illustration on the cover—a snake-haired woman with vampire fangs and blood-red talons—that gives you pause. Here's a collection of *Popeye* cartoons. You remember from your own childhood just how good the old, black-and-white *Popeye* shorts were, but—judging from the picture on the videotape package—these cartoons seem to be in color. Are they the original 1930s classics or the cheap, recently made imitations you've occasionally caught glimpses of on afternoon TV? You just don't know.

After about twenty minutes of doubt, perplexity, and

mounting frustration, you decide that you just don't have the time—or the patience—to continue the search. So you shrug your shoulders, give a small sigh of defeat—and ask the store manager for Volume Twelve of *He-Man and the Masters of the Universe*.

This scenario, typical of the experiences shared by millions of parents in our home video age, illustrates the need that *Kidvid* is designed to fill—the need for a thorough and reliable guide to the bewildering variety of video cassettes aimed at young children (ages three to ten).

In just a few years, the video cassette recorder has revolutionized the nature of home entertainment. For a couple of dollars—less than the price of a box of synthetically buttered popcorn at the neighborhood multiplex cinema—people can now rent a recent block-buster movie and enjoy it in the comfort of their own living rooms without having to endure long lines, cramped seats, and the incessant chatter of the couple across the aisle. As a result, people are simply not going to the movies as often as they used to. In the last several years, ticket sales have leveled off, and theater owners have begun to regard the VCR as the most serious threat to their livelihoods since the invention of TV. Meanwhile, TV executives take an equally dim view of the VCR phenomenon. The steady decline in the ratings of prime-time television shows is directly connected to the VCR's most significant feature—its ability to give viewers complete control over what they are watching. Instead of having to put up with whatever low-grade sitcom or mindless cop show is on at a given hour, the public now has the power to see exactly what it wants at any time it wants to—without the endless barrage of commercials.

For parents of young children, it is this single out-standing factor—the degree of control and free choice that the video cassette recorder allows them to exercise —that makes this high-tech marvel such a godsend.

Until the VCR came along, parents had virtually no choice when it came to their children's TV watching. True, they could say "no" to shows they found objectionable and limit the number of hours their kids spent in front of the set. But they couldn't choose what was going to be *shown* on the set. That decision was entirely in the hands of TV executives and corporate sponsors, whose main concern, by and large, has always been to make an easy buck by peddling the kind of cheap entertainment that appeals so powerfully to a child's undeveloped taste.

With a VCR, however, parents can be their own TV programmers, broadcasting only those shows they want their children to see. And parents have responded to this opportunity by turning children's cassettes (popularly known as "kidvids") into some of the hottest items in the flourishing video marketplace. Eight of the fifty best-selling cassettes of 1984 were animated movies, and kidvid titles accounted for over fourteen percent of the videotapes sold in 1985. New labels specializing strictly in children's tapes (Family Home Entertainment, Playhouse Video, Kid Time, Kideo) are springing up all the time. And even the most poorly stocked video rental shop is certain to have a healthy supply of cartoons, animated storybooks, and dramatized fairy tales.

So far, however, the booming sales of children's videos have probably benefited videomakers more than children. It's significant, for example, that the various volumes of *He-Man* cartoons are among the most popular kidvids around, having sold over 300,000 copies, even though they consist of precisely the same cartoons that are shown every day on TV. This striking (and rather sobering) fact suggests that a great many parents are not really taking full advantage of the tremendous opportunity that the VCR represents. Instead of exposing their children to better entertainment than can normally be seen on TV, they are, in many cases, simply using the VCR to supply them with highly concentrated doses of junk.

Since parents, as a rule, have their children's best interests at heart, the likeliest explanation for this phenomenon is that, when it comes to children's videos, most grown-ups just don't know what the best is. Everyone, of course, knows the classics: Disney's *Dumbo* and *Pinocchio, The Wizard of Oz,* and so on. But truly great children's films (like great films of any kind) are extremely rare, and the content (not to mention quality) of the vast bulk of available kidvid tapes is a mystery to most people.

The sheer number of children's tapes currently on the market makes it virtually impossible for parents to separate the good from the bad. The situation isn't helped by the exaggerated claims made by videotape distributors, who are mainly interested in turning a profit and are given to hyping their products in the most shamelessly misleading terms. Cut-rate, made-for-TV cartoons are strung together with a paltry bit of filler and advertised as "feature-length animated films." Inane juvenile melodramas, which disappeared within days of their initial theatrical releases, reappear on video cassette as "timeless motion picture classics." And every piece of kiddie schlock imaginable, from grade-Z Japanese monster movies to Czechoslovakian puppet films dubbed into incomprehensible English, is touted on its cover blurb as a "fun-filled fantasy that the whole family will enjoy."

Given how difficult it is to evaluate new and unknown tapes without actually watching them, it's no wonder that so many parents simply settle for the trite but familiar fare, the video junkfood, preferred by their kids—not only *He-Man and the Masters of the Universe,* but the whole dreary list of formulaic cartoons starring animated versions of hot-selling toys (*Strawberry Shortcake, G.I. Joe, The Care Bears,* and so on). There are scores, even hundreds, of better video cassettes available. But searching for them is a burden most parents simply aren't in a position to bear, particularly in an age when both adults in millions of American households are holding down jobs. To many parents, the great advantage of owning a VCR is precisely that it makes life easier by serving as an "electronic baby sitter." No child, of course, should simply be plunked down in front of the TV for long, unsupervised hours of video watching. But even when a VCR is being used to occupy only a small part of a child's free time, it is up to the parent to make sure that that time is well spent. After all, if the VCR *is* being treated as a baby sitter, then renting videotapes strictly to suit the undiscriminating tastes of young children is roughly equivalent to letting them select the form of child care they think is best for themselves. If offered a choice between a sitter who has strong feelings about nutritional matters and refuses to serve any snacks except fresh fruit, and one who would just as soon keep the kids pacified with a steady flow of ice cream, cookies, and potato chips, it's not hard to guess which alternative most children would pick. With video cassettes—as with everything else related to a child's well-being and development—it's the parent who has to make the right choice.

This book isn't meant to relieve parents of that responsibility. But it *is* designed to help them deal with it more easily and effectively by providing them with complete and accurate information about several hundred of the most commonly available children's videos. In addition to describing the contents of the cassettes in as much detail as space limitations allow, I have evaluated each one according to various criteria, depending on the nature of the program. Obviously, exercise tapes and instructional videos have to be judged by different standards than cartoons and feature films. In general, however, the reviews are designed to let parents know precisely how intelligent, entertaining, and skillfully made each videotape is. I have also paid close attention to matters of particular concern to most parents: excessive violence, sexual stereotyping, and the presence of images and fantasies that might be seriously disturbing to young children.

The lowest ratings have been reserved for those hopelessly inane videos (often consisting of recycled Saturday-morning cartoons) that traffic solely in frenetic, nonstop action and the most mindless form of slapstick. I have also been critical of the new breed of toy-inspired cartoons (*Strawberry Shortcake* and the rest) that, though often slickly produced, are pervaded by a crass, commercial sensibility and are aimed not at the hearts and heads of young viewers but straight at their parents' pocketbooks.

The best children's videos, on the other hand, are those that are not only enjoyable but also genuinely enriching, that nourish both the mind and the imagination, and that continue to provide meaningful pleasures even after repeated viewings. They tend to share another virtue, too. Videotapes like *The Secret of NIMH,* the 1939 version of *The Wizard of Oz,* the Cosgrove Hall production of *The Wind in the Willows,* and the animated adaptation of Raymond Briggs's *The Snowman* are derived from outstanding children's literature and offer parents a marvelous opportunity to foster an appreciation for reading in their daughters and sons. Young children love to see their favorite stories brought to life on screen. Conversely, discovering that a beloved cartoon or movie also exists as a book can be very exciting to them. Although the finest children's videos offer the same rewards as good children's literature—satisfying, emotionally meaningful stories presented in a rich, imaginative style—parents should take care to use video watching as a complement to, not a substitute for, reading.

In the heading of each review, I have provided only the information that seems most relevant to parents:

the name of the video's distributor, year of production, running time, suggested retail price (which may, of course, change at any time). The age guidelines are, of necessity, approximate, since children develop, intellectually and emotionally, at very different rates. Some ten-year-olds are perfectly happy watching Disney movies; others are already begging their parents to let them see movies like *Porky's* and *Friday the 13th.* Although the age recommendations at the start of each entry will give parents an idea of the tape's intended audience, they should rely on the review itself to judge how appropriate the cassette is for their particular child.

Finally, each heading rates the videotape according to a four-star system:

★	*Poor*
★★	*Average*
★★★	*Good*
★★★★	*Excellent*

With video watching rapidly becoming America's favorite family pastime, it is important for parents to find programs that will do something more than keep their kids sedated with an hour's worth of simpleminded entertainment. There is plenty of trash around, but there are also a significant number of genuine treasures, and a great many videos that, although not of the first rank, are very worthwhile. It's my belief that, with *Kidvid* as a guide, parents can turn the time their children spend in front of the VCR from a passive, largely unproductive experience into an actively rewarding one.

From conception to completion, this project has received the encouragement, guidance, and support of a great many people. I'd like to thank my friend Alan Karp, owner of the National Video store on Union

Turnpike in Jamaica Estates, Queens, for his consistent generosity. My consultant, Genevieve Kazdin, offered much good advice and suggested a number of ways to make this guide as useful as possible. Her assistance has been indispensable. As always, I am indebted to my friend and agent, Jonathan Dolger, for his unwavering sanity, good sense, and support. In its earliest stages, this project received important encouragement from Melissa Newman, and I am thankful to her for it. I am also deeply grateful to the people at Pocket Books, especially Bill Grose and my editor, Stacy Prince, whose enthusiasm for the project helped to make it a reality. My friends Terry Fischer, Judy Stone, Stephanie Spinner, and Beth Farb helped me out in various important ways. My thanks go to them all.

One of the nicest things about doing this book was coming into contact with so many kind and accommodating people in the video business, whose cooperation made my life much easier. I am especially grateful to the following individuals: Jane Ayer (MCA), Neal Baseman (Karl-Lorimar), Bob Blair (VCI), Tom Bishop (Family Home Entertainment), Susan Blodgett (CBS/Fox), Jim Brannigan (SQN), Bob Brown (Video City), Fran Cinneas (Showtime), Nick Clemente (Western Publishing), Cathy Cottrell (Active Home Video), Tom Devlin (Worldvision), Milo Duffin (King of Video), Ted Ewing (Blackhawk), Mike Finnegan (Warner Home Video), Joe Fleischman (Transworld), Murray Glass (Glenn Video Vistas), Kathie Gordon (CC Studios), Jim Gullo (Walt Disney Home Video), Ron Hall (Festival Films), Chris Hoffman (NTA), Paul Jacobson (Kid Time), Lynn Johnson (Paramount), Peggy Kovacs (Walt Disney Home Video), Bob Lampert (Unicorn Video), Fred Lasswell (Cartoony Enterprises), Cathy Mantegna (Children's Video Library), Brian Mareno (Active Home Video), Diane McGhee-Terry (Embassy), Meg Moore (Dudley-Anderson-Yutzy), Chris Morris (Prism), Sheila Morris (Karl-

Lorimar), Meg Murphy (SONY), Shari Nowack (Worldvision), John O'Donnell (SONY), John Riggio (Worldvision), Robin Schaffer (Unicorn), Lynn Singer (Family Home Entertainment), Richard Stadin (Mastervision), George Steele III (Pacific Arts), John Stepan (Video Gems), Andy Tannen (Ruder, Finn & Rotman), Pamela Tourangeau (Media Home Entertainment), Pamela Wah (Family Home Entertainment), and Kim Werz (MGM/UA).

Finally, as always, and for far too many reasons to enumerate here, I owe a huge debt of thanks to the incomparable Jonna Semeiks.

ABC Funfit

ABC VIDEO (1985), $29.95, 30 min.
5 and up, ★★★

This junior-level workout tape is good—but not as
good as it could have been. The problem mostly has to
do with its format. *ABC Funfit* was not designed
specifically for video. It is a three-minute television
show that airs twice each Saturday morning on
ABC-TV (where it is wedged in between the usual
mediocre cartoon fare). This video cassette assembles
ten of these three-minute segments, with mixed results.
The other workout tapes for children on the market
—*Tip Top! with Suzy Prudden* and *Mousercise*—begin
with warm-ups and stretches, then move through progressively more complicated routines, and end with
cool-down periods. By contrast, *ABC Funfit* simply
strings together a bunch of exercises. Each of the
segments is okay in itself—any child who performs all
the routines will unquestionably get a brisk, although
not overly strenuous, workout. But they don't really
constitute a coherent, carefully designed aerobics program.

Still, this tape has lots to recommend it. Hosted by
Mary Lou Retton—the sweetheart of the 1984 Olympics whose winning personality and irresistible smile
have made her a highly successful pitch-person for a
wide variety of products—*ABC Funfit* is lively and fun
to follow. To my eyes, Mary Lou herself seems to have
gotten a bit out of shape since her Olympics triumph
(each segment begins with a brief clip of her dazzling
gold medal–winning performance, and she looks decidedly more stocky than she did in 1984). But her
boundless energy and amazing physical dexterity make

her a very effective spokeswoman for the benefits of exercise.

ABC Funfit may not be the best kiddie fitness tape around. But any video that can get children onto their feet and engaged in some form of healthy physical activity is certainly worthwhile.

ABBOTT & COSTELLO CARTOON CARNIVAL

VCI HOME VIDEO (1967), $24.95, 60 min.
Ages 5–8, ★

Bill Hanna and Joe Barbera—the kings of cartoon schlock—are the perpetrators of these cheaply made shorts, produced for TV syndication in 1967 and starring cartoon caricatures of the famous comedy team. The characters look and talk like the originals (Bud Abbott—sounding like a very old man—supplies his own voice, and an actor named Stan Irwin does a creditable Costello imitation). But the original Abbott and Costello comedies—crude as they are—are infinitely superior to these brainless cartoons. Besides being terribly animated, they are completely devoid of plot, characterization, logic, and humor. Each five-minute episode is just a dopey excuse for a bunch of lamebrained action and dreary cartoon violence.

There are ten cartoons altogether in this collection. In "Germ Squirm," Bud and Lou are shrunken to microscopic size and chased around by a giant, hairy microbe. In "Wizardland," Bud and Lou find themselves in a magical fantasyland, where they are chased by a giant bearded genie. In "Cherokee Choo Choo," Bud and Lou are train conductors in the old West and are chased by a bunch of hostile Indians. Other episodes have them chased by everything from polar bears to the son of Kong. One cartoon, "Pinocchio's Double Trouble," promises, at the start, to be a nice change of pace, a humorous retelling of the classic story. It doesn't take long before it turns into (surprise!) another asinine chase, in which Costello, playing the part of the little wooden boy, is pursued by a "giant cannibal termite."

So much for plot. It's hard to describe the humor in these cartoons, since it doesn't exist. This show's idea of a witticism is to have Costello say to a genie named Mishmosh, "We'll make mincemeat out of you, Mishmosh." As for the violence: it is unremitting. Here is a complete synopsis of a cartoon called "The Indestructible Space Suit." Abbott and Costello are demonstrating their new space suit to the military (how or why Abbott and Costello have come to be in possession of this item is, characteristically, never explained). First, Abbott fires a cannonball, which hits Costello on the head. Then Abbott drops a safe on Costello's head. Next, Abbott drops Costello out of a helicopter (head first). Costello is then used as a human battering ram by a group of soldiers who try to break down a steel door with his head. When Costello complains that he can't straighten up, Abbott knocks him back into shape by bashing him under the head with a sledgehammer. Then he runs over Costello with a tank. To top it off, Costello is tossed into an explosives shack and blown up. Finis.

There are worse children's videos on the market than this one. But not many.

THE ABSENT-MINDED PROFESSOR

WALT DISNEY HOME VIDEO (1961), $69.95, 97 min.
5 and up, ★★★½

This high-spirited, live-action comedy (a big box-office hit when it was first released in 1961) stars Fred MacMurray as the brilliant but bumbling scientist, Ned Brainard, the kind of man whose housekeeper has to pin notes to his jacket to remind him that he's getting married that night—and who still forgets to show up for the ceremony. Unable to tear himself away from his lab, he sets off an explosion and awakens the next morning to find that he's missed his own wedding—for the third time. He also discovers a floating canister filled with a Silly Putty–like substance that can make anything, from a sneaker to an automobile, fly. He dubs this amazing stuff "flubber" (short for "flying rubber").

Ned spends much of the remainder of the film trying to win back his fiancée, Betsy, by convincing her of the importance of his find. Meanwhile, an unscrupulous businessman named Alonzo Hawk (Keenan Wynn), who has seen Ned tooling over the rooftops in a flubberized Model T, plots to steal Ned's discovery in order to sell it at a premium to the government. Needless to say, the film ends happily, with Hawk getting his comeuppance and Brainard and Betsy flying off into the clouds with a "Finally Married" sign attached to the rear of their airborne Tin Lizzie.

The Absent-Minded Professor is an extremely enjoyable film. Though it has a low-budget look to it (it was shot in black-and-white to make the wires in the flying sequences harder to detect), it is—like most Disney films—very polished technically. The flubber effects in particular are lots of fun. And while the sight gags are far from subtle (much of the film is like a live-action cartoon), they are often highly entertaining. One comic high point (so to speak) is the scene in which Brainard gets back at the villainous Hawk by attaching flubber to the soles of the scoundrel's shoes and turning him into a human pogo stick. Hawk keeps going higher and higher; it requires the combined efforts of the fire department and the university football team to save him from bouncing up and down on the sidewalk forever. (Keenan's pop—the great Ed Wynn—puts in a cameo appearance in this scene as the fire chief). Even better is a hilarious sequence involving a big college basketball game between the pint-sized players of Medfield College (Brainard's school) and a rival team of athletes twice their size. Brainard saves the day by ironing flubber onto the sneakers of the Medfield players, turning them into high-flying hot-shots who soar over their opponents, scoring baskets at will.

The Absent-Minded Professor may be a screwball comedy for kids, but parents will get a kick out of it, too. When people talk about films that offer wholesome, family fun, this is the kind of movie they have in mind.

THE ADVENTURES OF BLACK BEAUTY, Vol. 1

SONY (1972) $29.95, 50 min.
6 and up, ★★★

The Adventures of Black Beauty is not a retelling of Anna Sewall's classic children's book. Rather, this cassette contains two episodes from a handsomely produced British TV show that features Anna Sewall's world-famous stallion in a series of brand-new adventures.

In "The Fugitive," the black horse runs away from his owner's sadistic nephew. Injured and exhausted, he is discovered by the children of the new village doctor. The pretty young daughter, Victoria, falls madly in love with Black Beauty and begs her father to buy him, but the doctor can't afford the fifty-guinea price. In an exciting (if wholly predictable) climax, the owner falls ill, and the doctor—mounted on the swift-footed stallion—arrives just in time to save him. In gratitude, the owner gives the horse to the doctor's daughter.

The second episode, "The Pit Pony," also features a sadistic master and a mistreated horse. In this one, a sweet, shaggy pony named Barney has become too old to continue hauling carts in a coal mine and is going to be sold for dogmeat. A young boy named Billy, who loves the little pony, steals Barney from his owner and, with the help of Victoria and Black Beauty, saves the animal from the slaughterhouse.

Like so much of what's shown on TV, the shows in this series rely on rather obvious plot elements—cruel masters, noble children, last-minute changes of heart. In terms of story content, *The Adventures of Black Beauty* is rather bland and conventional. Still, what seems overly familiar to an adult is often fresh and compelling to a child. For the most part, this is a superior cassette. The acting, period costumes, and location photography are all first-rate (it was filmed on a country estate in Hartfordshire, England). Another nice thing about this show is that it manages to create drama and excitement without resorting to violence or slam-bang action. Best of all, we get to see Black Beauty perform a wide range of heroics—rescuing his mistress from quicksand, riding at breakneck speed to save a stricken man's life, putting a villain to rout. For kids who love books and movies about horses, this cassette is bound to be a treat.

Altogether, there are three volumes of *The Adventures of Black Beauty* (each containing a pair of episodes from the TV series) currently available.

THE ADVENTURES OF BUSTER THE BEAR

FAMILY HOME ENTERTAINMENT (1978),
$29.95, 52 min.
Preschool–6, ★★★

Buster the Bear's arrival in the Green Forest causes consternation among the other animals, especially Johnny Otter, who doesn't want to share the fish in the stream with Buster. This is one of several cassettes assembled from episodes of *Fables of the Green Forest*, a sweetly entertaining cartoon series based on the animal stories of children's author Thornton Burgess. (See review of *Fables of the Green Forest*.)

THE ADVENTURES OF CAPTAIN FUTURE, Vol. 1

FAMILY HOME ENTERTAINMENT (1980),
$29.95, 54 min.
6 and up, ★½

This anemic science-fiction cartoon features some slick, high-tech hardware—space ships, cyborgs, blaster guns, and the like. The settings, which range from asteroid belts to prehistoric landscapes, are also nicely rendered. In all other ways, though, this show is a dud. The characters are dull, the story is boring, the animation is extremely lackluster. You might not like the nerve-wracking level of violence in action shows like *G.I. Joe* and *Voltron,* but at least those cartoons fulfill one of the basic requirements of movies—they move. By contrast, *The Adventures of Captain Future* is not just sluggish—it's barely alive.

This show is sort of a kindergarten version of "Star Trek." Captain Future—a red-headed, all-American space hero—is the commander of a ship called the *Comet,* which belongs to an intergalactic organization known as the United Space Federation. Captain Future's courageous crew consists of a talking computer named Simon, who resembles a brain encased in a miniature UFO and who talks with the voice of the world's sexiest telephone operator; an intelligent, though irritable, cyborg whose name sounds like "Grug"; and a beefy, bald first mate named Otto, who wears a red undershirt and looks as though he'd be much more at home in a butcher shop or boiler room than at the command post of a futuristic spacecraft.

Like Captain Kirk and his pals, this frolicsome crew spends most of its time butting into the affairs of various alien life forms. This particular adventure begins when a specter, looking very much like the ghost of Hamlet's father, suddenly materializes on the deck of the *Comet.* This transparent figure—who identifies himself as a scientist from the lost planet Prometheus, which exploded one million years ago—begs Captain Future to travel back in time and try to save his civilization from destruction. Captain Future obliges, and the remainder of the tape is an elaborate, if not incomprehensible, story in which the captain and his gang find themselves back on earth during some prehistoric era, involved with dinosaurs, Martian soldiers, and a tribe of cavemen who are actually the descendants of ancient Promethean astronauts. Considering how complicated the plot is, nothing very interesting or exciting occurs. And the only mystery—whether or not the captain will be able to save the planet of Prometheus from destruction—is never resolved. I found the blurb on the cover of this cassette extremely misleading. Here's how it reads: "In this adventure, Captain Future and his crew use a time machine to go back a million years into the past to save a planet. Will they be able to change the past to save the future? You'll find out in this daring space story!" But in reality (since this cartoon show contains only two episodes of what turns out to be an on-going serial), you never do find out. To discover the answer, you have to rent Volume 2. Since Volume 1 is so dreary, your best bet is probably to avoid these lifeless cartoons altogether.

THE ADVENTURES OF FELIX THE CAT

MEDIA (1960), $29.95, 56 min.
Ages 5–8, ★

It's hard to imagine a worse set of cartoons than the ones collected on this cassette. This is a pity, since Felix was the first animated movie star—"the Charlie Chaplin of cartoon characters"—and his silent, black-and-white shorts are classics of early animation. This cassette, on the other hand, lumps together a bunch of made-for-TV color cartoons from the late fifties and early sixties. They are unbelievably bad.

To begin with, they are not just crudely drawn but

extremely ugly. The artwork looks as if it was executed by a severely untalented six-year-old with a set of faded magic markers. The level of humor would make the Three Stooges flinch with embarrassment. The voices (especially Felix's) are so grating that you begin to wish the talkies had never been invented. And, though Shakespeare probably didn't have these cartoons in mind when he spoke about a "tale told by an idiot," it would be difficult to come up with a better description of their plots.

Everything about these cartoons is offensive. They are full of unpleasant stereotypes. A child named Pointdexter, who is meant to be a typical intellectual, is portrayed as an obnoxious nerd in thick-lensed eye-glasses and a graduation cap permanently affixed to his head. American Indians are depicted as beak-nosed, arrow-shooting savages. There are details here that leave a viewer shaking his head in disbelief. When Felix returns to the Stone Age in a time machine, he encounters a dinosaur that breathes fire from its nostrils (nothing like conveying accurate scientific information to young minds). The violence is unrelenting and mindless. One cartoon consists of nothing but a string of nasty practical jokes that Felix and his neighbor play on each other during a Sunday afternoon. At one point, Felix drains the neighbor's back-yard pool and tries to trick him into diving to his death. The man retaliates by knocking Felix unconscious and attempting to run him over with a bulldozer.

This neighbor's name, incidentally, is "Rock Bottom"—a phrase that perfectly sums up the quality of this cassette.

There are two other cassettes in this series, which should also be avoided at all cost: *Felix in Outer Space* and *Felix's Magic Bag of Tricks*.

THE ADVENTURES OF HUCKLEBERRY FINN

MGM/UA (1939), $24.95, 89 min.
8 and up, ★★★

Mark Twain's book about the "ignorant village boy," Huck, who escapes from civilization in the company of the runaway slave, Jim, is regarded by many critics as the Great American Novel. Like so many films based on literary classics, this cinematic version of Twain's story is only a pale imitation of the original masterpiece. Still, it's an enjoyable and generally worthwhile children's movie.

The first half of the film follows the book fairly closely. When we first meet Huck (engagingly played by Mickey Rooney), he is living with the kindly Widow Douglas and her stern sister, Miss Watson. The women are doing their best to "civilize" the carefree country boy. Soon after we meet Huck, his brutish father appears on the scene and spirits the boy away to a lonely cabin in the woods. Huck engineers an escape and makes his way to a nearby island where he encounters Miss Watson's runaway slave, Jim. The two then start down the Mississippi River on a raft. Along the way, Huck and Jim have a variety of adventures, the majority of which, unfortunately, have been totally eliminated from the film (along with most of the book's uproarious humor). In fact, the only episodes that have been retained more or less in their entirety are those dealing with the Duke and the Dauphin, the two treacherous (though pricelessly funny) con artists Huck and Jim fall in with. The end of the movie—in which

Jim is returned to Missouri to stand trial for Huck's murder and Huck speeds to his friend's rescue at the helm of a steamboat—is a completely hoked-up bit of melodrama that bears no relationship at all to the book.

There is one other, much more unfortunate, way in which the movie differs from the book. Twain's novel is sometimes attacked for its supposedly racist attitudes. With the book, this accusation is wholly unjustified. A more legitimate charge of racism, however, can be leveled at the movie, since its portrayal of blacks, though sympathetic, is also very patronizing.

Nevertheless, in spite of its flaws and deficiencies, this movie has definite virtues. Though filmed in black and white, it's a handsome production that does a nice job of suggesting the idyllic nature of Huck and Jim's river voyage. Even more important, it manages to suggest the deep love that develops between the young hero and the black man—a relationship which is, of course, at the very heart of the story. Twain aficionados will certainly find things to dislike about this film, but it's a better than average family movie and a worthwhile introduction to one of America's (in fact, one of the world's) great books.

THE ADVENTURES OF LITTLE LULU AND TUBBY, Vols. 1 and 2

FAMILY HOME ENTERTAINMENT (1978), $29.95, 50 min.
Ages 5–8, ★★★

Little Lulu, the beloved comic book character, has been the star of two entirely different series of cartoons. *The Adventures of Little Lulu and Tubby* features episodes from the more recent, made-for-TV series. In comparison to the earlier cartoons (produced by Paramount in the 1940s), the ones collected here are very simply (some might say crudely) animated. Nevertheless, they have a great deal of charm and are full of the same gentle humor that made the comic books so endearing. (See reviews under *Little Lulu.*)

THE ADVENTURES OF REDDY THE FOX

FAMILY HOME ENTERTAINMENT (1978), $29.95, 52 min.
Preschool–6, ★★★

More charming cartoons from the series based on Thornton Burgess's popular animal tales. (See review under *Fables of the Green Forest.*)

THE ADVENTURES OF SINBAD THE SAILOR

FAMILY HOME ENTERTAINMENT (1975), $39.95, 87 min.
6 and up, ★★★

Like many Japanese cartoons, this full-length Arabian Nights adventure features some very elegant, graceful animation. The story itself, however, is slightly disappointing. Although it has an interesting beginning and an action-packed climax, its long middle section moves at a very slow pace. For the most part, it lacks the magic, excitement, and high adventure found in other movies of this kind (such as Ray Harryhausen's *The Seventh Voyage of Sinbad* or the 1940 version of *The Thief of Bagdad,* starring Sabu.) On the other hand, it doesn't contain anything that is likely to upset small children (as those other movies do).

At the start of the film, the dashing young hero, Sinbad, and his little friend, Ali, rescue a dying old man. The man gives Sinbad a map of a faraway island where a priceless treasure is hidden in an underground cave that is guarded by demons. Sinbad and Ali (along with the latter's adorable pet kitten) stow away on a ship and ultimately arrive in a distant kingdom, where, through a misunderstanding, they and several of their shipmates are imprisoned by the childlike sultan. Fortunately, the sultan has a beautiful daughter who falls in love with Sinbad at first sight; she helps him and his friends escape. Accompanied by the princess, Sinbad sails off to the treasure island, with the princess's former fiancé—the sultan's evil prime minister—in hot pursuit. At the end of the cartoon, Sinbad must battle an enraged giant roc, the sword-swinging prime minister, and a bunch of nasty creatures that resemble a flock of airborne jelly fish, before sailing off into the sunset with the princess.

Though this cartoon is a little flat for a Sinbad adventure, it contains a number of things that children will enjoy. There is an exciting (and beautifully animated) scene in which Sinbad rescues a cute baby whale from a swordfish. Later, the whale and his mother repay Sinbad by freeing his ship when it becomes entangled in a mass of seaweed. Ali and his pet kitten are endearing characters. So are two comical sailors—an Arabian Mutt-and-Jeff—who befriend Sinbad and share his adventures. Best of all is a memorable sequence in which the prime minister (who is versed in black magic) hatches a sinister "hell bat" from a basket of enchanted eggs. Although this scene is slightly spooky, it is one of the few genuinely magical moments in what is otherwise a well-made but slightly dull (and overlong) fantasy cartoon.

THE ADVENTURES OF ULTRAMAN

FAMILY HOME ENTERTAINMENT (1981),
$39.95, 90 min.
6 and up, ★½

Combine a dollop each of *Star Wars* and *Close Encounters of the Third Kind,* a tablespoon of *Superman,* a dash of pseudoreligious claptrap, and a whole bucketful of comic-book mayhem and you get *The Adventures of Ultraman,* a poorly animated sci-fi concoction made in Japan.

The hero is a handsome young space pilot named Scotty, who, along with a small band of buddies, fights to save the earth from the evil starlord, Barock. When Scotty is killed during an invasion early on in the cartoon, a gigantic UFO (copied detail for detail from the *Close Encounters* Mothership) descends from the skies and carries him off to a heavenly planet called Ultara, where he is promptly resurrected. The inhabitants, who dress in headbands and togas, bear a striking resemblance to ancient Greek gods, except for their leader, Mentor, who—with his robe, beard, and staff—is a dead ringer for Moses as portrayed by Charlton Heston. The religious subtext of this cartoon takes an even more confusing turn near the end, when the patriarchal Mentor is crucified by Barock, dissolved by a laser beam, and then reincarnated in the form of a small object that looks a lot like a floppy disk.

Anyway, it turns out that Scotty is himself a member

of this divine race (known as the Ultralords). Simply by opening his mind to the "common life Force" (sound familiar?), he is able to transform himself into the invincible Ultraman, a giant, costumed superhero who is given to striking graceful karate poses while zapping his adversaries with some kind of high-energy cosmic rays. There's plenty of zapping throughout this cartoon —along with blasting, shooting, punching, crashing, and exploding. In fact, the pyrotechnic effects are the best thing about it. Apart from *G.I. Joe*, I can't think of another cartoon with so many handsomely animated scenes of things getting blown up.

The Adventures of Ultraman might be a little weak on logic (also on plot, characterization, intelligence, and production values). But if you're looking for nonstop violence, destruction, and general pandemonium, you'll get your money's worth from this cartoon.

ALADDIN AND HIS WONDERFUL LAMP

CBS/FOX VIDEO (1985), $39.95, 60 min.
6 and up, ★★★★

This Arabian Nights fantasy lacks some of the dazzle and wit of the most inspired *Faerie Tale Theatre* productions. Still, it's a very entertaining program, distinguished by stunning costumes, lavish sets, and several extremely appealing performances.

Robert Carradine is very engaging as Aladdin, a shiftless but good-natured boy who is tricked by a cunning wizard (Leonard Nimoy) into retrieving a magical lamp from the depths of a mysterious cavern. The sequence in which the boy descends into this enchanted place is one of the highlights of the show. The shimmering walls of the cave are covered with the silhouettes of mythic beasts and various uncanny creatures, while the lamp itself sits inside the gaping mouth of a stone gargoyle. When Aladdin plucks his prize from its resting place, all these creatures seem to spring suddenly to life. It's a magical moment—not at all terrifying, but spooky enough to provide young viewers with some pleasurable chills.

The other potentially scary element in the story—the all-powerful genie who materializes when Aladdin rubs the lamp—is also very well handled. This blue-skinned, pointy-eared giant (wonderfully played by James Earl Jones) is a very menacing figure with a robust but distinctly diabolical sense of humor. (When Aladdin asks him to perform a task, the genie pleasantly offers to rearrange the features of the boy's face instead.) Jones, however, manages to turn this demonic figure into a charming, even lovable, character.

Equally charming is Valerie Bertinelli as Princess Sabrina, the sultan's daughter who becomes Aladdin's bride. To win her hand, Aladdin must pass a test. He must provide the sultan—a sweet but spoiled soul who dotes on his collection of priceless novelty items—with "an object more entertaining and imaginative than anything that now exists on earth." Aladdin is stymied for a while, but with the help of the genie, he comes up with his prize-winning device—a magical box with a window through which the viewer can watch colorful stories. In short, he invents TV.

This enjoyable and lavishly produced program is a worthy addition to the growing library of volumes in the first-rate *Faerie Tale Theatre* series.

(See review of *Faerie Tale Theatre* for a description of the series as a whole.)

ALADDIN AND THE WONDERFUL LAMP

MEDIA (1982), $19.95, 65 min.
Ages 6–9, ★★½

The artwork in this Japanese-produced animated feature is very impressive. The scenery in particular is stunning—lavishly detailed, gorgeously colored, highly imaginative. The cartoon does a beautiful job of conjuring up an Arabian Nights wonderland. In other respects, however, this cassette is a little disappointing. The story moves along at a very slow pace, the dubbed dialogue is stilted and awkwardly delivered, and there are a number of extremely spooky scenes that younger viewers might find hard to take.

The story follows the familiar legend of Aladdin, a street urchin who is enlisted by a wizard to descend into a mysterious cave and retrieve a magic lamp. With the help of the genie of the lamp, Aladdin wins a beautiful princess and builds a magnificent palace. When the evil wizard manages to steal the lamp and abduct Aladdin's wife, the hero sets out to find the sorcerer's castle. In the climactic segment of the film, Aladdin and his wife attempt to escape from the enchanted castle, with the villain in hot pursuit.

There are marvelous things in this cartoon: magic caves, living statues, mythical creatures (like the giant roc that comes to Aladdin's rescue at several points), genies, and flying carpets. There is even an adorable little desert mouse that Aladdin adopts as his pet and that young viewers will find irresistible. Unfortunately, the cartoon is also full of scary images. At one point,

Aladdin finds himself trapped in a dark tunnel full of giant snakes with glowing red eyes. At another, he must battle an army of fierce, warrior statues, brought to life by black magic. The genie himself, with his fangs, green skin, and booming voice, is a pretty unsettling figure. There is a moment when Aladdin, traveling across the desert on camel, encounters a patch of quicksand. Aladdin manages to escape but the camel sinks under the sand, its face contorted in agony. It's a very exciting—even powerful—scene for a cartoon, but it's pretty intense for young children. So is the climactic chase through the sorcerer's palace, a sequence with all the excitement—and terror—of a ride through a particularly spooky carnival funhouse.

This cassette has a lot to recommend it, but it should be approached with caution. If your child is sensitive to scary images in cartoons, this isn't the movie for him or her.

ALICE IN WONDERLAND

WALT DISNEY HOME VIDEO (1951), $79.95, 75 min.
Preschool and up, ★★★

Lewis Carroll fans object to this movie because it fails to capture the spirit and flavor of the original book. In their opinion, Disney has transformed one of the world's great fantasy stories into a piece of fluff. Though this criticism is valid—this animated version of *Alice* is unquestionably inferior to Carroll's classic—it is also a little unfair, since Hollywood adaptations of literary masterpieces hardly ever measure up to the originals.

A more serious shortcoming of this feature-length cartoon is that it simply isn't very interesting. Watching

Disney's greatest films—*Snow White and the Seven Dwarfs, Pinocchio,* and *Bambi*—we become totally caught up in the stories. In *Alice* there *is* no story—just a collection of mildly outlandish episodes that never add up to very much. As a result, it's difficult to get emotionally involved in what's going on. Alice herself is a pretty but insipid heroine, and her journey through Wonderland is the very slender thread that holds the movie together. In this film, the whole is definitely less than the sum of its parts.

On the other hand, some of these parts are marvelously done. A scene in a magic garden inhabited by bread-and-butterflies, dog-and-caterpillars, and a choir of singing flowers is pure enchantment. The story of "The Walrus and the Carpenter" (though it completely interrupts the flow of the action) is great fun. And the Mad Hatter's tea party has the wild, comic energy of a Marx Brothers sketch. There are wonderful characters (a hookah-smoking caterpillar, the Mad Hatter and March Hare, and the unforgettable Cheshire Cat); a few memorable songs ("I'm Late," "The Unbirthday Song," "All in a Golden Afternoon"); and, of course, some dazzling animation (the march of the soldier-cards is as masterful as anything the Disney artists ever pulled off).

It is also true that the absence of a strong, engrossing story line might be more of a problem for older viewers. Younger children, with their shorter attention spans, will find much to enjoy here (they may also be upset by a few things, especially the bloodthirsty Queen of Hearts, who is constantly screaming "Off with their heads," and the conclusion of the "Walrus and the Carpenter" sequence, in which all the cute baby oysters in their seashell bonnets get eaten up by the conniving Walrus).

All in all, Disney himself put it best when he said that the problem with his version of *Alice* is its lack of "heart." There are more than enough entertaining and imaginative bits here to keep young children happy, but the movie, on the whole, is pretty dull. (A much more successful Disney adaptation of the *Alice* adventures is the spirited 1937 Mickey Mouse short, *Thru the Mirror*, which is available on video cassette on the *Mickey and Donald Cartoon Collection*, Volume 1). Still, no one in the world has ever made better cartoons than the Disney studio during its "golden age," and even a disappointment like *Alice in Wonderland* is definitely worth seeing.

ALL ABOUT TEDDY BEARS

AVG (1985), $19.95, 30 min.
Preschool–7, ★★★

See review of *Read-Along Magic Videos*.

ANIMAL QUIZ, Vols. 1–9

WALT DISNEY HOME VIDEO (1983),
$39.95 each, 83 min. each
Ages 5–10, ★★★

Each volume of *Animal Quiz* consists of three segments of the TV series "New Animal World," one of those wildlife documentary shows that are perennially popular with kids. An affable fellow named Bill Burrod introduces and narrates each half-hour episode. In Volume One, viewers travel to Midway island, home of the black-footed albatross, whose clownish antics have earned it the nickname "gooney bird." Then we're off to the Indonesian island of Komodo for a look at the world's largest and most dangerous reptile, the Komodo Dragon. The final segment, "Zoo Babies," takes us on a visit with the baby animal population of the San Diego Zoo. Other volumes deal with everything from Mexican grizzly bears to Gibraltar apes to the elephants of Thailand. At the conclusion of each documentary, the host returns for a short, multiple-choice quiz that tests the audience's understanding of the program they've just seen.

Like other shows of this kind (such as Marlin Perkins's "Wild Kingdom"), "Animal World" is both informative and entertaining. The shows are spiced with humor and suspense. There's an amusing sequence in Volume One, for example, that shows the ridiculous three-point landings that have earned the gooney bird its nickname. A later sequence records a tense encounter between a research scientist and a carnivorous, nine-foot Komodo Dragon. The nature photography is impressive and the information is presented in an interesting, understandable way. Kids are sure to enjoy these programs—and learn from them, too.

Parents should note, however, that these tapes are not necessarily the best shows for repeated viewings. It's doubtful that the average child would be interested in seeing any one of these video cassettes more than once or twice. As a result, they are probably not worth buying. But they are certainly worth renting.

AQUAMAN

WARNER (1967), $24.98, 60 min.
Ages 6–9, ★★

The Monarch of the Ocean—accompanied by his teen-age ally, Aqualad, and their mascot, Tusky the walrus

—battles a host of underwater fiends in seven exceptionally monotonous Saturday-morning cartoons. (See review of *The Super Powers Collection*.)

ARCHIE

THORN/EMI (1978), $29.95, 60 min.
Ages 6–9, ★

The best that can be said for this cassette is that it doesn't contain any violence to speak of. Beyond that, it has no redeeming value whatsoever. The animation is cut-rate, the stories hopelessly dumb, and the humor abysmal.

The six cartoons on this tape feature the familiar gang from "Archie" comics—Veronica, Betty, Reggie, Jughead, and old carrot-top himself, plus a new addition, a shaggy mutt named Hot Dog. Each episode finds them in some inane situation, and usually culminates in a long, highly repetitive, and totally brainless chase sequence. The first cartoon on the cassette is typical: Veronica is on a "chivalry kick," so Reggie and Archie engage in a unicycle joust, using long poles with boxing gloves attached to the ends as weapons. When Archie is dismounted, he runs off and returns moments later, dressed in a full suit of armor and riding a swaybacked old plow horse. Reggie attaches a carrot on a stick to the horse's halter, and the nag takes off on a wild ride with Archie trying desperately to hang on. The cartoon ends (as most of them do) with a silly, if innocuous, song performed by "The Archies." (The music is the handiwork of Don Kirshner, the father of "bubble gum" rock).

Everything about this cartoon is lamebrained. How did Archie and Reggie become instant unicycle experts? Where did Archie get a full suit of armor?

Where (in the all-American suburb of Riverdale) did he get a plow horse? The humor is equally asinine and made even worse by the mindless use of a laugh track. (Here is a typical big yuk: Right before his duel with Reggie, Archie says, "Don't ever talk to a jouster when he's just about to joust." This inspired witticism produces a burst of canned laughter.) The characters even use incorrect grammar. Archie begins one cartoon (in which, for a change of pace, the characters take a wild ride in a hydrofoil, having already exhausted the possibilities of plow horses, biplanes, and jalopies) by saying to the audience, "Hi mates! Why don't you join the gang and I as we visit the Bay City Naval Base?"

In short, this collection of low-grade TV cartoons is a cassette to avoid. (The same goes for *Archie*, Volumes II and III, two more collections culled from the same TV series.)

AROUND THE WORLD IN 80 DAYS

ACTIVE HOME VIDEO (1984), $29.95, 70 min.
Ages 5–8, ★

This cartoon version of the Jules Verne classic is so bad that it's hard to sit through. The animation is flat and unimaginative, the characters have extremely grating personalities, and the comedy is completely inane.

The heroes of the film are the suave Englishman, Phineas Fogg, and his pint-sized French companion, Passepartout, who is given to exclaiming "Parlezvous!" whenever he's excited. As Fogg and his sidekick travel around the world, they are pursued by a comical villain named Fixx, who tries at every step of the way to sabotage their journey. One of the more irritating things about this cartoon is the way it equates humor with the mindless repetition of jokes that aren't funny to begin with. For example, whenever Fogg finds himself in a trap, he raises a finger and announces, "The motto of the wise is: Be prepared for surprises." Young children might well find this little rhyme clever, but even the most good-natured six-year-old is likely to start searching for something to throw at the screen after hearing Fogg's motto repeated for the twelfth time in as many minutes.

Even worse is the stupefyingly slow pace of this cartoon. In one respect, its creators have achieved something truly remarkable: they've managed to take a story about a high-speed race across the globe and turn it into an absolutely inert film—a movie that barely moves. Most of the first half of the film takes place in a cramped Greek hotel room, where Fogg and Passepartout are trapped during a severe storm. The second half is set largely in a haunted house in New Orleans. In short, what we have here is a version of *Around the World in 80 Days* that takes place, for the most part, inside two buildings.

This cartoon can be recommended only to parents who are interested in inducing a temporary catatonic state in their children.

Arthur and the Square Knights of the Round Table

ACTIVE HOME VIDEO (1984), $29.95, 80 min.
5 and up, ★★★

Arthur and the Square Knights of the Round Table is one of England's most popular cartoon shows—and for good reasons. It specializes in the kind of inspired silliness that the British excel in and that is as funny to grown-ups as to kids. This cassette contains eleven short cartoons, and every one of them is a delight: imaginative, fast moving, and extremely entertaining.

These rollicking medieval burlesques feature a large cast of zany characters: the evil sorceress Morgana, who is constantly hatching cockamamie schemes to thwart Arthur; her loyal if klutzy henchman, The Black Knight; the brave, noble, exceptionally dim-witted Sir Lancelot (who is like Dudley Do-Right in white armor); a wise-cracking jester; the pint-sized king himself; and assorted wizards, warlocks, and dragons (including the castle's cuddly mascot, Delbert, and a ferocious beast known as the Horrible Hootenany). The story lines are varied, inventive, and very funny. In "While Camelot Sleeps," the evil Morgana devises a fiendish plot to get her hands on the magical volume titled *Merlin's Book of Spells, Incantations, and Barbecue Cooking*. When Arthur holds auditions for a new town crier (the old one shouts "Twelve o'clock and all is well!" with such enthusiasm that he keeps the whole kingdom up all night), Morgana has the Black Knight apply for the job so that he can sneak into Merlin's chamber at night and steal the precious volume. (Like all her evil schemes, this one ends up failing miserably.) In another cartoon, Guenevere discovers an abandoned baby named Cuddles, who outweighs King Arthur by about thirty pounds and uses a mace as a rattle. At the end of the cartoon, Arthur punishes the Black Knight by tossing him in Cuddles's playpen ("I don't suppose you'd consider putting me in chains?" Blackie implores).

There's a smattering of head-bopping violence in these cartoons. If the mighty champion Lancelot is required to do battle with a dwarf king, you can be sure our hero will receive a serious pounding at the hands of his two-foot-tall opponent. In general, however, very little fighting goes on in the cartoons. They rely instead on sight gags (Arthur orders his men to lower the drawbridge, and they do—on his toe), verbal humor (invited to "break bread" with someone, the literal-minded Lancelot proceeds to rip the loaf into a pile of crumbs), and the comical personalities of the characters. Even the exaggeratedly zany style of the artwork is funny.

This is an excellent cassette to watch with the kids: you'll all have a good time.

BABAR, Vols. 1 and 2

VIDEO CITY (1985), $29.95 each, 60 min. each
Preschool–8, ★★★

You would expect a video adaptation of Jean DeBrun-hoff's much-loved Babar books to be animated, especially since their delightful, deliberately naive illustrations are so cartoonlike to begin with. So it comes as a surprise to discover that this French-made adaptation is not an animated film but a live-action series, starring a performer dressed in an elaborate elephant costume. It's even more of a surprise to discover that this approach works quite well. These cassettes are certainly no substitute for the books, but they do a very creditable job of capturing the look—and charm—of the original Babar stories.

In the first Babar book—*The Adventures of Babar* (1933)—the little elephant leaves the jungle (after his mother is killed by a hunter) and makes his way to a city. There he meets a rich Old Lady who gives him money to buy some clothes. After outfitting himself with a handsome green suit and a derby hat, Babar goes to live in the Old Lady's house, where he becomes quite polished and educated. At the end of the story, he returns to the Great Forest and becomes king of the elephants.

Each of these cassettes consists of eleven five-minute episodes that, taken together, tell much the same story. Unfortunately, Volume One opens halfway through the tale, with Babar trying on his green suit at the tailor's (children unfamiliar with the book may well be confused by how abruptly the story begins). Every episode is a brief, gently amusing elaboration of one of the incidents in the original book. When Babar first dines with the Old Lady in *The Adventures of Babar,* for example, we simply see him sitting at a table, lifting a glass of wine in his trunk. In the video version, this episode is developed into a brief skit in which Babar is taught certain elementary rules of etiquette (for example, the crudeness of using one's trunk to suck soup directly from the tureen) by the Old Lady. The humor is understated but very sweet, and DeBrunhoff's marvelously childlike drawing style is skillfully recreated in the colorful sets and costumes. Babar in particular is extremely well done. He moves a bit stiffly, but his costume is perfect. Even more important, this cassette does a wonderful job of capturing Babar's personality, his irresistible mixture of lordly dignity and childlike innocence.

No child should be deprived of the pleasures of the original Babar books. These cassettes, engaging as they are, are in no way an adequate alternative. But children who already know and love Babar will enjoy seeing him brought to life on these charming cassettes.

BATMAN

WARNER (1968), $24.98, 60 min.
Ages 6–9, ★★

These five crudely animated "Batman" adventures
—part of Warner Home Video's "Super Powers
Collection"—find the dynamic duo doing battle with
their usual lineup of "kookie criminals." Although they
strike the same campy tone as the popular "Batman"
TV series, these cheap cartoons aren't nearly as entertaining.

(See review of *The Super Powers Collection*.)

BEANY AND CECIL, Vols. 1–6

RCA/COLUMBIA (1961–63), $24.95 each, 60 min. each
Preschool–7, ★★★

These made-for-TV cartoons from the early 1960s are
better than most. Created by Bob Clampett (a major
figure in the history of American cartoons who developed such characters as Tweety Bird, Daffy Duck, and
Porky Pig during his years as an animation director at
Warner Brothers), the "Beany and Cecil" shorts are
fast paced, funny, and very charming.

Each of these volumes contains six ten-minute cartoons, starring the lovable Sea Sick Sea Serpent, Cecil;
his sweet little pal, Beany (a tow-headed kid in a
propeller beanie); Uncle Captain Huffenpuff; and a
cast of strange and colorful characters (including the
cackling baddie, Dishonest John, and the dreaded

Three-Headed Threep, a prehistoric caveman with the heads of Moe, Larry, and Curly). The animation, though not great, is lively and appealing, and the cartoons are full of sight gags, slapstick, and the kind of terrible puns that young kids in particular find totally hilarious. (In an episode set in a haunted hotel, Beany is handed a dinner menu whose "Boo Plate Special" consists of Fright Chicken, Bashed Potatoes, and I Scream for dessert.) Parents should note that there is also a good deal of casual violence here, in the free-wheeling style of the old-time Warner Brothers cartoons. Almost every episode features a fair amount of punching, slapping, bopping, clubbing, and tossing around. Still, though the level of the humor may, at times, be pretty primitive, it's never crude or mean. (At one point, after Cecil is clobbered by a hammer-head shark, a character turns to the camera and innocently asks, "Do you think there's too much violence on TV?")

All in all, these video cassettes offer sweet, high-spirited fun for the kiddies and a nostalgia trip for baby-boom parents (who may well have fond memories of Beany and Cecil from their own childhoods, and who will get a kick out of all the topical references to such fifties idols as Peter Gunn, Davy Crockett, The Kingston Trio, and Ed "Kookie" Byrnes).

THE BEAR WHO SLEPT THROUGH CHRISTMAS

FAMILY HOME ENTERTAINMENT (1983),
$29.95, 60 min.
Preschool–8, ★★★

The hero of this endearing, made-for-TV cartoon is a cute little bear named Theodore Edward (Ted E. for short) who has always hibernated through Christmas. For once, he is determined to stay awake and see what the holiday is all about. His coworkers at the Organic Honey factory—who believe that there is no such thing as Christmas—laugh at him for his gullibility, and his hardheaded boss (whose office is decorated with a sign that reads, "There's Money in Honey") cautions him about fooling around with "philosophical concepts" like Santa Claus. But Ted E. won't be dissuaded. When his friends all jet off (via Bear Air) for their annual hibernation vacation, he sets out for the big city, where he finally discovers the true meaning of Christmas in the dingy apartment of a little girl whose family is too poor to afford presents.

This is a sweet, well-made cartoon, animated in a charming, whimsical style and featuring a very engaging performance by Tommy Smothers as the voice of Ted E. Bear. Another standout performer is Arte Johnson, who does an amusing turn as the voice of Professor Werner von Bear, an ursine expert on Santa Claus, who refuses to believe that a bear can discover the significance of Christmas without a few government grants to bankroll his research. The story is sweet without being overly sentimental, and its intelligence and humor will appeal to adults as well as children.

To fill out the cassette (the cartoon itself runs under thirty minutes), the packagers have added two read-aloud stories, "Ted E.'s Thanksgiving" and "Christmas Comes to Monster Mountain." The first concerns Ted E.'s efforts to build a float for the Honey Bowl Parade. In the second, the plucky little bear rescues Santa Claus from the clutches of Count Dracula. Both of these stories are narrated by Patty Bear, anchorbear for the Bearwitness News (broadcast from beautiful downtown Bearbank), while picture-book illustrations are shown on the screen. This segment of the cassette is little more than bland (if harmless) filler. Still, the main feature is good enough to make this a kiddie tape worth renting.

BEAROBICS

AVG (1985), $19.95, 30 min.
Preschool–7, ★★★

See review of *Read-Along Magic Videos*.

THE BEAST OF MONSIEUR RACINE AND OTHER STORIES

WESTON WOODS/CC STUDIOS (1985),
$29.95, approx. 40 min.
Preschool–8, ★★★

In addition to the title story (by Tomi Ungerer), this wonderful cassette—Volume Two of the outstanding *Children's Circle* series—features animated adaptations of Pat Hutching's *Rosie's Walk*, Marjorie Flack and Kurt Weise's *The Story of Ping*, and Tomi DePaola's *Charlie Needs a Cloak*.
(See review of *The Children's Circle*.)

THE BEATRIX POTTER COLLECTION

AVG (1985), $19.95, 30 min.
Preschool–7, ★★★

See review of *Read-Along Magic Videos*.

BEAUTY & THE BEAST

FAMILY HOME ENTERTAINMENT (1984),
$29.95, 60 min.
Ages 6–9, ★★★

"Beauty and the Beast" is one of the most lovely and moving of all fairy tales. This animated adaptation (based on the classic 18th-century version by Madame Leprince de Beaumont) is a straightforward, slightly pedestrian cartoon. There's nothing fancy or even particularly imaginative about it. Still, by sticking closely to the original story, it manages to convey a good deal of its power and appeal, and ends up being a pretty satisfying children's film.

One of the best things about this cartoon is the character of the Beast, who is portrayed as a kind of wolfman in aristocrat's clothing. When enraged, he's a fearsome figure. Young viewers, in fact, are likely to find him pretty hair-raising at times, particularly when he first appears in the film, growling in rage because one of his prized roses has been plucked by Beauty's father. A later scene—in which Beauty's brothers ride to her rescue and are confronted by a mass of black storm clouds that forms itself into the ferocious countenance of the Beast—is also unsettling. For most of the film, however, Beast is a kind and gracious creature, whose devotion to Beauty (and despair at being unable to win her love) is touchingly conveyed by the actor who provides the character's voice.

This film has its flaws. Although the settings (particularly the Beast's enchanted castle) are nicely rendered, the animation on the whole is wooden and one-dimensional. And while the Beast is a memorable creation, Beauty (who is described in the original story as a "charming, sweet-tempered" person) comes across as something of a simp. At the start of the film, her father learns that his entire fortune has been wiped out at a single blow. Seconds later, a lightning bolt completely demolishes their home. As the family stands there amidst the wreckage of their lives, Beauty pipes up brightly, "Well, at least we still have each other!"

Still, "Beauty and the Beast" is one of the world's great stories. Even in the form of this middling cartoon, its enchantment comes through.

BEAUTY AND THE BEAST

CBS/FOX VIDEO (1983), $39.95, 60 min.
6 and up, ★★★★

This exquisite production is one of the very best of Shelley Duvall's *Faerie Tale Theatre* presentations. Klaus Kinski's Beast is both a fearsome and a poignant figure—a creature compounded of rage, self-loathing, and a touching, tormented love. As Beauty, Susan Sarandon is ravishing. It's easy to see why the Beast is willing to give up his life for her. Even more important, she makes Beauty's growing attachment to the hideous creature seem completely convincing and inevitable.

Visually, this program is extremely impressive, thanks to Roger Vadim's splendid direction and a hauntingly lovely production design inspired by Jean Cocteau's famous 1946 film version. The Beast's enchanted castle—which seems always to be bathed in moonlight—has the uncanny quality of a dream, and several of the scenes are truly unforgettable. Perhaps the most memorable—and moving—occurs when the Beast, having succumbed to his wildest instincts and torn apart a deer, appears at Beauty's window one night, his clothes splattered with blood. Beauty regards him with contempt. "Forgive me for being a beast," he cries out in an agony of self-hatred. "Close the curtain. Your look is hurting me."

Most of the *Faerie Tale Theatre* shows do a commendable job of storytelling. This one does more: it manages to evoke the dark, visionary atmosphere that surrounds the greatest fairy tales. Younger children might find the Beast a scary figure (Kinski is an actor of such ferocious intensity that he can be unsettling even when he's not playing a monster). But older children are sure to find this program completely enthralling.

(See review of *Faerie Tale Theatre* for a description of this series as a whole.)

BECOMING REAL FOREVER

AVG (1985), $19.95, 30 min.
Preschool–7, ★★★

See review of *Read-Along Magic Videos*.

THE BERENSTAIN BEARS PLAY BALL

EMBASSY (1983), $24.95, 25 min.
Preschool–8, ★★★

THE BERENSTAIN BEARS' COMIC VALENTINE

EMBASSY (1982), $24.95, 25 min.
Preschool–8, ★★★

THE BERENSTAIN BEARS' EASTER SURPRISE

EMBASSY (1981), $24.95, 25 min.
Preschool–8, ★★★

THE BERENSTAIN BEARS MEET BIG PAW

EMBASSY (1980), $24.95, 25 min.
Preschool–8, ★

These recycled TV specials do a nice job of capturing the charm of the beloved Berenstain Bears, stars of a phenomenally popular series of children's books by the husband-and-wife team of Stan and Jan Berenstain. The animation itself isn't anything special, and it's easy to tell that these half-hour films first saw life on network TV (there are periodic fade-outs where the commercial breaks originally came). For TV cartoons, however, they are extremely well done. They are bright, funny, full of life and personality, and are told in rhymed language that is charming and intelligent. And they are able to deal with relatively complex issues (everything from the importance of sharing to the "miracle of birth") in a reassuring, sweet-tempered, and (in every case but one) thoroughly common-sensical way.

The bears themselves are four lovable, very human animals who are meant to represent the typical, American nuclear family. Actually, in our age of high divorce rates and two-income households, this family seems a little out of date—a throwback to fifties TV sitcoms. Papa Bear is a blustering (if well-meaning) bumbler who thinks he knows it all and generally makes a complete mess of things. Mama is a quiet and self-effacing housewife who is the voice of moderation and sanity. Brother and sister tend to be a bit more in step with the times. In *The Berenstain Bears Play Ball,* for example, Papa's heart is set on having his son become a baseball star. It is sister, however, who turns out to be the natural and who even gets to sing a feminist-flavored song called "I Want It All." On the whole, these are delightful and warm-hearted cartoons with a lot to recommend them. However, there is one important exception that parents should be alerted to.

That exception is the cassette called *The Berenstain Bears Meet Big Paw.* This Thanksgiving special deals with the legendary creature—the bears' version of Sasquatch—who, it is said, will appear and wreak destruction on Bear Country if its inhabitants ever grow "selfish and greedy." As it turns out, the bears have become just that. Although they live in a virtual paradise—a beautiful land where the grapes spit out their own seeds and the worms happily leap onto fish hooks—they hoard their goods behind big fences and refuse to share anything with the needy. Up to this point there is nothing wrong with this cartoon: Its

attack on selfishness and greed is a perfectly appropriate Thanksgiving message.

The problem arises in the second half. When news
arrives that Big Paw is on the way, the inhabitants of
Bear Country grab whatever weapons are at hand and
(like the villagers in old Frankenstein movies) march off
to meet the monster. At this point, Mama breaks into a
Broadway-style song-and-dance routine whose message
is that we shouldn't automatically be suspicious of
strangers. And when Big Paw ends up rescuing Brother
Bear and Sister Bear from certain death, the moral is
reinforced: don't assume someone is bad simply because he's a stranger.

In an ideal world, this would be a noble and worthy
sentiment. Sadly, we live at a time when many parents
must try to teach their children (who are only too ready
to believe that everyone is a friend) the opposite
lesson—i.e., to be wary of strangers. The terrifying
reality of child abduction and abuse makes this a
necessary evil. As a result, some parents may well
object to this tape, since they may feel that its message
is not simply inappropriate but potentially dangerous.
It's an unfortunate but unavoidable fact that, in today's
society, telling children that "a stranger is just someone
you haven't met yet" is not the wisest lesson to teach.

BILL COSBY'S PICTUREPAGES,
Vols. 1–4

WALT DISNEY HOME VIDEO (1985),
$49.95 each, 55 min. each
Preschool, ★★½

Bill Cosby's PicturePages is an instructional show for
preschoolers that combines teaching with Cosby's spe-

cial brand of humor and charm. In short segments (each is only a few minutes long), Cosby introduces young viewers to such basic concepts as short/tall, over/under, open/closed, bottom/top, etc. The "PicturePage" itself is a visual aid designed to help children master each concept by having them identify matching objects. With the help of his special felt-tip pen (named Mortimer Ichabod Marker), Cosby helps his preschool audience make the right connections. Each mini-lesson follows precisely the same format.

Cosby, of course, is famous for his rapport with young children (it's a quality that has made him, among other things, such a successful spokesman for products like Jello and Coke), and his easygoing charm is one of the best things about this show. Little kids are sure to be enthralled by his ability to communicate so warmly, directly, and naturally with them. With his funny faces, silly stories, and warmhearted clowning around, he comes across as the world's funniest and most lovable uncle. And the lessons themselves should certainly help preschoolers with such simple concepts as push/pull, square/circle, and sounds/smells.

There are, however, several problems with this show. Because it was designed (apparently) as a TV series, it contains awkward references to earlier segments. In the middle of Volume One, for example, Cosby—introducing the difference between rectangle and triangle—reminds viewers that "last week we learned about a shape called a square." This remark is bound to confuse any four-year-old who is watching Volume One for the first time. More seriously, this program is obviously meant to be interactive. At the start of each segment, Cosby refers to a PicturePage number, and he makes it clear that the viewers at home are supposed to be following along in their own Picture-Page workbooks. With the release of Volume Three in June, 1985, Disney Home Video did, in fact, begin to distribute workbooks through local dealers, but an informal survey of my own neighborhood video stores suggests that these books are by no means generally available. This is particularly unfortunate because each segment begins with a short, animated introduction telling the kids to get out their pencils and crayons so they can draw along in their own PicturePage books. *Bill Cosby's PicturePages* is a worthwhile program, but unless your children have the accompanying workbooks, they are bound to find it a bit disappointing.

BLACK BEAUTY

WORLDVISION (1978), $24.95, 49 min.
5 and up, ★★★

For a made-for-TV cartoon, this animated adaptation of Anna Sewall's classic children's novel is surprisingly good. As far as technique goes, there isn't anything especially distinguished about it. Produced by Hanna-Barbera, it relies on the kind of flat, limited animation common to Saturday-morning cartoons. On the whole, however, this film has a very nice look to it. The settings in particular—the meadows and farms, cobblestoned streets and rain-swept forests—are handsomely rendered and give the cartoon the appearance of a tastefully illustrated children's book. More important, the story itself is skillfully dramatized and briskly paced. And the actors who perform the voices do an exceptionally good job of bringing the characters to life. The result is a cartoon that is consistently gripping, and, at times, quite moving.

As in Sewall's book, the noble, sweet-tempered Beauty is the narrator of the tale. We follow him from the idyllic days of his colthood through his many triumphs and tribulations, beginning with his move to Birtwick Park, where he meets the jolly little pony Merrylegs and the doomed, embittered mare Ginger, who warns Beauty of the cruelty of men. Later, Beauty is sold to the Earl of Wickshire, whose sadistic groom, Reuben Smith, ruins Beauty's knees in a careless accident. Beauty experiences many reversals of fortune before his story is over—his life is packed with joys and sorrows, adventure and suspense. Inevitably, this cartoon condenses or cuts out some parts of Sewall's story, while others (such as the death of Reuben Smith) have been needlessly altered, presumably to make the story more suitable for young viewers.

On the whole, however, this above-average cartoon does a solid job of capturing the pathos and drama that have made Sewall's book a favorite for over a century.

THE BLACK STALLION

CBS/FOX VIDEO (1979), $79.98, 103 min.
6 and up, ★★★½

The Black Stallion is possibly the most beautifully photographed family film ever made. Every shot has the richness, texture, and meticulous composition of a fine oil painting. If anything, the film is almost *too* pretty. It is so self-consciously arty that some children might find it a bit slow going in spots. On the whole, however, it is a powerful and moving film that completely avoids the sticky sentimentality that mars so many other movies about young children and their beloved animals.

The first hour of the film is genuinely magical. The time is 1946. A young boy named Alex Ramsey

41

—whose face has the wholesome sweetness of a Norman Rockwell portrait—is traveling on a cruise ship with his father off the North Coast of Africa. Also on board is a wild Arabian stallion, cruelly mistreated by its owners. When the ship goes down during a tempest, Alex saves himself from drowning by grabbing onto the horse, which carries him onto a deserted island. The remainder of this opening section (which is played without dialogue) is a classic adventure fantasy—part *Robinson Crusoe*, part *My Friend Flicka*. Living alone and free on his sunlit tropical isle, Alex learns to survive with nothing more than his wits and his father's pocket knife. He also wins the trust—and ultimately the love—of the untamed black stallion. It's a child's idyll, gorgeously filmed and directed, and parts of it (especially the scenes in which Alex first rides the galloping horse through the blue ocean spray) are both exhilarating and intensely lyrical.

The second half is a bit more conventional, but —again, thanks to Carroll Ballard's artful direction and the continuously stunning cinematography of Caleb Deschanel—it achieves real power, especially during the climactic sequence. After being rescued by some fishermen, Alex returns to his home town, along with "The Black." There, he is taken under the wing of an ex-jockey, Henry Dailey (beautifully played by Mickey Rooney). This section of the film concerns the efforts of Alex and Henry to train The Black for a match-race against the two fastest thoroughbreds in the country. You've undoubtedly seen scenes like this one a dozen times before, but it's a measure of the filmmakers' skill that this concluding race sequence (predictable though its outcome is) packs a real emotional wallop.

BLACKSTAR, Vols. 1–3

FAMILY HOME ENTERTAINMENT (1981),
$29.95, 60 min. each
Ages 5–9, ★★

Blackstar, a Saturday-morning, sword-and-sorcery cartoon that ran on CBS for a year, beginning in the fall of 1981, is very similar to *He-man and the Masters of the Universe.* This is not surprising, since the same company, Filmation, is responsible for both programs. There *are* a few differences between the two sword-slinging heroes. Blackstar has dark hair and rides on a snarling, green dragon-steed named Warlock, whereas He-Man is blond and rides on a snarling, green tiger named Battle Cat. And the bad guys in *Blackstar*—a square-jawed, alien tyrant called The Overlord and his bestial minions—aren't nearly as colorful as Skeletor and his sinister crew. Still, the two shows offer basically the same package of bad animation, weak stories, lame dialogue, corny jokes, and repetitive (not to say unremitting) action.

Blackstar is actually an American astronaut who, after being "swept through a black hole," finds himself on the "ancient alien planet" of Sagar. There, he is befriended by a crew of tree-dwelling dwarves, who are a blatant rip-off of J.R.R. Tolkien's hobbits (in a burst of daring originality, the filmmakers have named these creatures trobbits). Although these seven little men (who are also reminiscent of Walt Disney's Seven Dwarves) are meant to have distinctive personalities, it's impossible to tell them apart. The only memorable one is a crotchety, white-bearded character who sounds exactly like Alvin the Chipmunk doing a Walter Bren-

43

nan imitation. In most of the episodes (each cassette contains three), the trobbits are threatened in some way by the evil Overlord. It is left to Blackstar and his two allies—an enchantress named Mara and an elf-warrior named Clone, who can transform himself into a variety of scary-looking creatures—to come to the little folk's rescue. This inevitably involves endless, running battles between the good guys and a constant parade of minimally imaginative fantasy monsters (one-eyed dinosaurs, giant dragonflies, "antler bats," flying gargoyles, etc.). It's all very noisy and empty headed. And the bargain-basement animation is highly repetitious: it's entirely possible to see the identical shot of Blackstar leaping onto the back of his winged dragon-steed a half-dozen times in the course of a single twenty-minute episode.

On the whole, *Blackstar* isn't even as good as *He-Man and the Masters of the Universe*—which is to say it isn't very good at all.

BON VOYAGE, CHARLIE BROWN

PARAMOUNT (1980), $29.95, 76 min.
5 and up, ★★★

Charlie Brown, Linus, Snoopy and the rest of the crew travel to Europe as exchange students in this full-length animated feature, which is guaranteed to gladden the hearts of "Peanuts" lovers, young and old.

(See review of *A Boy Named Charlie Brown*.)

THE BOX OF DELIGHTS

SIMON & SCHUSTER VIDEO (1984), $29.95, 120 min.
8 and up, ★★★★

The winner of three British Academy of Television Awards, this splendid BBC production is one of the most magical and inventive fantasy programs available for children. It is also one of the most beautifully made. It combines the elegant, tasteful look of a "Masterpiece Theatre" production with the imaginative sweep of works like C.S. Lewis's *The Lion, the Witch and the Wardrobe* and the movie *Time Bandits*. Add to that mixture the wonder and charm of fairy tales like "Jack and the Beanstalk" and "Tom Thumb," plus a dash of Dickens's *A Christmas Carol* and you have some idea of the richness and excitement of this thoroughly enchanting video.

The time is 1934. The hero of the story is a young British schoolboy named Kay Harker, who, while traveling home on a train for the Christmas holidays, finds himself caught up in a series of fantastic adventures. A gang of scoundrels, disguised as curates and led by a vicious sorcerer named Abner Brown, is attempting to gain control of The Box of Delights, an ancient object with wondrous powers. The Box is in the possession of a mysterious, white-bearded puppeteer, a "Punch-and-Judy man" named Cole Hawlings, who turns out to be a five-hundred-year-old wizard. Hawlings entrusts the Box to young Kay, who makes use of its magical powers to travel through time, shrink himself down to the size of a mouse, and journey into an enchanted forest in the company of a mighty hunter named Herne. The program is packed with outstanding special effects sequences. Among the most memorable are a journey Kay makes to the time of King Arthur; a trip into Herne the Hunter's "Wild Wood," where the young boy undergoes a series of breathtaking metamorphoses; a thrilling ride on a toy sailboat; and several Tom Thumb-like adventures in which Kay, reduced to pocket size, makes his way through the dark dungeons of the villain's medieval fortress. In the end, the evil Abner (who has attempted to sabotage the Christmas Eve services at the local cathedral by imprisoning the bishop, along with all the choir boys) is defeated, and the story ends with a glorious holiday celebration.

Marvelous as it is, *The Box of Delights* is not really suitable for very young viewers. The highly literate script can be difficult to follow in places, partly because of the sophisticated level of the diction and partly because of the heavy British accents of the performers. Moreover, the storyline itself is fairly complex. There are also a few unsettling images: red-winged demons, a spooky talking brass head, and one or two scary nightmares that leave Kay in a cold sweat. But for children eight and older—and for their parents as well—this first-rate program is sure to be a very special viewing experience.

A BOY NAMED CHARLIE BROWN

CBS/FOX VIDEO (1969), $39.95, 80 min.
5 and up, ★★★

Charlie Brown and the rest of the "Peanuts" gang made their big-screen debut in this delightful, feature-length film. Like the various "Peanuts" specials on TV (most of which are also available on video cassette), it is short on plot and long on sweetness, charm, and humor.

At the start of the film, we see Charlie Brown failing at his usual occupations—kite flying, ball playing. He can't even get his toy boat to float in the bathtub. He seeks psychiatric help from Lucy, whose novel form of therapy is to project slides of Charlie Brown's failures onto a screen and force him to watch. With Linus's encouragement, Charlie Brown enters the school spelling bee, determined to prove that he is not a born loser. Much to his (and everyone else's) amazement, he wins—only to discover (to his horror) that he must represent his school in a televised, nationwide contest. As he boards the bus to head off for the big city, his friends gather around to bid him goodbye and shout out words of encouragement. "Return victorious, Charlie Brown!" they cry. "Or don't come back at all!" adds Lucy. There's a moment of suspense when it looks as though Charlie Brown might actually emerge a winner, but, true to form, he blows it at the last minute. The cartoon ends sweetly, though, when—with the help of his pal Linus—Charlie realizes that there's more to life than winning contests.

This movie is made in the same style as the TV specials—and, in fact, although it was made for theatrical release, it is probably better suited to the small screen. The animation is simple but slick and does a perfect job of bringing Charles Schulz's drawings to life. There is a lovely jazz score by Vince Guaraldi and some not-so-great songs by Rod McKuen. To give the film a little more pizzazz than the usual "Peanuts" special, its creators have tossed in some imaginative effects: each song or musical number is performed to the accompaniment of an ingenious visual sequence. For example, when Snoopy pulls out his stereo set to play the national anthem before a big ball game, the screen explodes into a kind of op-art montage of stars and stripes. Later on, Schroeder's performance of Beethoven's "Pathétique" sonata is accompanied by a succession of lyrical, vaguely psychedelic images: monks, flowers, tombstones, stained glass windows, cathedrals, ocean waves, and various abstract shapes.

Still, in the last analysis, what makes this movie (and all the other "Peanuts" cartoons that have been produced since) so enjoyable are the charm of its characters and its wealth of vintage Charles Schulz jokes and situations: Snoopy flying his Sopwith Camel, Linus experiencing severe withdrawal symptoms after loaning Charlie Brown his security blanket, Lucy attributing Charlie Brown's spelling success to the words he's given—failure, incompetent, insecure, unconfident. ("Of course!" cries Lucy, each time Charlie Brown gets one right. "That's a word he's well acquainted with!"). "Peanuts" fans young and old will find this film a delight.

There are three other feature-length "Peanuts" movies available on video cassette: *Snoopy Come Home; Race for Your Life, Charlie Brown;* and *Bon Voyage, Charlie Brown.* Like *A Boy Named Charlie Brown,* each is essentially a collection of comic vignettes, strung together on a (somewhat slender) story line and full of Charles Schulz's special charm.

THE BOY WHO LEFT HOME TO FIND OUT ABOUT THE SHIVERS

CBS/FOX VIDEO (1983), $39.98, 60 min.
6 and up, ★★★★

Based on the Grimm Brothers' tale, "The Story of the Youth Who Went Forth to Learn What Fear Was," this thoroughly delightful—but potentially disturbing

—*Faerie Tale Theatre* dramatization stars Peter Mac-Nicol as young Martin, a boy immune to fear. While the other villagers in his tiny Transylvanian town live in a perpetual state of dread (just hearing an owl hoot is enough to make them turn pale with terror), Martin merely scoffs at their superstitions. He simply cannot be scared.

Convinced that there is something seriously wrong with himself, he decides to find out the meaning of fear and sets out to discover something that will give him the shivers. Eventually, he happens upon an inn (called "The Stake and Brew"), where he learns of a challenge issued by the ruler of the realm: any man able to survive three nights inside the king's haunted castle will win a great treasure plus the hand of the beautiful Princess Amanda. Martin accepts the challenge and spends three highly eventful nights inside the spook-infested place. But nothing he sees—from a living, bat-winged gargoyle to a decapitated zombie that uses his own head as a basketball—fazes him in the least. In the end, he wins both prizes. It is not until his fiancée begins painting a blissful picture of their future (big wedding, lots of children, etc.) that Martin finds himself quaking in fear. (In the original story, it takes a bowl of fish poured down the hero's back to get him to shudder).

Like the Grimm Brothers' original, this first-rate production is essentially a comical ghost story, with the humor and horror existing in more or less equal proportions. Peter MacNicol gives a sweetly appealing performance as the fearless hero, and the other cast members—including Christopher Lee as King Vladimir, David Warner as the innkeeper, and Frank Zappa as a hilariously repulsive hunchback named Attila—are equally outstanding. This is also one of the most sumptuously designed of the *Faerie Tale Theatre* programs, with sets inspired by the artwork of Breughel and Gustav Doré.

For all its virtues, however, parents should be warned that this video cassette contains some of the creepiest images on any kiddie tape around. At one point, for example, Martin is threatened by some ax-wielding zombies, who look like a bunch of extras from *Night of the Living Dead*. One of them throws a hatchet at Martin, who catches it, laughs, and casually tosses it over his shoulder. Landing across the zombie's wrist, it chops off his hand, which is immediately grabbed by another ghoul, who lifts it hungrily to his mouth. At another point, a zombie tries to unsettle Martin by sticking out his tongue, which has a wriggling beetle attached to the end of it. (Martin remains undaunted. "So what?" he says. "It's just a bug.")

It's possible that young Martin's blithe indifference to the horror around him may communicate a healthy lesson to children—that there is no real need to fear ghoulies and ghosties and things that go bump in the night. On the other hand, it's also possible that some of the spookier images in this program may give young viewers themselves a serious case of the shivers.

(See review of *Faerie Tale Theatre* for a description of this series as a whole.)

BRIGHTY OF THE GRAND CANYON

ACTIVE HOME VIDEO (1967), $39.95, 90 min.
8 and up, ★★★

This well-made adventure movie—based on a book by Newbery Award winner Marguerite Henry—is distinguished by its majestic Western scenery (it was shot on location in and around the Grand Canyon), solid acting, and a story that is continuously absorbing. This isn't a film for very young viewers: they will have trouble following the action, and there is one fairly brutal murder scene that could easily upset them. But older children will find this colorful movie exciting, suspenseful, and quite moving in spots.

The hero of the film is a lop-eared, shaggy burro called Brighty, who is adopted by a lovable prospector nicknamed the Old Timer. When the Old Timer is murdered by a bushwhacking claim jumper named Jake Irons, Brighty sets out to find the miner's friend, Jim Owens, a famous hunter and wilderness guide (played by the late, great Joseph Cotton). The second half of the film concerns the efforts of Jim, Brighty, and a young boy named Homer to track down the killer and bring him to justice.

The film moves along at a brisk clip and is full of stirring and dramatic episodes: an exciting sequence in which Jim takes Teddy Roosevelt on a hunting expedition; a rousing battle between the plucky little burro and a mountain lion; the climactic encounter between Jim and Jake on the edge of a canyon cliff. There are also a number of tender and heartwarming moments. The Old Timer's love for Brighty is especially sweet—a circumstance which makes the cold-blooded killing of the prospector particularly upsetting (the bad guy knocks the old man to the ground, shoots him twice in the back, then hurls the body off a high cliff). It's true that the viciousness of this crime adds emotional intensity to the story: you can't wait to see the villain get what's coming to him. Still, the sequence seems unnecessarily shocking. In all other respects, however, *Brighty of the Grand Canyon* is wholesome and enjoyable fare—a handsomely photographed and very satisfying family film.

THE BROTHERS LIONHEART

PACIFIC ARTS (1976), $39.95, 120 min.
8 and up, ★★★★

The place: a turn-of-the-century Swedish city. A nine-year-old boy named Karl, terminally ill with tuberculosis, tells his older brother, Jonathan, that he is afraid of dying and of being buried in the ground. To comfort him, Jonathan tells Karl that only his outside will be laid in the earth. His inside will fly away to a place called Nankeola, a fairy-tale world of black knights and white doves, medieval fortresses and fire-breathing dragons. Shortly afterwards, Jonathan himself is killed while saving Karl from a fire. Karl lingers for a few days. Then, after suffering a final, terrible fit of coughing, he closes his eyes and finds himself reunited with Jonathan in the enchanted realm of Nankeola.

So begins *The Brothers Lionheart*, a lovely, live-action film made in Sweden and extremely well dubbed into English. Written by Astrid Lundgren (the author of *Pippi Longstocking*), the story is about the struggle between the heroic inhabitants of Cherry Valley (who adopt Jonathan and Karl) and the evil lord Tengil, who has conquered the neighboring valley and imprisoned the rebel leader, Orvar, in the bowels of a mountain prison. There are very few family films as stunningly photographed as this one. The opening section, set in the real world of Sweden, is filmed in sepia tones and has the look of an antique daguerreotype. When the action shifts to Nankeola, the movie (somewhat like *The Wizard of Oz*) bursts into radiant color. The whole film is a visual treat, full of lyrical images. Even the scenes set in Tengil's evil kingdom—a wasteland of black rocks and deep gorges—have a stark, haunting beauty.

The film contains all the standard elements of this kind of fantasy adventure: swordplay, heroic quests, medieval dungeons, and a fight-to-the-death with a dragon. There is also a certain amount of violence (including one uncharacteristically brutal scene in which the traitor, Jossi, is branded with the mark of his evil master). For the most part, however, this film is completely different from such raucous American counterparts as *Dragonslayer* and *Conan the Destroyer*. It moves along at a stately pace, and there is a muted, dreamlike quality to it. (If Ingmar Bergman decided to make a sword-and-sorcery adventure for kids, it would probably look something like this.) Its emphasis is not on fighting and bloodshed but on the magical beauty of the landscape, the courage and decency of the freedom fighters, and—most of all—the deep and genuinely touching love of the two Brothers Lionheart. This is a superior cassette.

THE BUGS BUNNY/ROAD RUNNER MOVIE

WARNER (1979), $59.95, 90 min.
5 and up, ★★★

Warner Brothers cartoons—featuring such animated superstars as Bugs Bunny, Daffy Duck, Elmer Fudd, Porky Pig, and Wile E. Coyote—are not everyone's cup of tea. Many parents regard them as the epitome of nonstop action and senseless cartoon violence. There's no denying that this feature-length film is basically a collection of extended running battles (between Elmer and Bugs, Bugs and Daffy, Daffy and Marvin Martian, Wile E. Coyote and the Road Runner, etc.), and that no opportunity is missed to explode a keg of TNT under a character or send someone soaring off a cliff. It's also true that many of these cartoons (or ones very much like them) can be seen most weekend mornings on TV's "Bugs Bunny/Road Runner" show. So if you dislike cartoons specializing in breakneck action and pie (or dynamite)-in-the-face humor, or if you simply want to use your VCR to expose your children to things they can't ordinarily see on TV, this video cassette isn't for you.

On the other hand, many people (myself included) regard Golden Age Warner cartoons like the ones compiled here as mini-masterpieces: classic works of Hollywood animation (and comedy). This film strings together ninety minutes worth of shorts, all created under the direction of animation great Chuck Jones. Included are such gems as "Duck Dodgers in the 24½ Century") which finds a futuristic Daffy armed with a disintegrating gun that—what else?—disintegrates when fired); "What's Opera, Doc?" (in which Elmer, decked out in a Viking get-up, pursues Bugs around a stage while singing such famous Wagnerian lyrics as, "Be vewwy quiet/I'm hunting wabbits"), and the legendary "Duck Amuck" (in which Daffy is tormented by a malicious, unseen animator, who turns out to be Bugs). There is also a lengthy, hilariously funny "Road Runner" cartoon in which the ever-hopeful, infinitely ingenious, and utterly inept Coyote attempts to capture his fast-moving foe with a host of mail-order contraptions, all of which (naturally) end up backfiring on him.

To link these cartoons together, the filmmakers have provided some new, animated footage: an introduction in which Bugs offers a humorous history of chases from prehistoric days through the silent movie era, plus a guided tour through the portrait gallery of his posh Beverly Hills mansion. While animation purists might regard this material as so much boring filler, Bugs's introduction actually makes an interesting point, reminding us that these brash, boisterous, exuberant cartoons fit into a tradition of movie comedy that extends back to the days of Mack Sennett's Keystone Kops.

Other Warner Brothers cartoon collections include: *Friz Freleng's Looney Looney Looney Bugs Bunny Movie, Bugs Bunny's 3rd Movie: 1001 Rabbit Tales, Daffy Duck's Movie: Fantastic Island,* and (perhaps best of all) the seven volumes of *The Looney Tunes Video Show.*

BUGS BUNNY'S 3RD MOVIE: *1001 RABBIT TALES*

WARNER (1982), $59.95, 74 min.
5 and up, ★★★

Another compilation of Warner Brothers cartoons linked together with some new animation. (See review of *The Bugs Bunny/Road Runner Movie.*)

CAPTAIN SCARLET VS. THE MYSTERONS

FAMILY HOME ENTERTAINMENT (1967),
$39.95, 90 min.
7 and up, ★★★

This British-made science fiction series (which was syndicated in this country in the late 1960s) concerns an organization named Spectrum, whose agents, led by the heroic Captain Scarlet, do battle against a mysterious force of Martian invaders, known (appropriately) as the Mysterons. Though the premise sounds pretty juvenile, the show is played absolutely straight. The story is full of drama, action, and suspense. There is also a fair amount of very realistic violence—characters are shot, burned to death, killed in car wrecks and plane crashes. What is most noteworthy about this program, however, is that it is all done with puppets.

The stars of *Captain Scarlet* are beautifully sculpted marionettes that appear to speak and move around entirely by themselves (the method used to bring these figures to life is described by the producers as "Super Marionation," which seems to involve manipulating the puppets with concealed rods and extremely fine wires that can't be detected on screen). The puppets have extremely handsome—and uncannily realistic—faces, with moving eyes and mouths. It's true they don't change expressions much—but then, neither does Sly Stallone. After a short while, thanks partly to their wonderfully subtle gestures and partly to the terrific performances by the actors who supply the voices (Scarlet himself sounds exactly like Cary Grant), these small, plastic figures seem completely alive.

The puppets aren't the only exceptional thing about this show. Every bit as remarkable is the world they inhabit. *Captain Scarlet* features some of the most breathtaking scale-model sets and props ever created for TV. The work of special effects wiz Derek Meddings (who later went on to create even more spectacular props for such blockbuster movies as *Live and Let Die* and the *Superman* films), the sets for this program constitute nothing less than an entire world in miniature. Everything—from tree-lined freeways to sand-swept deserts, from a hotel room in Paris to a military complex on Mars—is recreated with staggering precision, down to the smallest detail. Technically, this program is a wonder—a state-of-the-art puppet adventure full of marvelous effects.

For a kiddie program, *Captain Scarlet* is extremely exciting, full of high-speed chases, high-tech battles, assassination attempts, and extraterrestrial intrigue. Occasionally, the plot is a little hard to follow, and many parents may well regard the violence as unsuitable for younger children (there are times when the show seems like a James Bond movie acted out by puppets). But if you're on the lookout for an intelligent, beautifully made science fiction program with interesting characters, an engrossing plot, and wonderful effects, you might give this show a try.

THE CARE BEARS IN THE LAND WITHOUT FEELING

FAMILY HOME ENTERTAINMENT (1983),
$29.95, 60 min.
Preschool–9, ★★½

The Care Bears (like Strawberry Shortcake) are characters concocted by the American Greeting Card Corporation to sell merchandise (cards, dolls, books, etc.) to little girls. It is ironic that—though these characters are meant to be the incarnation of warmth, feeling, and love—they are, in reality, cute 'n' cuddly in the most calculated and even coldblooded way. Still, the corporate masterminds who fabricated them obviously know their business: these multicolored little salesbears are a marketing phenomenon.

To be fair, this cartoon could be a lot worse. The

story concerns a young boy named Kevin who is angry and unhappy over his family's plan to move to a new neighborhood. Muttering "I don't care about anything," he wanders off to a dark and sinister park, where he is abducted by the evil Professor Coldheart, carried off to a creepy castle, and forced to drink a potion which transforms him into one of the Professor's crew of froglike slaves. Learning of Kevin's predicament, the Care Bears fly down from their heavenly kingdom, Care-a-lot, and set off on a peril-filled journey to Coldheart's castle in order to rescue Kevin.

There are some nice, fairy-tale touches here. At one point, the bears find themselves in a forest of talking trees similar to the one Dorothy and her friends travel through in *The Wizard of Oz*. And the story of the heroic quest—the journey through a dangerous land to save a captive friend—has a universal appeal.

Still, this cartoon sounds much more dramatic and interesting than it really is. Part of the problem is simply the Care Bears themselves. They have no personality whatsoever—just adorable names (Tenderheart, Cheerbear, Funshine, etc.), pastel-colored fur, and identifying symbols on their stomachs (Tenderheart has a heart, Funshine has a sun, Friendbear has flowers, and so on). The message of this cartoon—that it's okay to have feelings—is also a little puzzling. What child *doesn't* have feelings? Real fairy tales, which are much less simple-minded than this piece of fluff, help children *deal* with their feelings. All this cartoon really has to offer are the kinds of bright, cheerful images and sugar-coated sentiments found on greeting cards. It's not terrible, just thoroughly bland: as sticky-sweet and insubstantial as a mouthful of cotton candy.

Since the Care Bear adventure runs only thirty minutes, the packager has padded out this one-hour tape with four old Warner cartoons, featuring Porky Pig, Tweety Bird, and others. Although these cartoons (from the late 1930s through the early 1950s) are clearly intended as filler, they are in every way superior to the feature presentation. True, they contain a few moments of old-style Looney Tune violence (at one point, Tweety Bird shoves a lit stick of dynamite into the face of his feline adversary). And a 1953 cartoon called "Plop Goes the Weasel" contains a fairly offensive stereotype of a Southern mammy. But all in all, these cartoons are inventive, bursting with energy, and completely hilarious. One in particular, starring a pair of cats modeled on Abbott and Costello, is a comic gem. It's worth renting the tape just to see this cartoon.

The Care Bears are also featured on *The Care Bears Battle the Freeze Machine*, a one-hour tape containing another half-hour animated Care Bears adventure followed by two read-aloud stories.

THE CARE BEARS MOVIE

VESTRON (1985), $79.95, 75 min.
Preschool–9, ★★½

Apart from its length, this animated feature (a big hit when it was released theatrically during Christmas, 1984) is no different from the half-hour Care Bears cartoons produced for TV. It's pretty to look at: the animation (done by Canada's acclaimed Nelvana studio) is limited but very slick, and the settings —particularly the Care Bears' heavenly home, Care-a-lot, and a fairy-tale jungle called the Forest of Feelings —have a lush, radiant quality. But the warmth of all the Care Bears combined can't conceal the essentially coldblooded nature of this movie. The best children's books and films have the dense, engrossing substance of a dream. By contrast, *The Care Bears Movie* is nothing but a commercially manufactured fantasy, contrived by marketing experts whose only concern is to make a product so sweet, mild, and inoffensive that it will appeal to the largest possible number of young, unformed tastes. The resulting confection is a film with no real story development—just the same, clichéd plot used in every other cartoon of this type—and characters who, like the toys they are based on, are cute but possess no distinctive personalities.

The (minimal) story concerns a lonely magician's assistant, named Nicholas, who is taken over by an evil spirit and begins casting spells that turn people into loveless, uncaring beings. With their celestial kingdom shaken by cloud quakes and their Care-o-meter (which measures love and friendship) plummeting at a precipitous rate, the Care Bears set out to defeat the evil spirit, which they eventually do by unleashing an irresistible blast of rainbows, stars, and hearts from their cute little bellies. That's about it as far as plot goes. There are some nice songs by sixties folk-rockers Carole King and John Sebastian, and Mickey Rooney provides a competent, professional narration. In general, however, this movie—though unquestionably gentle and warmhearted—is depressingly unimaginative. (It also contains a small but glaring bit of good old-fashioned sexism. There's a little boy named Jason who wants to be a jet pilot when he grows up; meanwhile, his sister, Kim—the only girl in the movie—intends to be a nurse. You'd think that, in 1985, it would be okay to show a girl who wants to become a doctor.)

The best thing in the movie is a sky-sailing cloud-ship that carries the bears on a quest down a celestial river. Fans of the Bears will also get a kick out of a bunch of adorable nonbear characters—including a pink elephant, a little penguin, and a lion called Braveheart —whom the ursine heroes meet on their journey and who, at the end of the film, are welcomed into the Care Bears family as honorary Care Bears Cousins. Braveheart and his friends are sweet enough creations. Still, it's hard to escape the suspicion that their cinematic debut was designed to coincide with their appearance (in the form of overpriced, plastic figurines) on the shelves of toy stores.

CASPER THE GHOST

NTA (1940s), $19.95, 40 min.
Preschool–9, ★★★

Many people remember Casper the Friendly Ghost as a popular 1950s comic book character and, later, as the star of a half-hour Saturday-morning cartoon show that ran on ABC throughout most of the 1960s. Originally, however, Casper appeared in a series of beautifully animated shorts produced by Famous Studios in the 1940s. This cassette—part of NTA's excellent *Cartoonies* series—brings together three of these charming (if somewhat repetitious) cartoons, beginning with Casper's debut film, "The Friendly Ghost."

In this endearing 1945 short, we are introduced to the gentle, round-headed little specter, who likes to sit around reading *How to Win Friends* at night while his more conventional buddies are out terrorizing the neighborhood. Packing up all his worldly (or rather, otherworldly) possessions in a little bundle, Casper sets off in search of a friend, but every creature he approaches—a rooster, some hens, a mole, a cat, and a mouse—flees in horror. Heartbroken, Casper stretches out across a railroad track, but (being dead already) he can't even manage to kill himself. In the end, he is befriended by a little brother and sister, who don't seem the least bit bothered to have a transparent playmate. The other two Casper cartoons on this cassette follow the same exact formula, with only slight variations. In "There's Good Boos Tonight" (1948), Casper leaves his graveyard home and goes off (again) in search of a friend. After introducing himself to (and scaring the daylights out of) a number of animals (this time a calf, a cow, and a skunk) he sits down to weep ("I wish I were dead," he cries). Just then, a cute little fox named Ferdie bounds out of the bushes, and he and Casper become best friends. In a heartwrenching conclusion, Ferdie is killed by a hunter. Casper is inconsolable—until Ferdie, now a ghost himself, pops out of the ground and is reunited with Casper. The final Casper short, "A Haunting We Will Go" (1949), is a virtual scene-for-scene remake of "There's Good Boos Tonight," with a little duck named Dudley substituting for Ferdie the Fox. Though adult viewers might be put off by the lack of variety in the plot lines, young children—who love seeing (or hearing) the same story over and over—are sure to find these amusing, warm-hearted cartoons very appealing.

Alternating with the Casper shorts are three musical cartoons. Two of them are part of Famous Studios' "Screen Song" series, also from the 1940s. Each of these cartoons consists of a sing-along number (complete with a bouncing white ball over the lyrics) preceded by a short comic sketch that is thematically related to the song. In "Ski's the Limit," a humorous travelogue about Switzerland fades into a performance of a catchy little tune called "I Miss My Swiss Miss, My Swiss Miss Misses Me." "Stork Market" begins with a tour of a baby factory as a lead-in to the popular song, "Pretty Baby." The last cartoon on the cassette is a splendidly animated Max Fleischer short called "Peeping Penguins" (1937), in which a bunch of the young birds get into deep trouble by ignoring their mother's warning, delivered in a song called "Curiosity Killed the Cat."

THE CHARMKINS

FAMILY HOME ENTERTAINMENT (1985),
$19.95, 30 min.
Preschool–8, ★★

Using cartoons to sell toys and other merchandise to young children is a pretty deplorable practice. But using the *same* cartoon, over and over again, seems even worse.

The Charmkins is another half-hour, toy-based cassette containing all the depressingly predictable elements found in other cartoons of this ilk. First, there is the standard, brightly colored fantasyland, known in this cartoon as Charmworld—a place full of flowers, sunshine, and a bunch of relentlessly cheerful characters, the Charmkins, who are all named after flowers (not to be confused with Strawberry Shortcake's little pals, the Berrykins, who are named after fruits). Bordering this greeting-card utopia is the usual kingdom of darkness, here called Gloomy Swamp, which is ruled by a cackling, creepy killjoy named Dragonweed. This "King of Weeds" (whose voice is supplied by Ben Vereen) hates the sweet little Charmkins because he is never invited to their "flower festivals" and also because he is the only sane person in the cartoon. He is certainly the only character with a distinctive personality. The plot, such as it is, is set in motion when Dragonweed kidnaps Ladyslipper, the adorable little ballerina-Charmkin. In the end, a few of her friends journey into the Gloomy Swamp and defeat Dragonweed, using the only weapons permitted in this kind of cartoon: rainbows, songs, and the irresistible force of the hero's overpowering cuteness.

Many parents approve of cartoons like these because they are so "positive." And it's certainly true that they contain nothing violent or remotely disturbing. But they also contain nothing challenging, original, or imaginative. They are pure pap. Of course there's nothing wrong with sweet sentiments. But these cassettes (which are really just the same sugary confection, repackaged each time in a slightly different form) reflect a very cynical attitude on the part of the producers. The assumption behind a cartoon like *The Charmkins* (and *Rainbow Brite in "Peril in the Pits"* and *The Care Bears in the Land Without Feelings* and *Strawberry and the Baby Without a Name*) is that the only things little girls are interested in, or capable of relating to, are rainbows, flowers, and cute little characters with tiny voices and big, round eyes. Good kiddie videos (like good children's books) stimulate and enrich young imaginations. Cartoons like this one, on the other hand—with their relentless, mechanical repetition of the same formulaic elements—can only end up stifling them.

CHATTERER THE SQUIRREL

FAMILY HOME ENTERTAINMENT (1983),
$29.95, 60 min.
Preschool–6, ★★★

Big-mouthed Chatterer learns some important lessons about humility and freedom in these episodes from the charming cartoon series, *Fables of the Green Forest*. (See review under *Fables of the Green Forest*.)

THE CHILDREN'S CIRCLE, Vols. 1-6

WESTON WOODS/CC STUDIOS (1985),
$29.95 each, 40–45 min. each
Preschool-8, ★★★★

For thirty years, a movie production company called
Weston Woods, located in a small Connecticut suburb,
has been transforming critically acclaimed children's
books into equally outstanding short films. Up until
recently, these wonderful little movies were distributed
only to libraries and schools. That two dozen of them
have finally been collected on six videotapes (with more
on the way) is an occasion for rejoicing. Without
question, *The Children's Circle* is the finest series of
children's cassettes on the market today.

Each volume contains four wonderfully animated
stories based on award-winning picture books. Unlike
the Disney studio, which has always imposed its own
style on its source materials, Weston Woods is committed to making animated adaptations that stick scrupu-
lously close to the originals. The work of some of the
finest contemporary children's-book illustrators (artists
like William Steig, Tomie DePaola, Ezra Jack Keats,
Tomi Ungerer, and Maurice Sendak) is represented,
and brilliantly brought to life, on these cassettes.
Charmingly narrated and set to delightful background
scores, these video storybooks are a pure joy.

Another nice thing about them is that they aren't
meant to replace the experience of reading. On the
contrary, they are intended to give children a lively
sense of the riches to be found in books. At the same
time, they demonstrate, once and for all, that children's
stories communicated through the medium of video

don't have to be crudely made and mindlessly scripted —that they can, in fact, be every bit as imaginative and artful as stories told in print. If you are looking for a high-quality alternative to the usual run of low-grade, Saturday-morning cartoons, you owe it to yourself —and even more important, to your kids—to get hold of these cassettes.

The six currently available titles are:

Volume I: Doctor De Soto and Other Stories. The main feature on this cassette, based on a book by William Steig, was nominated for a 1984 Academy Award as Best Animated Short Film. It concerns a kind-hearted mouse-dentist, who has to figure out a way of dealing with a singularly ungrateful patient—a crafty fox who, once his dental work is done, plans to repay the good doctor by eating him. Also on this cassette: H.A. Rey's *Curious George Rides a Bike,* Tomi Ungerer's *The Hat,* and Quentin Blake's *Patrick.*

Volume II: The Beast of Monsieur Racine and Other Stories. This cassette leads off with Tomi Ungerer's delightful tale of a retired French tax collector who befriends a bizarre but gentle creature—a four-legged beast that looks like a cross between a baby elephant, a sheepdog, and an anteater. Also included: Pat Hutchin's *Rosie's Walk,* Marjorie Flack and Kurt Weise's *The Story of Ping,* and Tomie DePaola's *Charlie Needs a Cloak.*

Volume III: Smile for Auntie and Other Stories. The main feature—which was named the Outstanding Film of the Year at the London Film Festival—is an absolutely hilarious skit about a middle-aged auntie who is determined to coax a smile from an infant who is just as determined not to give her one. This cassette also features adaptations of: Robert McCloskey's *Make Way for Ducklings,* Ezra Jack Keats's *The Snowy Day,* and Eugene Field's *Wynken, Blynken and Nod* (as illustrated by Barbara Cooney).

Volume IV: The Foolish Frog and Other Stories. Pete Seeger (in a typically exuberant performance) is the singer/narrator of this rollicking, animated folksong about a farmer who invents a tune so irresistibly catchy that no one (including the chickens and cows) can resist singing and dancing along. This toe-tapping short is followed by Arlene Mosel and Blair Lent's *Tikki Tikki Tembo,* Tomie DePaola's *Strega Nonna,* and Gail E. Haley's *A Story—A Story.*

Volume V: Teeny-Tiny and the Witch-Woman and Other Scary Stories. This volume is every bit as wonderful as the other cassettes in this series, but parents should be advised that it contains material which some small children may find disturbing. The title story in particular—a variation of "Hansel and Gretel," based on a book by Barbara Walker and Michael Foreman —is a very spooky tale about three brothers who venture into a creepy forest and end up in the clutches of a cannibalistic witch-woman, a grotesque-looking hag whose house is decorated with the bones of her previous victims. The other animated stories on this cassette are: Dick Roughsey's *The Rainbow Serpent,* Paul Galdone's retelling of *The King of Cats,* and *A Dark, Dark Tale* by Ruth Brown. (Please Note: This volume is recommended only for children six years and older.)

Volume VI: The Three Robbers and Other Stories. A trio of brigands terrorize the countryside until they encounter a charming little girl named Tiffany in "The Three Robbers," a prize-winning short based on a book by Tomi Ungerer. Also included: *Leopold the See-Through Crumbpicker* by James Flora, *The Island of the Skog* by Steven Kellog, and *Fourteen Rats and a*

Rat-Catcher, written by James Cressey and illustrated by Tamasin Cole.

CHILDREN'S SONGS AND STORIES WITH THE MUPPETS

PLAYHOUSE VIDEO (1985), $59.95, 56 min.
Preschool and up, ★★★½

A video collection of favorite bits from TV's phenomenally popular "Muppet Show" series. (See review of *Jim Henson's Muppet Video.*)

A CHRISTMAS CAROL

VESTRON (1978), $59.95, 72 min.
8 and up, ★★½

See review of *Great Expectations.*

CINDERELLA

CBS/FOX VIDEO (1984), $39.98, 60 min.
6 and up, ★★★½

Like all the shows in the *Faerie Tale Theatre* series, this graceful and amusing version of *Cinderella* is a classy production in every way.

Even dressed in rags and covered from head to toe in soot, Jennifer Beals (of *Flashdance* fame) is very fetching as the cruelly mistreated heroine. Decked out in her radiant ball gown, she's a true vision of loveliness. Unfortunately, as an actress, she is more or less a complete dud. The opposite is true of Matthew Broderick as Prince Henry. Broderick (the boyish star of *WarGames*) is a very engaging actor, but he looks more like an usher at a movie theater than a handsome fairy-tale prince.

Nevertheless, though the leads leave a bit to be desired, this is a charming and romantic dramatization, enlivened by the high-spirited performances of Jean Stapleton, as a fairy godmother with a Southern accent and a penchant for teasing, and Eve Arden as Cinderella's cheerfully malicious stepmother. (When Cinderella asks why her stepmother uses her so badly, Arden says pleasantly, "The answer is quite simple, dear. You see, nature has been kind to you. You've been blessed with incredible beauty, a sweet disposition, and a loving heart. These are qualities that are totally absent in myself and my stepdaughters. Therefore, in order to balance the scales of nature, which have been unfairly tipped in your favor, we treat you like dirt.")

Children—and parents, too—will enjoy this lavishly produced and consistently entertaining video.

(See review of *Faerie Tale Theatre* for a description of this series as a whole.)

THE COMIC BOOK KIDS, Vol. 1

KID TIME VIDEO (1981), $49.95, 60 min.
6 and up, ★★★

The title of this cassette is a little misleading, since comic books don't really play a big part in this program.

It's not an animated show, either (the title makes it sound as if it might be yet another witless Saturday-morning cartoon). Instead, *The Comic Book Kids* turns out to be a lively, extremely enjoyable musical-adventure series, performed with lots of panache by a cast of little-known but talented actors, all of whom seem to be having a terrific time.

Comic books serve merely as a plot device—a way of (literally) getting into each story. The stars are a pair of high-spirited adolescents named Carrie and Skeets, whose older friend, a perpetually frazzled comic-book artist named Marvin, works in the studio of the irascible Burt Bonnix (Joseph Campanella, the only "name" actor in the show). In the introductory episode, Marvin has created a new character—a wizard named Phantos —though he hasn't figured out a good situation to place him in. By means of a slightly strained plot contrivance, Skeets conjures Phantos off the page. The wizard, whose land is being ravaged by a dragon named Drako, pleads with Skeets and Carrie to return with him to his world. To make the journey possible, he gives each of them a sequin-and-jewel-encrusted "transporter belt" (which looks like something Elvis Presley might have worn during a show at Caesar's Palace). The kids help defeat Drako and, in gratitude, Phantos insists they keep the magic belts.

Each subsequent episode (there are two half-hour shows per volume, with four volumes currently available) follows the same format: Skeets and Carrie find a drawing on Marvin's board and use their magic belts to step inside the story. In Episode Two, "Ghost to Ghost," the kids enter a haunted house and help a character named Janet, whose scheming aunt is trying to trick the girl out of her inheritance. Other shows find them involved with pirates, cowboys, extraterrestrials, fairy-tale characters, and a number of legendary figures, from Bigfoot to Robin Hood.

There are lots of nice things about this show. Though the stories are a little conventional, they are well paced and performed with real gusto by the cast. The villains in particular are an irresistible crew, and are made to seem even more delightful by the first-rate songs they get to perform. Each show features a couple of musical numbers, and they tend to be surprisingly good, with strong melodies and witty lyrics. The sets are also very charming. Though they don't look as if a great deal of money has been lavished on them, they are bright, clever, and quite stylish.

In essence, these musical-comedy-adventure shows are videotaped mini-plays. At a time when so much children's programming is as empty-headed and mechanical as a GoBot, it's refreshing to see a show that captures some of the pleasures of live theater—one that stars neither an animated superwarrior nor a cute 'n' cuddly cartoon doll, but a cast of professional singer-actors putting on a delightful performance on simple but cleverly designed stage sets. *The Comic Book Kids* doesn't pretend to be educational—it just tries to entertain. In comparison to so many current children's shows, it is entertainment of a superior kind.

COUNTRY MUSIC WITH THE MUPPETS

PLAYHOUSE VIDEO (1985), $59.95, 57 min.
Preschool and up, ★★★½

Johnny Cash, Roy Clark, Mac Davis, John Denver, Crystal Gayle, Loretta Lynn, Roger Miller, and Roy Rogers and Dale Evans are the stars of this video anthology culled from "The Muppet Show" TV series. (See review of *Jim Henson's Muppet Video*.)

CURIOUS GEORGE, Vols. 1–3

SONY (1972), $24.95 each, 30 min. each,
Preschool–7, ★★★

These three cassettes—starring the mischievous little monkey created by H.A. Rey and beloved by several generations of young readers—have an appealing simplicity. Minimally animated, they are less like cartoons than picture books with partially moving illustrations. Each story is presented as a series of full-color drawings with a voice-over narration. For children, this technique is the video equivalent of having a grown-up read aloud to them from a Curious George book. Every so often, one of the characters in a drawing (usually George) comes to life and performs some simple movement. This technique may not seem very interesting to older viewers, but young children are sure to be charmed by it.

Each volume in this series contains six five-minute stories that essentially follow the same plot. George's owner, the Man in the Yellow Hat, suggests an outing —to an art show, an aquarium, a ballet. Within minutes, George, impelled by his unquenchable curiosity, manages to create a serious disturbance. In the end, however, he redeems himself by performing a good (sometimes heroic) deed and is forgiven by everyone.

These cassettes, scripted by various writers and edited by H.A. Rey's wife, Margret, do a nice job of capturing the spirit of the original stories, although they tend to sanitize George's character a bit (in the books, more emphasis is placed on the trouble he gets into and less on his redeeming behavior). The artwork also faithfully reproduces Rey's memorable style.

Nothing can serve as a substitute for the original Curious George books; they are acknowledged classics. But these endearing videotapes make a nice supplement to them.

SONY has also released a feature-length (83 min.) Curious George cassette, containing twelve more of the simian scamp's animated adventures.

DAFFY DUCK'S MOVIE: FANTASTIC ISLAND

WARNER (1983), $39.95, 78 min.
5 and up, ★★★

A Warner Brothers cartoon anthology, starring Daffy Duck, Speedy Gonzalez, Porky Pig, Pepe LePew, the Tasmanian Devil, and others. The cartoons are tied together with newly animated material that satirizes TV's "Fantasy Island." (See review of *The Bugs Bunny/Road Runner Movie*.)

THE DANCING PRINCESSES

CBS/FOX VIDEO (1984), $39.98, 60 min.
6 and up, ★★★½

This story of six overprotected princesses who escape each night into a secret fantasy world is the most purely romantic of all the *Faerie Tale Theatre* productions. Investigating an exorbitantly high bill from the royal cobbler, the king—a widower who knows nothing about raising girls—discovers that his beautiful daughters (Jeanetta, Dinetta, Musetta, Wanetta, Coretta, and Loretta) have been going through a half-dozen new pairs of dancing slippers every night. Thoroughly baffled, he issues a royal decree: that whosoever can discover the princesses' secret shall marry the daughter of his choice and become the heir to the throne. The mystery is ultimately solved by a dashing ex-soldier, who, with the help of an invisible cloak, follows the sisters into an underground fantasyland—a radiant dream forest where they are met each night by six handsome princes who take them dancing under the moon.

Lesley Ann Warren and Peter Weller play the romantic leads in this lavish adaptation of the Grimm Brothers story "The Shoes That were Danced to Pieces." Younger children may find it a bit slow-moving, but older children—and their parents—will be thoroughly enchanted.

(See review of *Faerie Tale Theatre* for a description of this series as a whole.)

DANGERMOUSE, Vols. 1–3

THORN/EMI (1982–85), $29.95 each, 60 min. each, **5 and up, ★★★**

It's easy to see why *Dangermouse* has become a cult favorite in England. This action-packed, tongue-in-cheek adventure cartoon—whose suave, rodent hero is a cross between Mickey Mouse and James Bond —combines the sublime silliness of Monty Python with a very dry, distinctly British sort of wit. Packed with wild puns, sophisticated dialogue, and sly visual references to film ranging from *Alien* to *The Yellow Submarine,* it is one of those highly intelligent and entertaining cartoon series that (like the old "Rocky and Bullwinkle" show, which it resembles) can appeal equally to children and adults.

Dressed in a white jumpsuit and rakish eyepatch, Dangermouse—"the world's greatest secret agent" —lives in a secret hideaway located in a mailbox on Baker Street. His constant companion is a roly-poly little coward named Penfold. Together, they battle the fiendish frog, Baron Silas Greenback, the criminal mastermind behind some of the most infernally clever schemes ever devised by man (or amphibian). In one episode, the Baron attempts to flood the world with exploding custard. (Dangermouse saves the day by zooming off into space and bringing back an extraterrestrial "custard mite" that gobbles up the nasty stuff before it covers the globe.) In another, Greenback uses a malevolent charm, stolen from a primitive South American tribe, to bring "ghastly bad luck" to anyone it is pointed at. (Colonel K—Dangermouse's boss—is zonked with its rays while sitting at his desk, and an elephant immediately falls on his head.)

There is much here for little children to enjoy: lots of fast-paced action (but no real violence), slapstick humor, and all kinds of silly shenanigans. On the other hand, much of the humor (and vocabulary) will go over their heads. "Look friend," Dangermouse tells a chattering extraterrestrial at one point, "I speak thirty-four languages—but gibberish isn't one of them." (The heavy British accents also make some of the dialogue hard to understand.) There is a disgruntled announcer whose voice comes on during the breaks between episodes. At one point, in an effort to "raise the standards of the show," he offers to sing an aria from *Die Fledermaus,* then has second thoughts because he's "had enough of mice for awhile." Throughout it all, the dashing rodent remains supremely unflappable, in the best secret agent tradition. "They've got us!" cries the quivering Penfold when he and DM find themselves trapped on board an enemy spaceship. "Only as long as the door is locked," our hero replies shrewdly.

Because this is one of those rare cartoons that adults can enjoy as much as (in fact, maybe even more than) youngsters, it has the great virtue of encouraging parents to sit down with their kids and watch something together (instead of simply plopping the kids down in front of the TV and leaving them there for a few hours).

DASTARDLY & MUTTLEY

WORLDVISION (1969), $39.95, 53 min.

Ages 5–9, ★★

Dastardly & Muttley is standard, Saturday-morning kiddie fare—a flashy, hyperactive cartoon show featuring goofy characters, endless high-speed chases, and lame, kindergarten-level humor.

The stars of the cartoon are the four supposedly wacky members of the villainous Vulture Squadron: a quivering coward named Zilly; an oddball named Clink, who wears a Moe Howard hairdo and is subject to a "comical" speech impediment (his words are punctuated with a strange assortment of whistles, beeps, grunts and other sound effects); the mustachioed leader, Dick Dastardly; and the team mascot, Muttley, a shaggy dog with a hoarse chuckle and a vivid imagination. This quartet—the self-proclaimed "scourge of the skyways"—zooms around in a bizarre selection of antique biplanes trying to catch a patriotic carrier pigeon named Yankee Doodle Pigeon. That's the whole plot of the show (summed up in its theme song, "Stop That Pigeon!"). The result is like a cross between *Those Magnificent Men in Their Flying Machines* and a *Road Runner* cartoon, though without the wit or visual inventiveness of either.

There are eight Dastardly & Muttley cartoons on this video cassette. Most of them are nothing more than extended chase sequences. A typical sight gag will have Muttley perched on the upper wing of a biplane, attempting to smash the pigeon with a boulder but dropping it on Dastardly's head by mistake. The verbal humor is of an equally high order. When Dastardly threatens the cowardly Zilly, he cracks, "I'll cook your goose, you chicken." Later, going to put his coat in the closet, he asks Muttley to bring him an "empty hanger," so Muttley hooks an airplane hangar to a truck and pulls it over.

While there isn't much violence here, there are small bits of physical cruelty that seem even meaner than the kind of head-bonking humor found in many other cartoons. When Dastardly gets annoyed at Muttley, he likes to tear the medals off the dog's chest (Muttley wears them pinned to his fur) or snap the mutt's flying goggles in his face. A few of the cartoons focus on Muttley, a daydreamer who likes to imagine himself in exciting situations: as Fletcher Christian on board the *Bounty*, a fairy-tale hero climbing a beanstalk, or a magician known as the Marvelous Mutt-Dini. These cartoons provide a welcome relief from the relentless commotion of the chase episodes, but they're not much better in terms of intelligence or humor.

DAVID COPPERFIELD

VESTRON (1978), $59.95, 72 min.
8 and up, ★★½

This cartoon version of the Dickens classic is part of Vestron Video's well-intentioned but rather dull *Charles Dickens Collection*. See review of *Great Expectations*.

DAVY CROCKETT, KING OF THE WILD FRONTIER

WALT DISNEY HOME VIDEO (1955), $79.95, 88 min.
6 and up, ★★★½

If you are a member of the baby-boom generation, you're sure to have fond and vivid memories of this famous frontier adventure. When it was first shown in three parts on the old "Disneyland" TV show, it set off one of the biggest fads of the 1950s. At the height of the Crockett craze, it seemed as though every young boy in America had a coonskin cap on his head, a toy flintlock rifle in his hands, and "The Ballad of Davy Crockett" on his lips.

The film (spliced together from the original TV episodes) follows Davy from his days as an Indian fighter through his experiences as a congressman to his glorious death at the Alamo. The movie is packed with action and adventure, and presents a shining, heroic vision of our national past that, though highly idealized, is intensely appealing. Davy himself, as played by Fess Parker, is an embodiment of all-American virtues. He is a boyishly handsome, rugged individualist, who —devoted though he is to his wife and family—is constantly setting off with his friend Georgie Russell (Buddy Ebsen) to follow the call of duty. A crack shot and rough-and-tumble frontier brawler, Davy is the quintessential fighting man of peace. His skill with his fists and his long-rifle, Ol' Betsy, don't in any way diminish his sweetness, piety, and innocence. Like all real American heroes, he is answerable to no man but himself. His credo (frequently cited throughout the movie) is simple: "Be sure you're right, then go ahead."

This is an exciting and handsome production, which —in spite of some evident corner-cutting (whenever Davy and Georgie spot some wildlife, the film cuts to an obvious insert from a Disney nature film)—holds up quite well. There are, however, two things about it that might well make some parents uneasy. First, it contains an exceptional amount of violence. It is packed with scenes of people being shot, stabbed, tomahawked, bayonetted, and beaten to a pulp. Second, it presents a pretty insulting picture of American Indians, who are, for the most part, portrayed as either helpless children or savage beasts.

Apart from these flaws, Disney's *Davy Crockett, King of the Wild Frontier* is a highly entertaining frontier action film, featuring the kind of old-fashioned, all-American hero that has become more or less extinct in the world of contemporary kiddie entertainment (which has been taken over by invading armies of GoBots, Transformers, and Masters of the Universe).

Also available from Walt Disney Home Video: *Davy Crockett and the River Pirates*.

DAVY CROCKETT ON THE MISSISSIPPI

WORLDVISION (1976), $39.95, 49 min.

6 and up, ★★½

In the nineteenth century, when he first achieved the status of a true American folk hero, Davy Crockett was known as a backwoods brawler, two-fisted Indian fighter, and flamboyant braggart. Walt Disney did a lot to clean up Davy's image in the phenomenally popular TV shows of the 1950s (which still stand as the definitive version of the Crockett legend, at least as far as any member of the baby-boom generation is concerned). *Davy Crockett on the Mississippi*—a made-for-TV cartoon from Hanna-Barbera—takes this process even further, transforming the King of the Wild Frontier into the world's most wholesome boy scout and big brother. The results, while honorable, are pretty dull. The animation is (predictably) very flat and stiff, and the story goes to such lengths to avoid anything that smacks of violence that it ends up being extremely insipid.

In this story, Davy—accompanied by his lovable pet grizzly bear, Honeysuckle (who provides the comic relief, such as it is)—meets up with a young Huck Finn look-alike named Matt Henry, who is on his way to live with his Uncle Clarence. Davy and Matt make the journey down river together, undergoing many exciting experiences, from a flash flood to an encounter with hostile Shawnees to an attack by a fierce mountain lion. Unfortunately, none of these adventures amounts to very much. For example, after a long, suspenseful build-up in which we are shown the snarling mountain lion stalking Crockett and his companions, the animal finally springs onto Davy's back. Davy simply flips the big cat off, raises a hand in warning, and says something like, "Hold it, big fella, you're outnumbered." The cat then bows its head and slinks away. Every episode follows the same pattern. There is a threat of danger, which is instantly resolved in the most nondramatic way possible. The hostile Indians change their mind and decide not to attack. A band of river pirates is vanquished when Davy and his pal Mike Fink (portrayed here as a big, lovable lunk in a knitted cap) knock the villains off a boat with a piece of stretched rope. A wild boar chases Davy up a tree, then turns around and leaves.

It is clear that the makers of this cartoon have taken a great deal of trouble to eliminate any potentially offensive action and violence from the story. On one level, this is an understandable and even admirable thing to do. The only trouble is that the Davy Crockett story is—and has always been—interesting primarily as a two-fisted, frontier legend, full of action, heroism, and high adventure. If Disney's *Davy Crockett* suffers somewhat from an excess of violence, this one goes to the opposite extreme. It's simply too clean-cut for its own good. You won't find anything objectionable here, but you won't find much of interest, either.

THE DEVIL AND DANIEL MOUSE

WARNER (1978), $29.98, 24 mins.
6 and up, ★★★

A separate cassette devoted just to this award-winning animated fable from Canada's acclaimed Nelvana studio. (See review of *Nelvanamation*.)

DISNEY CARTOON COLLECTIONS

WALT DISNEY HOME VIDEO (1928–61),
various prices and running times
Preschool and up, ★★★★

For parents and children—not to mention animation buffs—being able to buy or rent vintage Walt Disney cartoons is one of the best things about owning a VCR. Over the past few years, the folks at the Disney Studio have released a treasure trove of cartoon collections under an assortment of titles. Theoretically, a number of these cassettes—which were sold as "limited editions" for short periods of time—are no longer available. But you can still find rental copies in many local video stores.

The average cartoon collection from Walt Disney Home Video is something of a mixed bag, containing both certified classics and fairly run-of-the-mill selections. However, even the most mediocre Mickey Mouse short is a tour de force compared to almost any cartoon being made today. And the best of them —cartoons like "The Band Concert," "Mickey's Fire Brigade," and "The Boat Builders"—are not only masterpieces of animation but inspired screen comedies, as brilliantly timed and hilariously funny as the shorts of Keaton or Chaplin.

One caveat: for all their innocence and charm, many Disney shorts contain a fair amount of casual, comic violence. In a typical cartoon collection, your child might see Goofy being socked in the head with a two-by-four, Donald having his tail feathers singed by a hot waffle iron, and Pluto getting his nose mauled by an irate crab. This kind of minor physical cruelty has been a staple of humor since people first began swapping jokes, but if you firmly object to exposing young children to it, you'll have to be careful about which of these cassettes you rent (or purchase).

Following are the titles of the various cartoon collections that have been released to date, along with a brief run-down of their contents.

1. MICKEY MOUSE & DONALD DUCK CARTOON COLLECTIONS, Vols. 1–3

$49.95 each, 41–44 min.

Each of these cassettes contains six vintage cartoons, featuring Mickey, Donald, Pluto, Goofy, and Chip 'n' Dale. Among the gems to be found on these tapes are "Thru the Mirror" (1936), a brilliantly imaginative version of Lewis Carroll's *Through the Looking-Glass*, with Mickey in the role of Alice; "The Moose Hunters" (1937), a hilarious bit of animated slapstick, starring Mickey, Donald, and Goofy as the world's most endearingly inept sportsmen; and "Lend a Paw" (1941), an Academy Award–winner about Pluto's struggle to overcome his jealousy of a cute little kitty Mickey takes into his home.

2. CARTOON CLASSICS, Vols. 1–11

$49.95 each, 41–55 min.

Each of these handsomely packaged volumes contains six or seven selections. They vary somewhat in quality, but there are plenty of genuine classics here, and most of the cassettes contain at least one cartoon that either won or was nominated for an Academy Award.

Volume One: Chip 'n' Dale, featuring Donald Duck. Six rollicking cartoons from the 1940s and 50s, including "Chip 'n' Dale" (an Academy Award nominee for 1947), "Three for Breakfast" (1948), "Winter Storage" (1949), and "Corn Chips" (1951).

Volume Two: Pluto. Six shorts starring Mickey's lovable orange mutt: "Pluto's Fledgling" (1948), "The Pointer" (Academy Award nominee, 1946), "Private Pluto" (1943), "The Legend of Coyote Rock" (1945), "Bone Trouble" (1940), "Camp Dog" (1950), and "In Dutch" (1946).

Volume Three: Disney's Scary Tales. Seven spooky cartoon treasures, including "The Haunted House" (a 1928 black-and-white Mickey Mouse short), "Pluto's Judgment Day" (1935), and "The Skeleton Dance" (1928), the first of the "Silly Symphonies" (this black-and-white animated fantasy, in which several skeletons emerge from their graves and perform a little dance, is generally regarded as one of the best cartoons ever made; it's an extremely charming film, though it's conceivable that some youngsters might find it a little unsettling).

Volume Four: Sport Goofy. With his usual grace and dexterity, Goofy demonstrates how not to play a variety of sports, including tennis, baseball, and hockey.

Volume Five: Disney's Best of 1931–1948. A splendid collection of six animated shorts that were either nominated for or won Academy Awards: "Mickey's Orphans" (1931), "Flowers and Trees" (1932), "The Country Cousin" (1936), "The Ugly Duckling" (1939), "Truant Officer Donald" (1941), and "Mickey and the Seal" (1948).

Volume Six: More Sport Goofy. Six more classic how-not-to demonstrations from cartoonland's klutziest athlete.

Volume Seven: More of Disney's Best, 1932–1946. Six more brilliantly animated cartoons, all of which were either Oscar nominees or winners as Best Cartoon Short Subject: "The Three Little Pigs" (1933), "The Tortoise and the Hare" (1934), "The Old Mill" (1937), "The Brave Little Tailor" (1938), "Donald's Crime" (1945), and "Squatter's Rights" (1946). (*Note:* "The Three Little Pigs" is one of the most famous of all Disney shorts, thanks partly to its theme song, "Who's Afraid of the Big Bad Wolf?" It's a wonderful, justly celebrated cartoon, but the wolf himself is a pretty scary character. And his final comeuppance, though well-deserved—he slides down the chimney and lands in a vat of boiling turpentine—has been known to upset more than one little viewer.)

Volume Eight: Sport Goofy's Vacation. Goofy takes a much-needed break from his disastrous athletic career and embarks on a series of equally disastrous vacations in six delightful cartoons, including the 1961 Oscar nominee, "Aquamania."

Volume Nine: Donald Duck's First 50 Years. Six animated milestones in Donald Duck's career, beginning with his 1934 screen debut in "The Wise Little Hen." Also included: "Donald and Pluto" (1936), the first cartoon starring Donald; "Don Donald" (1937), which marks the debut appearance of Daisy Duck; "Donald's Nephews" (1938), the cartoon that first introduced Huey, Dewey, and Louie; "Donald's Double Trouble" (1946), a hilarious short in which Donald persuades a suave look-alike to court Daisy in his stead; and "Rugged Bear," an Oscar nominee from 1953.

Volume Ten: Mickey's Crazy Careers. Containing such animated masterpieces as "The Clock Cleaners" (1937), "Magician Mickey" (1937), "Mickey's Fire Brigade" (1935), and "The Band Concert" (1935)—which many cartoon buffs regard as the single greatest Disney short ever made—this first-rate anthology is arguably the finest volume in the *Cartoon Classics* series.

Volume Eleven: The Continuing Adventures of Chip 'n' Dale, Featuring Donald Duck. Seven more cartoons starring the chipmunk tricksters and their fowl-tempered nemesis. Included is the 1949 Oscar nominee, "Toy Tinkers."

---

3. LIMITED GOLD EDITION CARTOON CLASSICS, Seven volumes

1928–59, $29.95 each, 47–52 min. each

Released in the summer of 1984, these classily packaged videotapes were on sale for a limited time only. You can't buy them anymore, but many local video stores still carry rental copies. With one exception *(Disney's Best: The Fabulous '50s)*, each cassette contains seven cartoons plus a brief prologue featuring Walt Disney.

Mickey. The world's most famous rodent is the star of these vintage shorts. Animation buffs will appreciate the inclusion of the historic 1928 sound cartoon, "Steamboat Willie," while children will delight in such classic Mickey Mouse comedies as "Mickey's Grand Opera" (1936), "The Worm Turns" (1937), "Mr. Mouse Takes a Trip" (1940), and "Symphony Hour" (1942).

Minnie. A tribute to Mickey's sweetheart, who made her debut in the 1928 black-and-white cartoon "Plane Crazy," which leads off this program. Also included: "Mickey's Rival" (1936), "The Nifty Nineties" (1941), "First Aiders" (1944), "Bath Day" (1946), "Mickey's Delayed Date" (1947), and "Figaro and Frankie" (1947).

Pluto. Mickey's big-hearted (if slightly slow-witted) mutt is the sweetly befuddled hero of these seven engaging cartoons: "Pluto Junior" (1942), "Pluto at the Zoo" (1942), "Canine Casanova" (1945), "Pluto's House Warming" (1947), "Cat Nap Pluto" (1948), "Pluto's Heart Throb" (1950), and "Wonder Dog" (1950).

Donald Duck. A charming anthology starring the character with the shortest temper and worst elocution in the Disney universe. Probably the best cartoon in this collection is the one least likely to be appreciated by children—the 1939 "The Autograph Hound," which features wonderful, animated caricatures of stars like Clark Gable, Greta Garbo, and the Ritz Brothers. Needless to say, these are names and faces that will mean absolutely nothing to your kids. Still, there's plenty here for them to enjoy, including "Donald's Cousin Gus" (1939), "The Riveter" (1940), "Drip Drippy Donald" (1948), and "The New Neighbor" (1953).

Daisy. A delightful collection of seven vintage cartoons chronicling the rocky romance of those two supremely excitable love birds, Donald and Daisy: "Mr. Duck Steps Out" (1940), "Cured Duck" (1945), "Crazy Over Daisy" (1946), "Dumb Bell of the Yukon" (1946), "Donald's Dilemma" (1947), "Sleepy Time Donald" (1947), and "Donald's Dream Voice" (1948).

Silly Symphonies. Though none of the familiar Disney characters are present in these highly imaginative shorts, children should thoroughly enjoy this cassette all the same. The best of the bunch is probably "The Flying Mouse" (1934), a beautifully animated fable about a young mouse who learns to accept his limitations (there are, however, a few potentially disturbing elements in this cartoon, including a caveful of extremely unpleasant bats). The other selections are: "Birds in the Spring" (1933), "The China Shop" (1934), "The Cookie Carnival" (1935), "Woodland Café" (1937), "The Moth and the Flame" (1938), and "Farmyard Symphony" (1938).

Disney's Best: The Fabulous '50s. A compilation of four slightly longer cartoons, including the 1953 Oscar winner, "Toot, Whistle, Plunk, and Boom," a witty, inventive short—animated in a jazzy, highly stylized manner—which traces the evolution of music from prehistoric days to the present. Also included: "Pigs is Pigs" (an Academy Award nominee in 1954), "Noah's Ark" (1959), and "Lambert, the Sheepish Lion" (1951). Though the last is probably the least interesting in terms of animation and graphic style, young children will probably enjoy this endearing story (about a lion who grows up believing he's a lamb) the most.

4. LIMITED GOLD EDITION II CARTOON CLASSICS, Seven volumes.

(1933–60), $29.95 each, 45–50 min. each

Following the success of the first "Limited Gold Edition" video cassettes, the Disney studio released a second series in the summer of 1985. Once again, these tapes were only on the market for a few months, but rental copies can still be found on the shelves of many neighborhood video shops. The seven titles are:

Disney's Dream Factory. A collection of six "Silly Symphonies" from the thirties—"Old King Cole" (1933), "The Pied Piper" (1933), "Music Land" (1935), "Three Blind Mouseketeers" (1936), "Merbabies" (1938), and "Wynken, Blynken and Nod" (1938).

Donald's Bee Pictures. Seven cartoons chronicling the ongoing battle between the hotheaded Duck and his insect nemesis, Spike the Bee: "Inferior Decorator" (1948), "Honey Harvester" (1949), "Window Cleaners" (1950), "Bee at the Beach" (1950), "Bee on Guard" (1951), "Let's Stick Together" (1952).

From Pluto with Love. The further adventures of Mickey's best friend: "Pluto's Playmate" (1941), "T-Bone for Two" (1942), "Rescue Dog" (1947), "Pluto's Surprise Package" (1949), "Sheep Dog" (1949), "Cold Turkey" (1951), and "Plutopia" (1951).

How the Best Was Won. Of the five outstanding cartoons on this tape, four—"Building a Building" (1933), "Three Orphan Kittens" (1935), "Ferdinand the Bull" (1938), and "Goliath II" (1960)—were Oscar nominees. (Two of them—"Three Orphan Kittens" and "Ferdinand"—won.) Also included: "Funny Little Bunnies" (1934).

Life with Mickey. An entertaining—if somewhat uneven—selection of Mickey Mouse comedies: "Shanghied" (1934), "Mickey's Polo Team" (1936), "Alpine Climbers" (1936), "Mickey's Circus" (1936), "Mickey Down Under" (1948), "R'Coon Dawg" (1951).

An Officer and a Duck. Six cartoons of World War II vintage, dealing with Donald's life as a soldier: "Donald Gets Drafted" (1942), "Vanishing Private" (1942), "Sky Trooper" (1942), "Fall Out" (1943), "The Old Army Game" (1943), and "Home Defense" (1943).

The World According to Goofy. More misguided instruction and inspired silliness from cartoonland's most lovable lunkhead: "Goofy's Glider" (1940), "Baggage Buster" (1941), "How to Be a Sailor" (1944), "They're Off" (1948), "Home Made Home" (1951), "Man's Best Friend" (1952), and "How To Dance" (1953).

DOCTOR DE SOTO AND OTHER STORIES

WESTON WOODS/CC STUDIOS (1985),
$29.95, approx. 40 min.
Preschool–8, ★★★★

This cassette, the first volume in the superb Children's Circle series, contains four wonderfully animated adaptations of award-winning children's books: William Steig's *Doctor De Soto*, H. A. Rey's *Curious George Rides a Bike*, Tomi Ungerer's *The Hat*, and Quentin Blake's *Patrick*.

(See review of *The Children's Circle*.)

DR. SEUSS—THE CAT IN THE HAT/DR. SEUSS ON THE LOOSE

PLAYHOUSE VIDEO (1974), $29.98, 51 min.
Preschool–8, ★★★★

DR. SEUSS—THE LORAX/THE HOOBER-BLOOB HIGHWAY

PLAYHOUSE VIDEO (1974), $29.98, 51 min.
Preschool–8, ★★★★

Dr. Seuss fans of all ages will be delighted with these animated anthologies of classic Seuss stories. Written by Dr. Seuss (Theodore Geisel) himself and coproduced by animation greats Friz Freleng and Chuck Jones, these colorful cartoons are extremely faithful to Seuss's wonderfully idiosyncratic artwork and zanily inventive language. In addition, they contain a number of whimsical songs with lyrics by—you guessed it—Dr. Seuss.

"The Cat in the Hat" is the vintage Seuss fantasy about two housebound young children and the irrepressible, top-hatted trickster who relieves the kids' rainy-day boredom by turning their house upside down. "Dr. Seuss on the Loose" is a mini-collection of three short tales: "The Sneetches," an amusing—and instructive—fable about prejudice; "The Zax," a brief, pointed sketch about the folly of stubbornness; and "Green Eggs and Ham," Seuss's beloved tale of a fellow who obstinately refuses to try a new dish—only to discover, when he finally relents, that he really loves it.

The second Seuss collection contains two stories. In "The Lorax"—a comic fable with a serious, conservationist message—a money-hungry industrialist named the Once-ler ignores the pleas of the title character (a small fuzzy creature who "speaks for the trees") and ends up converting a beautiful country into a dark, polluted wasteland. In "The Hoober-Bloob Highway," the heavenly baby-dispatcher, Mr. Hoober-Bloob, uses a celestial video machine to show a little human-to-be what it means to be alive. It's a charming, warmhearted tale about life's problems and pleasures.

These handsomely produced video cassettes are two of the best children's programs around.

DR. SEUSS FESTIVAL

MGM/UA (1970/1966), $49.95, 48 min.
Preschool–8, ★★★★

This cassette contains two cartoon versions of Dr. Seuss classics, both originally made for TV and directed by former Warner Brothers animation great, Chuck Jones (who is probably best known as the creator of the "Road Runner" cartoons).

"Horton Hears a Who" leads off the program. This is the story of a kindhearted elephant named Horton, who hears a voice coming from a dust speck one day. Discovering that the speck is the home of a race of microscopic beings called Whos, Horton vows to protect them because "a person's a person, no matter how small." The elephant's heroic efforts to save his unseen friends from his nasty jungle neighbors (who think Horton is crazy) form the crux of this genuinely heartwarming story, which is narrated by Hans Conried.

The second cartoon is based on Dr. Seuss's holiday classic "How the Grinch Stole Christmas." Narrated by Boris Karloff, it concerns a mean-spirited creature called the Grinch who decides to spoil Christmas for the inhabitants of Who-ville. Disguising himself as Santa Claus, he sneaks into town on Christmas Eve and makes off with everything connected with the holiday —stockings, gifts, trees, decorations, even the food for the big Christmas feast. Believing that by stealing these goods he has effectively prevented the arrival of Christmas, he stands on a mountain peak above town and eagerly waits for the inhabitants of Who-ville to wake up and discover that Christmas hasn't come. But the next morning, much to his astonishment, he hears sounds, not of sadness, but of joy and celebration coming from the village, and he realizes that Christmas doesn't depend on presents and decorations—that the holiday spirit "doesn't come from a store," but from the heart.

Both these cartoons were coproduced by Dr. Seuss, who also wrote the teleplays. Not surprisingly, they follow the original books very closely. There are, however, a few minor alterations. In "Horton Hears a Who," for example, there is a subplot (not to be found in Seuss's book) about a scientist living on the dust speck who has invented a machine to prove that other worlds exist beyond Who-ville. And "How the Grinch Stole Christmas" contains several slapstick routines between the Grinch and his dog Max that seem much closer in spirit—and style—to Chuck Jones's "Road Runner" cartoons than to Dr. Seuss's book. For the most part, however, this cassette is so entertaining, intelligent, and full of worthy sentiments that only a die-hard Dr. Seuss purist—or a Grinch—would find fault with it.

DOROTHY IN THE LAND OF OZ

FAMILY HOME ENTERTAINMENT (1981),
$29.95, 60 min.

Ages 5–9, ★★★

The feature presentation on this cassette is a slight but charming half-hour cartoon about Dorothy's further adventures in the magical land of Oz. Although the animation is limited, the artwork—and particularly the background scenery—is very pretty and imaginative. And though the story is not especially eventful or exciting, it does feature a few vivid characters, including one—a pumpkinheaded yokel named (appropriately) Jack Pumpkinhead—who is every bit as amusing and colorful as the immortal Cowardly Lion, Tin Woodman, and Scarecrow (who put in cameo appearances).

At the beginning of the story, the Wizard ("played" by Sid Caesar, who also does the voice of a very funny talking mince pie named U.N. Krust) shows up at the farm of Dorothy's Uncle Henry and Auntie Em. It seems that, after returning from Oz, the former wiz has tried—unsuccessfully—to make a career for himself as a fair-ground balloonist. When he inflates his latest masterpiece—a gigantic green balloon in the shape of a turkey—Dorothy and Toto grab hold and are soon blown back over the rainbow and set down in Winkle Country, just west of the Emerald City of Oz. There she meets the lovable bumpkin, Jack Pumpkinhead, who tells her about the new menace that has risen up in the land since the Wicked Witch was destroyed: an evil sorcerer named Tyrone the Terrible Toy Tinker. Tyrone plans to bring an army of lead soldiers to life and use it to conquer all of Oz. In order to accomplish this scheme, however, Tyrone needs Jack's keg of magical "life powder." In what is the only truly dramatic (and potentially frightening) part of the cartoon, Tyrone appears, grabs the magic powder, and uses it to turn Dorothy's silly-looking turkey balloon into a living bird-monster, the Green Gobbler. In the second half of the cartoon, Dorothy and Jack journey to Tyrone's dark fortress, located in a volcanic crater. On the way, they meet a couple of other characters who join them in their quest to defeat Tyrone: Hungry Tiger (who, like his predecessor, the Cowardly Lion, seems ferocious but is really a marshmallow inside) and Tik-Tok, a mechanical wind-up man who plays the Tin Woodman role in this cartoon (though he doesn't have any of the latter's charm or personality). Naturally, things turn out fine at the end. All in all, *Dorothy in the Land of Oz*—which has been recommended by the National Education Association—is a perfectly nice cartoon, capturing much of the appeal of L. Frank Baum's creations.

To give this cassette more substance, its packager has supplemented the main feature with a selection of five old color cartoons. Whoever chose these cartoons must be a student of American animation, since four of them represent significant moments in cartoon history. First, there is the 1939 Warner Brothers cartoon, "Prest-O, Change-O," in which a couple of mutts, running from the dogcatcher, take refuge in a magician's house and have to contend with a wacky rabbit who is the direct forebear of Bugs Bunny. Then there is the 1946 *Terrytoon* cartoon, "The Talking Magpies," which marks the earliest appearance of the characters who were soon to evolve into Heckle and Jeckle. (Parents should note that this cartoon contains a hefty dose of slapstick violence, with the mischievous magpies bashing Farmer

Al Falfa over the head with giant mallets and blasting him in the face with his own double-barreled shotgun.) Also included are the first Casper the Friendly Ghost cartoon and Chuck Jones's influential (and absolutely hilarious) 1942 parody, "The Dover Boys at Pimento University." The only really questionable choice here is the 1936 Max Fleischer cartoon, "The Cobweb Hotel." It's a wonderful piece of animation, and grown-up cartoon buffs will undoubtedly be delighted to see it. But its main character, a monstrous, grotesquely ugly spider who runs a hotel that is really an elaborate fly trap, is scary enough to give nightmares to any child.

DRAW AND COLOR YOUR VERY OWN CARTOONYS RIGHT ALONG WITH UNCLE FRED

PLAYHOUSE VIDEO (1985), $19.98, 60 min.
Ages 4–8, ★★★★

Uncle Fred (the *nom de video* of Fred Lasswell, artist-writer of the *Barney Google* and *Snuffy Smith* newspaper comic strips) is the creator and delightfully endearing host of this first-rate instructional tape. With his oversized red beret, big round eyeglasses, and goofy grin he looks a bit like a cartoony himself. And his playfully silly manner makes everything he does a lot of fun to watch.

What's best about this tape, however, is that kids don't simply sit back and watch it. They become actively, creatively involved with it. Using the simplest of tools—a pencil, a few sheets of paper, and a handful of crayons—Uncle Fred shows them how to draw twenty amusing "cartoonys": whimsical, freehand sketches of subjects that range from the very simple (a daisy, an apple, an elephant's foot) to the slightly more complex (an elephant showering in a lake, a suburban house with a white picket fence, a little boyfriend bringing flowers to his girl). Though the drawings are quite professional and loaded with charm, Uncle Fred's emphasis isn't on producing polished pieces of art. On the contrary, he is constantly urging his audience to keep things "funny and fast," to make their sketches "nice, easy, and breezy." As a result, young viewers come away from this tape not only with some useful knowledge about basic artistic principles (shape, composition, spatial relationships, and so on) but also —and even more important—with a strong sense that artistic creation is a form of exuberant, imaginative play.

In this way, *Draw and Color Your Own Cartoonys* manages to compensate for the major, built-in limitation of most instructional videos. Once you've done the average do-it-yourself tape a few times, there isn't much point in doing it again. But *Draw and Color Your Own Cartoonys* instills lessons that stay with children for a long time after they've exhausted all the projects on the tape. My own children watched this video avidly for a couple of weeks (even my youngest daughter who, at the time, was too small to do the actual art work, loved watching Uncle Fred and trying to guess what pictures were going to emerge from the circles, wiggles, and lines he was putting on screen). Afterwards, my six-year-old continued to apply the principles she'd learned from Uncle Fred to her own original drawings, producing all kinds of funny and imaginative "cartoonys."

This is one of the best interactive videos around for young children. Your kids will have a great time with it—and learn something, too.

DTV—ROCK, RHYTHM & BLUES

WALT DISNEY HOME VIDEO (1984), $29.95, 45 min.
5 and up, ★★★

This Disney take-off on MTV-style music videos is lots of fun. Each of the dozen or so songs on the tape is accompanied by a clever montage of clips from assorted Disney cartoons, which relate (though often tenuously) to the lyrics. As Marvin Gaye and Tammi Terrill sing "Ain't No Mountain High Enough," we see footage of Pluto scaling a snow-covered peak, Mickey piloting a plane over the summit of a mountain, Bongo the Bear perched on the edge of a high cliff, etc. A sequence in which the Big Bad Wolf chases after Goldilocks is set to the Supremes' "Stop! In the Name of Love." Various cartoon couples—Mickey and Minnie, Donald and Daisy, Bambi and Faline—exchange kisses to the tune of Hall and Oates' "Kiss on My List," and so forth.

Setting Disney cartoons to rock music in this way produces some genuinely amusing moments (perhaps the funniest is the footage of the ballerina hippos from *Fantasia*, which is set to the Jackson 5's "Dancing Machine"). The editing here is so ingenious that the cartoons seem to have been animated with these songs in mind.

Buoyant and clever as it is, however, this tape —along with the others in this series—is essentially a novelty item, and doesn't really stand up to repeated viewings. It's certainly worth renting. Your kids will undoubtedly get a kick out of it. But if you're looking for something more substantial and enduring, stick to the original, uncut Disney cartoons (plenty of which have been made available by now).

The other titles in this series are: *DTV—Golden Oldies*, *DTV—Love Songs*, and *DTV—Pop & Rock*.

DUMBO

WALT DISNEY HOME VIDEO (1941), $84.95, 63 min.
Preschool–9, ★★★★

Compared to animated epics like *Pinocchio* and *Snow White and the Seven Dwarfs*, *Dumbo* is a modest, unpretentious movie—but no less charming or affecting for that. In fact, it is one of the best and most moving of all the Disney cartoon features.

The hero is an adorable baby elephant whose freakishly oversized ears make him a laughingstock in the eyes of the other elephants (wittily portrayed as a group of tongue-clucking, middle-aged gossips). Dumbo's mom, Mrs. Jumbo, is lovingly protective of her new baby, and when some obnoxious schoolboys start to taunt him, she becomes enraged and spanks one of them with her trunk. Her anger panics the crowd, and she is subdued, locked up in a boxcar, and branded a "Mad Elephant." Heartbroken and alone, Dumbo is taken under the wing of a friendly mouse named Timothy, who discovers (with the help of some happy-go-lucky crows) that the little elephant has a miraculous power—his ears can function as wings. The story ends with the flying elephant becoming the star of the circus and an international showbiz sensation.

Like most full-length Disney cartoons, *Dumbo* contains its share of potentially upsetting moments. The sight of a baby elephant forcibly kept from his mother plays powerfully on the separation anxieties common to small children. Another scene—in which Dumbo accidentally guzzles down a trough full of liquor and hallucinates a procession of spooky pink elephants—is dazzlingly executed. However, parts of it are genuinely nightmarish. Some viewers also regard the black crows as racist caricatures (though, in fact, they don't seem particularly stereotyped, and—in terms of their wit, good sense, and generosity—they are certainly among the most attractive characters in the film).

All in all, *Dumbo* is a small-scale but big-hearted movie, with a great deal of warmth, humor, and appeal.

DUNDERKLUMPEN

VIDEO GEMS (1979), $39.95, 85 min.
Ages 5–8, ★★★

This sweet-tempered but rather slow-moving fantasy film—a Swedish production dubbed into English —skillfully uses both real and animated characters in a kind of kiddie version of *A Midsummer Night's Dream.* Shot on location on a lovely wilderness lake in the "land of the midnight sun," the movie involves a vacationing family from Stockholm. One magical, midsummer evening, while father and mother relax on the porch, Dunderklumpen—a tubby little cartoon character in coveralls, gold earrings, and a big, floppy hat —sneaks into the children's bedroom and (like Santa Claus in reverse) stuffs a bunch of toys into his backpack and absconds with them. When the stolen toys cry out for help, the father (a bearded bear of a man named Beppe Wogers, who also wrote the story) and his angelic-looking son, Jens, pursue Dunderklumpen into the forest.

And that's about it as far as plot is concerned. Parents who don't like their children exposed to cartoon violence will probably find this movie quite appealing, though others might feel that it goes too far in the opposite direction, since (in spite of a package blurb that describes it as "dazzling" and "exciting") there is very little action of any kind in the film. Dunderklumpen and his kidnapped companions (a rag doll, a teddy bear, a lion, and a rabbit) travel through the woods, where they encounter a number of colorful characters and pause periodically to break into song and dance. The music (composed by jazz great Toots Thielemans) is consistently catchy, and the animated characters are a genuinely enchanting crew. Among the most charming are the childlike Dunderklumpen, who has run off with the toys because he is lonely and wants to be their friend; Dumb-One, a rattle-brained rabbit who might be the first cousin of Lewis Carroll's March Hare; Lionel, a feisty little lion in oversized, polka-dotted boxer shorts; One-Eye, the "rotten, nasty" villain who turns out to be a sensitive guy gone astray; Jorm, a living, tree-covered mountain, who likes nothing better than to curl up in a lake and take a nap; and a nattily dressed, supremely unflappable bee who bears a passing resemblance to Lou Costello and talks like a New York City cab driver.

Although there is a slender story line involving One-Eye and a stolen treasure chest, nothing very dramatic happens. The movie rambles along amiably to a heartwarming conclusion in which One-Eye learns (or rather rediscovers) that life's true treasures are freedom, happiness, and nature. While some children will find this film a pretty slow-going experience, others will be captivated by its endearing cast of animated characters, its sweet humor and entertaining score, and the natural beauty of its wilderness setting.

THE EASTER BUNNY IS COMING TO TOWN

CHILDREN'S VIDEO LIBRARY (1977), $29.95, 60 min.
Preschool–8, ★★½

This slight, rather bland holiday film has its charms, but there's nothing very special about it. Probably its best feature is its likable use of puppet animation. The characters are cute and colorful little puppets, made to seem alive by means of stop-motion photography (a kind of three-dimensional flip-book effect, in which a small figurine is filmed a frame at a time, with slight changes in its position made between each exposure).

The story itself is pretty thin and not very interesting —the kind of thing a parent might make up off the top of his or her head to tell the kids at bedtime. It is narrated by Fred Astaire, who appears in puppet form in the movie as a train conductor on board the Little Engine that Could (what this fabled little locomotive has to do with the story of Easter is anybody's guess). The train is delivering bags of mail to the Easter Bunny—mostly letters asking questions about the origins of various Easter beliefs and rituals: Where does the Easter Bunny come from? Why do we color eggs on Easter? Why are Easter flowers called lilies? and so on. The story that follows—a frothy little fairy tale about a town called Kidville and a clever rabbit named Sunny, who turns out to be the furry mastermind behind the various holiday traditions—is a whimsical (if occasionally strained) attempt to answer these questions. Interspersed throughout the film are some pleasant, if not especially memorable, songs.

On the whole, this film is an almost exact video equivalent of the holiday confections (jelly beans, chocolate rabbits, and the like) that Sunny the Bunny invents: it's a sweet nothing, not intended to stimulate or enrich, but simply made for quick, easy, and mildly pleasant consumption.

THE EMPEROR'S NEW CLOTHES

CBS/FOX VIDEO (1984), $39.98, 60 min.
6 and up, ★★★★

Dick Shawn is pricelessly funny as the supremely vain and self-involved Emperor who cares about nothing but clothes and spends all his time primping before mirrors. This ruler is so smitten with himself (he gives his reflection fond little kisses and eliminates the defense budget so he can spend more money on cummerbunds) that he makes the evil stepmother in "Snow White" look positively self-abasing.

When a couple of roving con artists named Morty and Bo (Art Carney and Alan Arkin) stumble onto one of the emperor's weekly fashion shows—at which the king models his latest outfits before a crowd of down-trodden peasants (whose taxes pay for his wardrobe) —they hit upon a brilliant ploy. Passing themselves off as the greatest tailors in the land, they offer to weave an extraordinary fabric that is invisible to anyone who is either unfit to hold office or hopelessly stupid. Needless to say, when the rascals appear with a wardrobe of invisible clothes, no one—neither the emperor nor any of his hangers-on—is willing to admit that he cannot see a thing. The climactic procession, in which the king, dressed in nothing but red satin bloomers, displays his new clothes to his incredulous subjects, is extremely funny. In the end, Morty and Bo turn out to have a streak of Robin Hood in them (they take the gold they have finagled from the emperor and donate it to the starving peasants). Meanwhile the emperor learns that being a king means more than looking the part.

With its lavish Louis XIV sets and costumes, its outstanding performances by Arkin, Carney, and Shawn, and its clever, amusing script, this delightful dramatization is one of the best shows in the *Faerie Tale Theatre* series.

(See review of *Faerie Tale Theatre* for a description of the series as a whole.)

FABLES OF THE GREEN FOREST

MEDIA (1971), $29.95, 40 min.
Preschool–6, ★★★

This short, engaging film consists of two twenty-minute cartoons featuring characters created by popular children's author Thornton Burgess. What makes this cassette so nice for younger viewers is that it tells interesting, imaginative stories about an endearing bunch of forest creatures who have distinctive, very human personalities. They're not just bland, sugary greeting card characters.

In the first story, "Whose Footprint is That?" a possum named Uncle Billy (who looks and sounds as though he just stepped out of a Pepperidge Farm commercial) develops a powerful hankering for fresh eggs. Sneaking off to Farmer Brown's hen house, he indulges in a prehibernation feast, falls asleep, and awakens to find himself trapped in the coop. How he manages to escape is the crux of this amusing, mildly suspenseful tale. In the second cartoon, "Johnny's Hibernation," Peter Rabbit (a sweet but somewhat dim bunny who seems to have studied with the same voice coach as Bullwinkle) throws a farewell party for his forest friends who are about to go into hibernation. Everything goes smoothly until a couple of uninvited guests (a fox and a weasel) try to crash the party. But it all turns out well in the end.

This movie has none of the shortcomings of so many other kiddie cartoons. The characters—Peter, Uncle Billy, Johnny Chuck, Sammy Jay, Jimmy Skunk and other denizens of the Green Forest—are cute but not cloying. There are no frenetic chases, dumb jokes, or exploding cigars—just a pair of sweet, gently humorous cartoons with the charm of old-fashioned bedtime stories.

Family Home Entertainment also offers a number of one-hour cassettes containing episodes from the *Fables of the Green Forest* cartoon show. Currently available titles include: *The Adventures of Buster the Bear*, *Chatterer the Squirrel*, *Johnny Woodchuck's Adventures*, *The Adventures of Reddy the Fox*, and *Sammy Blue Jay*.

FAERIE TALE THEATRE, 26 volumes

CBS/FOX VIDEO (1982–85), $39.98 each, 60 min. each
6 and up, ★★★–★★★★

The brainchild of actress Shelley Duvall, *Faerie Tale Theatre* was inspired by Duvall's desire to make the classic fairy tales come alive for modern audiences. Enlisting the help of her show business friends—actors, directors, designers—Duvall began producing these hour-long dramatizations in 1982. The resulting programs, originally shown on cable TV and subsequently released on video cassette, have been very popular both with viewers and critics. And deservedly so. These outstanding productions, featuring terrific casts, first-rate scripts, and splendid designs (often inspired by the artwork of classic fantasy illustrators) are among the best children's programs around.

This is not to say that every show is a masterpiece. In attempting to breathe new life into these aged tales, the writers often huff and puff a little too hard. Some of the shows are much too clever and sophisticated for their own good. They possess an irreverent tone that, at times, comes perilously close to parody. Others simply seem strained. Purists object to the liberties that are taken with the material. But folk narratives have been told and retold, modified and adapted, for centuries. To treat them as sacred relics or precious literary antiques is to rob them of their vitality. By retelling these classic tales in terms that are relevant to our age, *Faerie Tale Theatre* is simply doing what good storytellers have always done, which is to adapt their material to their own particular time and place.

In spite of their occasional flaws, the shows in the *Faerie Tale Theatre* do a remarkably good job of capturing the magic, wonder, and deeper emotional meanings of the great fairy tales. Even at their most playful, they remain surprisingly faithful to the shape, texture, and spirit of the stories. They also vary widely in mood and atmosphere. While some possess the cheery, childlike exuberance of a Disney cartoon, others are intensely romantic, and a few are full of the darkness and terror that are also a feature of many fairy tales. One of the best things about these shows is that they are meant to appeal to viewers of all ages, so that parents and children can watch and enjoy them together.

To date, there are twenty-six titles in this series. For descriptions of the individual programs, see the following reviews:

Aladdin and His Wonderful Lamp
Beauty and the Beast
The Boy Who Left Home to Find Out About the Shivers
Cinderella
The Dancing Princesses
The Emperor's New Clothes
Goldilocks and the Three Bears
Hansel and Gretel
Jack and the Beanstalk
The Little Mermaid
Little Red Riding Hood
The Nightingale
Pinocchio
The Pied Piper of Hamelin
The Princess and the Pea
The Princess Who Never Laughed
Puss in Boots
Rapunzel
Rip Van Winkle
Rumpelstiltskin
Sleeping Beauty
The Snow Queen
Snow White and the Seven Dwarfs
The Tale of the Frog Prince
The Three Little Pigs
Thumbelina

FANGFACE

WORLDVISION (1978), $39.95, 44 min.
Ages 6–9, ★½

Fangface (originally a Saturday-morning cartoon series
that ran for a year on ABC in the late 1970s) is a
hopelessly dumb suspense/comedy/horror show—a
kind of animated version of such poverty row pictures
as *Bela Lugosi Meets a Brooklyn Gorilla* and *The
Bowery Boys Meet the Monsters*. As a matter of fact,
two of its main characters—a stocky adolescent named
Pugsy (who speaks Brooklynese) and his lamebrained
sidekick, Fangs (who wears a baseball cap with its brim
turned backwards)—bear a striking resemblance to
Leo Gorcey and Huntz Hall. The main gimmick in this
cartoon is that Fangs is actually a werewolf. When he's
shown a picture of the moon, his eyeballs spin in circles,
smoke spouts from his ears, his face begins to bulge,
and he is transformed into a lovable lycanthrope, who,
when excited, exclaims "Oooo! Oooo!" in the manner
of the immortal Joe E. Ross (Ritzik on the old Phil
Silvers show and Officer Gunther Toody in the late,
still-lamented "Car 54, Where are You?")

Fangface himself is a fairly amusing creation, but he's
the only part of the show that is even remotely appealing. Everything else about it is completely inane. In
each episode (there are three on this cassette), Fangs,
Pugsy, a black girl named Kim, and an all-American
type named Biff get involved in a mystery that features
a Hollywood-style monster. In the first, the gang battles
a blue-skinned, incredible Hulk look-alike called the
Heap. In the second, they are captured by a tribe of
apemen in Viking costumes. The last finds them bat-

tling a revivified mummy. The action is crude and incessant, the animation is cheap, the "humor" is awful. Most offensive is the absolutely mindless use of canned laughter. To pick just one example at random: at one point in the first cartoon, Fangs says, "Pugsy and I are partners." Pugsy replies, "I'd rather be partners with the Heap!" This hilarious witticism is followed by a burst of guffaws from the laugh track.

In short, *Fangface* is an example of Saturday-morning programming at something close to its worst. There's no real excuse for renting it, since the whole point of owning a VCR, if you're a parent, is precisely to offer your children something better than this kind of animated schlock.

THE FANTASTIC ADVENTURES OF UNICO

RCA/COLUMBIA (1983), $39.95, 90 min.
6 and up, ★★

This feature-length cartoon, produced in Japan and skillfully dubbed into English, is exciting, colorful, beautifully animated—and totally unsuitable for young children. Although the hero of the film—the big-eyed baby unicorn, Unico—is, as the announcer says, "cute as cute can be," a number of the other characters border on the grotesque. More seriously, parts of this cartoon are so scary and violent that a number of the children I watched it with sat through whole sections of it with their hands over their eyes.

The story itself is a strange mixture of Greek myths and Grimms' fairy tales. Unico is a small, white-furred creature with a thatch of red hair, a chubby face (more human than horse-like), and the magical ability to make people "lighthearted and happy." Jealous of his gifts, the gods decide to banish him to the dreaded Isle of Oblivion, but the kindhearted West Wind carries him instead to a misty land where he can live without attracting the notice of the gods. Carried off from his mother and set down in the land of mist, Unico encounters the first of the film's exceptionally spooky places: a dark, sinister temple, inhabited by a living statue—a towering stone demon with the wings of a bat, the face of a gargoyle, and a terrifying voice, who begins attacking Unico with lightning bolts (it was at this point that the younger members of my home audience started hiding their eyes).

The second section of the movie finds Unico in the company of a cute black-and-white kitty named Katy, who is looking for a witch to turn her into a human being. Their journey leads them to an enchanted forest straight out of a Grimm Brothers tale, where they arrive at the cottage of a white-haired crone. This old lady, with warts all over her face and an enormous red nose that looks like a diseased salami, is exceptionally unpleasant to look at. Thanks to Unico, Katy gets her wish and is changed into a pretty young woman, though she still retains some of her feline habits. In one particularly stomach-turning scene, she chases a very realistically rendered cockroach across the cottage floor, catches it in her hands, and is about to pop it into her mouth when Unico reminds her that young girls don't snack on bugs.

But the worst is yet to come. Katy is seduced by a dashing young baron, who turns out to be a Bluebeard-like villain. Flying to Katy's rescue, Unico knocks the evil baron off the roof of his castle. The young man plummets through the air and—in a scene that seems more suitable to a *Friday the 13th* movie than a kiddie cartoon—is impaled (quite graphically) on a spire.

This, however, is not the end of the baron. Rising from the spire, he assumes his true shape—a huge, horrific demon—and a dramatic battle ensues. Unico ultimately wins by transforming himself into a magnificent flying white horse, but not before we've been treated to enough shots of the gigantic, tusked fiend to provide impressionable youngsters with a year's supply of nightmares.

Technically, this is a very impressive cartoon. The animation is graceful, rich in detail, and luminously colored. The character of Unico is also very appealing, particularly to young children. But the situations the little creature finds himself in seem grotesquely inappropriate for small viewers.

FAT ALBERT AND THE COSBY KIDS

THORN/EMI (1982), $29.95, 60 min.

6 and up, ★★★

As TV cartoons go, *Fat Albert and the Cosby Kids* is several cuts above average. Instead of shrill gags, frenetic action, and cheap, prefabricated fantasy, it relies on the same qualities that have made Bill Cosby himself such a popular performer: gentle, warmhearted humor, a powerful empathy with children, and a talent for turning the everyday situations of middle class life into the stuff of comedy.

Each of the three cartoons on this cassette follows the same format. Cosby appears at the beginning in a brief live-action prologue that lays out the theme of the cartoon. In the first, the kids (Dumb Donald, Harold, Rudy, Mushmouth, Bucky, Bill and his kid brother Russell, and, of course, Fat Albert) play hooky, with predictably disastrous results. In the second, Bill and Russell are sent to the hospital for tonsillectomies. The final segment finds the kids hero-worshiping a stuck-up teen named Scrap Iron, who treats them with contempt (though he's happy to take advantage of their adoration). Cosby reappears at several points to spell out the message (don't cut school, don't be afraid of hospitals, don't look up to someone who looks down on you), and each cartoon ends with the kids performing a rock song whose lyrics reinforce the moral of the tale. All in all, this is an engaging cassette that does a nice job of teaching kids worthwhile lessons while entertaining them.

There are, however, two problems with this cassette. First, it contains nothing that children can't see all the time on commercial TV (in the New York City area, for example, "Fat Albert and the Cosby Kids" is broadcast daily). Second, these cartoons use canned laughter as mindlessly as the most inane TV sitcom. Considering the care and thoughtfulness that seem to have gone into the making of this show (its closing credits list a three-member "Educational Advisory Panel"), it's surprising that its producers would rely on a device that both cheapens the humor and insults the intelligence of the audience.

Also available: *Fat Albert*, Volumes II and III, two additional cassettes featuring episodes from this popular TV cartoon show. Volumes I and III are an hour long; Volume II runs only 23 minutes.

FELIX IN OUTER SPACE

MEDIA (1984), $29.95, 55 min.
Ages 5–8, ★

FELIX'S MAGIC BAG OF TRICKS

MEDIA (1984), $29.95, 60 min.
Ages 5–8, ★

Two more shoddy collections from the bottom of the TV cartoon barrel. (See review of *The Adventures of Felix the Cat*.)

THE FOOLISH FROG AND OTHER STORIES

WESTON WOODS/CC STUDIOS (1985),
$29.95, approx. 40 min.
Preschool–8, ★★★★

Pete Seeger sings and recites the title story on this thoroughly delightful cassette from the outstanding *Children's Circle* series. (See review of the *Children's Circle*.)

FREE TO BE . . . YOU AND ME

CHILDREN'S VIDEO LIBRARY (1974), $29.95, 44 min.
Preschool–8, ★★★★

Parents should consider it one of their main responsibilities to make sure that their children see this terrific, truly uplifting videotape. A project of the Ms. Foundation for Women, *Free to Be . . . You and Me* consists of a collection of wonderfully entertaining songs, stories, skits, and cartoons that deal with a variety of issues, but that all have the same basic intent—namely, to help kids see the rich possibilities that life has to offer and to encourage them to be everything they are capable of becoming.

With material provided by writers like Lucille Clifton, Dan Greenburg, Carl Reiner, Shel Silverstein, and Charlotte Zolotow, and a stellar cast of performers —including Marlo Thomas, Alan Alda, Harry Belafonte, Mel Brooks, Roberta Flack, Dustin Hoffman, Michael Jackson, Kris Kristofferson, and Dionne Warwick —*Free to Be . . . You and Me* comes with the most impressive credentials of any kiddie tape on the market. And the quality of the results matches the talent of the participants. The program is composed of a bunch of short, consistently delightful segments, each one addressed to a particular childhood concern. A charming duet by Michael Jackson and Roberta Flack, for example, deals with coming to terms with your physical imperfections and being happy with the way you look. Another song, performed by Marlo Thomas and Harry Belafonte, reminds children that mommies and daddies are people, too. It also emphasizes that women can be anything they want to be, from doctors to construction workers. This feminist message is reinforced in a number of the segments. There's a charmingly animated cartoon, for example, about a princess whose father (in the traditional way of fairy-tale kings) wants to hold a contest to see who will win his daughter's hand in marriage. The only trouble is that his daughter isn't so sure she wants to get married—and certainly not before she has a chance to live her own life for a while. Throughout the program, in fact, kids are encouraged to reject the narrowly defined sex roles our culture tries to impose on all of us—boys as well as girls. There's a very amusing cartoon about a little girl who wants nothing more out of life than to be treated like a dainty, "sweet young thing"; she comes to an appropriately bad end when she runs into a pack of hungry tigers who are only too eager to oblige. In another, equally engaging cartoon, Alan Alda narrates the story of a boy named Dudley Pippin, whose dearest wish is to own a doll. Elsewhere on the tape, Rosie Greer —looking mountainous as he perches on a stool and strums a guitar—sings a song that informs little boys that it's okay to cry. Other parts of the program deal with more general issues: the importance of friends, feelings about siblings, the need for interracial harmony.

Free to Be . . . You and Me is, without question, one of the very best videotapes available for kids. Funny, exuberant, wise, and reassuring, it is, in a word, a must-see for children and parents alike.

FRIZ FRELENG'S LOONEY LOONEY LOONEY BUGS BUNNY MOVIE

WARNER (1981), $69.95, 79 min.
5 and up, ★★★

Another feature-length anthology of vintage cartoons linked together with new animation and starring Bugs Bunny, Daffy Duck, Yosemite Sam, Porky Pig, Foghorn Leghorn, and Tweety and Sylvester. (See review of *The Bugs Bunny/Road Runner Movie*.)

THE FROG PRINCE

MUPPET HOME VIDEO (1982), $49.95, 50 min.
Preschool–7, ★★★★

Jim Henson applies his Muppet magic to the famous
fairy tale of "The Frog Prince" and the result, unsurprisingly, is pure enchantment.

The title character is a dashing young man named Sir
Robin the Brave, who has been transformed into a
woebegone little frog by the evil witch Taminella.
Showing up at the pond of Kermit the Frog one
morning, Robin explains that unless he is kissed by a
beautiful princess he will remain a frog forever. (Kermit, slightly incensed, wants to know what's so bad
about being a frog. "When you're a frog, you've got it
all," he cries. "The lily pads, the stagnant water, the
whole quagmire!") Soon afterward, Robin meets a
young princess who has also been bewitched by
Taminella—everything the girl says comes out back-
ward, so that no one can understand a single word.
Meanwhile, Taminella has persuaded the none-too-
bright King Rupert that she is his long-lost sister. With
the princess suffering from her terrible affliction, Taminella is next in line to inherit the kingdom—unless
she can be stopped by the princess, Robin, and
Kermit.

This program is packed with sweetness, wit, and the
Muppets' very special brand of charm. It has a marvelous cast of characters (kids should get a particular kick
out of Taminella's hulking slave, Sweetums), bright,
enchanting settings, and a bunch of delightful songs
(including a hilarious paean to froghood called "It's

Ever So Jolly Just Being a Frog"). Like virtually every Muppet production, this tape can be enjoyed by everyone from preschoolers to grown-ups. It's a pleasure from beginning to end.

FUN AND FANCY FREE

WALT DISNEY HOME VIDEO (1947), $49.95, 76 min.
Preschool–9, ★★★½

Fun and Fancy Free is something of a hodgepodge, an animated feature patched together from various pieces (including an extended live-action sequence starring Edgar Bergen and his famous ventriloquist dummies, Charlie McCarthy and Mortimer Snerd). It doesn't really hold together as a feature, but the individual parts are very entertaining.

Jiminy Cricket is used to string the different segments together. Hopping and singing his way across a living room, the "happy-go-lucky" insect comes upon a pair of sad-looking toys—a teddy bear and a doll. In an effort to cheer them up, he puts on a record called *Bongo the Bear,* a "musical story" narrated and sung by Dinah Shore.

Bongo is the first of the film's two animated featurettes. It's a slight but endearing story (written by Sinclair Lewis) about a circus "wonder bear" who hears the call of the wild one day and escapes from his boxcar into the woods. There he falls in love with a winsome female bear who responds to Bongo's affection by slapping him. Heartbroken, Bongo retreats into the forest, little realizing that a solid slap in the face is a bear's natural way of saying, "I love you." By the time he discovers this fact, his beloved

117

has fallen into the clutches of a towering brute named Lumpjaw. In the end, Bongo defeats his foe in a freewheeling battle and wins the hand of the fair, furry maid.

The film then cuts back to Jiminy, who discovers a birthday invitation lying on a bureau and hops next door, where the festivities are under way. The host turns out to be Edgar Bergen, who is entertaining the rest of the party—the birthday girl, plus Bergen's wise-cracking alter ego, Charlie McCarthy and the sweetly moronic Mortimer Snerd—with a ventriloquist routine. After some humorous banter between Bergen and his puppets, the second of the film's animated segments is introduced, an entertaining version of "Jack and the Beanstalk" starring Mickey Mouse, Donald Duck, and Goofy. This sequence is unquestionably the high point of the film. It's a delightful adaptation, full of thrills, laughs, and classic Disney touches. (The dimwitted villain, Willie the Giant—who seems less like the cannibalistic ogre of the fairy tale than a colossally overgrown baby—is an especially funny creation.)

The whole of this film may be less than the sum of its parts, but the parts are extremely well done. *Fun and Fancy Free* is a very charming movie that kids are sure to enjoy.

THE FURTHER ADVENTURES OF SUPERTED

WALT DISNEY HOME VIDEO (1984), $49.95, 49 min.
5 and up, ★★½

The crime-fighting teddy bear and his spotty companion return in six new adventures (see review of *The*

Premiere Adventures of Superted). All the ingredients that make the first volume of this series so enjoyable are here: colorful stories, classy animation, priceless comedy, and the same unforgettable cast of delightfully oddball characters.

Parents should be warned, however, that, unlike its predecessor, this tape contains two segments that may not be suitable for younger, more impressionable viewers: "Superted and the City of the Dead"—in which a character pries open a sarcophagus lid and a truly terrifying mummy leaps straight out at the viewer—and "Superted at Creepy Castle," which takes place in an eerie Transylvanian setting straight out of a Dracula movie.

On the whole, this second collection of Superted cartoons is every bit as intelligent and entertaining as the first. In certain ways, it is better (the artwork, for example, is even more sumptuous). Unfortunately, it can't be given a wholehearted recommendation, since some children may well find themselves sitting through stretches of it with their hands over their eyes.

THE GIGGLESNORT HOTEL, Vols. 1–7

KARL-LORIMAR HOME VIDEO (1975–77),
$39.95 each, 60 min. each
Preschool–7, ★★★

Young children will be amused by these tapes—and even learn a few things from them. The Gigglesnort Hotel is a ramshackle establishment, owned by a crusty old fellow named Captain Gigglesnort and inhabited by a colorful crew of charming puppets. There is Dirty Dragon, the coal-eating, smoke-breathing janitor; a zany bellhop, Weird, who looks like the first cousin of

Tweedledum and Tweedledee; a hillbilly buzzard named Maynard; a living lump of clay called Blob (whose girlfriend is a statue of Florence Nightingale), and a bunch of other lovable characters. The only human in the show is the affable hotel manager, Bill Jackson (the creator of the series), who mans the desk, operates the switchboard, and does his best to deal with the swirling craziness around him.

Each cassette contains two half-hour episodes that revolve around various themes and are designed to offer both entertainment and low-key instruction. In "Fire Safety," for example, Dirty Dragon and his girlfriend, Layla, go out on a date to a Godzilla movie, come home for a Kerosene Fizz nightcap, and become locked in a goodnight kiss that fills the hotel with smoke. This comical situation serves as the occasion for some basic fire safety lessons. Another episode, "Puppy Parenthood," deals with the responsibilities of pet care. Perhaps the funniest segment is "Tender is the Man," in which the male puppets become obsessed with a TV detective named Harry Bigshoulders and start emulating their idol by acting like male chauvinist pigs. "Let's go out in the street and swagger," Dirty cries. Blob decides to bring his date a football instead of a bouquet of flowers, and Maynard goes home and forces his girl to watch pro wrestling on TV. The women respond to this mistreatment by forming a club, whose motto is "Shoving people around isn't acting like a real man; it's acting like a jerk." In the end, Dirty and his pals learn their lesson: that real masculinity means the ability to be sturdy, strong—and tender.

The sets in this show are simple but amusing (the fire extinguisher on the wall of the hotel lobby is a giant, squirting lapel flower), the puppets are very endearing, and the lessons are communicated in an understated but effective way. The humor itself ranges from the relatively sophisticated to the hopelessly silly. In one

120

episode, Weird—who has been told that he can have a pet as long as it doesn't "get out of hand"—solves the problem by adopting a giant foot. This is the sort of gag five-year-olds find hilarious (even if it seems totally inane to anyone past first grade).

This is far from a great kiddie cassette but it's a very likable one, offering sweet laughs and some simple but important messages.

G.I. JOE: A REAL AMERICAN HERO

FAMILY HOME ENTERTAINMENT (1983), $39.95, 100 min.
5 and up, ★★½

This feature-length cartoon—yet another animated spin-off of a hot-selling line of toys—is the Saturday-morning TV equivalent of a movie like *Indiana Jones and the Temple of Doom* or *The Road Warrior*. It is a hyperkinetic, high-velocity, action film consisting entirely of nonstop, slam-bang action. For what it is, it's very well done, and it's easy to see why young boys in particular would find it extremely exciting. Though the animation is limited, there's nothing stiff or plodding about it. On the contrary, this cartoon never moves at anything less than full blast. If you're looking for something sweet and edifying, you won't find it here. *G.I. Joe* doesn't pretend to be anything but what it is: a state-of-the-art, kiddie-level zap-'em-up, with all the flash, fireworks, and speed (and educational value) of a supercharged video game.

The original G.I. Joe action figure was a two-fisted, all-American dogface. In our age of commando chic, however, he has undergone a transformation into a paramilitary type named Duke, who leads "America's daring, highly trained, special mission force"—code-named "G.I. Joe"—in a never-ending battle against the "ruthless terrorist organization" known as Cobra. In this movie, the evil masterminds of Cobra—the blank-faced Cobra Commander and the sinister Destro, a heavily muscled individual with a metallic head and the voice of Darth Vader—attempt to take over the world with something called a M.A.S.S. device, which can shoot dissolving beams anywhere in the world. To foil this fiendish plot, the G.I. Joe team has to build its own M.A.S.S. device, which requires Duke and his assorted sidekicks—Snake Eyes, Tripwire, Stalker, Short Fuse, Scarlet, Torpedo, and about two dozen others—to locate the rare "catalytic elements" that fuel the machine. This rather rudimentary plot is simply an excuse for stringing together a continuous series of air battles, commando attacks, underwater clashes, and armored assaults—all featuring lots of high-tech, futuristic weaponry. The fighting begins in the first sixty seconds with a screaming sneak attack on the G.I. Joe air base and it doesn't quit until the climactic assault on Cobra Castle. The action is incessant and moves all across the globe, from mountain to jungle, polar region to volcanic plain. There are battles with robot warriors, giant tube worms, Indian gladiators, polar bears, and, of course, with Cobra's vast and faceless army of blue-suited storm troopers.

This cassette has one undeniable virtue: it's much less sexist than, say, the average *Strawberry Shortcake* cartoon. Though most of the interracial G.I. Joe team members are men, there are a few female heroes among them, most prominently, a crossbow-carrying redhead named Scarlet, who plays an important role in the film. Essentially, this G.I. Joe cassette is a cross between *Star Wars* and *The A-Team* (as in the latter, there is a very high level of violence here, though no one ever gets killed or even hit with one of the endless rounds of ammunition fired off in the course of the fighting). If action, adventure, and lots of excitement are what you're looking for in a kiddie cartoon, this tape has them all. On the other hand, if you are opposed to either animated violence or the highly questionable new practice of using flashy cartoons to peddle merchandise to children, you won't find much of value here.

Also available: *G.I. Joe: A Real American Hero —The Revenge of Cobra* ($39.95, 99 mins.). In addition, Family Home Entertainment has released five half-hour *G.I. Joe* episodes, selling for $14.95 apiece: *Countdown for Zartan, Red Rockets Glare, Hi-Freak, Cobra Stops the World,* and *Satellite Down.*

GOLDEN BOOK VIDEOS

GOLDEN BOOK VIDEO (1985),
$9.95 each, 30 min. each
Preschool–6, ★★★

See review of *Three Richard Scarry Animal Nursery Tales.*

GOLDILOCKS AND THE THREE BEARS

CBS/FOX VIDEO (1983), $39.98, 60 min.
6 and up, ★★★

In spite of some entertaining performances by Alex Karras, Hoyt Axton, John Lithgow, and Tatum

O'Neal, this comical version of "Goldilocks and the Three Bears" is one of the least successful of the *Faerie Tale Theatre* productions. The problem is the script. At their best, the programs in this series manage to breathe new life into familiar folk tales by infusing them with a modern sensibility. At times, this approach produces some jarring anachronisms, but, on the whole, it works very well. The problem with this particular program is not that it tampers with the tale of Goldilocks, but rather that the changes it makes in the story don't add anything new, interesting, or meaningful to it. It's a jokey adaptation with a bunch of strained jokes.

Tatum O'Neal, outfitted in a glaringly phony wig of heavy blond curls, is convincingly real as the spoiled, petulant title character, who is given to sneaking off into the woods when she should be home doing her schoolwork. Carole King, extremely wan as Goldilocks's mother, spends her days sewing a needlepoint sampler that reads, "My Life is a Tapestry" (an allusion to King's hit album of the 1970s and the kind of adult in-joke that is a hallmark of *Faerie Tale Theatre*). John Lithgow is incapable of giving a bad performance, but he's basically wasted here as Goldilocks's dad, who does nothing but sit on his porch swing reading lurid stories from the local scandal sheet.

The heart of the fairy tale—Goldilocks's experiences inside the home of the three bears—occupies about ten minutes of story time. To fill up the rest of the hour, the writers have come up with an uninspired continuation of the tale, in which Goldilocks moves in with the bears and is tracked down by a park ranger (Hoyt Axton). A good deal of time is taken up with glimpses of the bear family at work and play. Alex Karras's Poppa Bear (here named Lardo) is a lovable lug who resembles a walking shag carpet, and his wife and son, Cubby, are equally appealing. But their springtime activities—such as opening a roadside honey stand—aren't particularly interesting to watch.

All in all, this video cassette, though mildly charming, falls surprisingly flat. Of course, even the worst *Faerie Tale Theatre* productions have things to recommend them: ingenious costumes and wonderful sets (the production design of this program is based on the artwork of Norman Rockwell), first-rate casts, and interesting (if uneven) attempts to make age-old stories come alive for modern audiences. For the most part, however, this "Goldilocks" is a disappointment.

(See review of *Faerie Tale Theatre* for a description of the series as a whole.)

GONZO PRESENTS MUPPET WEIRD STUFF

PLAYHOUSE VIDEO (1985), $59.95, 57 min.
Preschool and up, ★★★½

The Great Gonzo is the host of this antic collection of classic bits from TV's hugely popular "Muppet Show" series. (See review of *Jim Henson's Muppet Video*.)

GREAT EXPECTATIONS

VESTRON (1978), $59.95, 72 min.
8 and up, ★★½

This Australian-produced animated feature, part of Vestron's *Charles Dickens Collection*, sticks close to the details of the original novel. All the major characters are here: the young hero Pip; his childlike brother-in-law Joe; Miss Havisham, the half-crazed old maid who was abandoned by her lover on her bridal night; her lovely but coldhearted protégé, Estella; Abel Magwitch, the convict-with-a-heart-of-gold; and more.

Everything, in fact, is here—except the heart and soul of Dickens's book. Watching this well-intentioned film is less like seeing a video dramatization of the original novel than an animated book report that offers up the bare bones of the story but can't begin to duplicate the experience of actually reading it. Dickens is a classic writer precisely because the world he creates is so rich, intense, and full of life—packed with drama, humor, pathos, mystery, and wonder. His novels are peopled with the most vividly drawn cast of larger-than-life characters in literature.

Animated in a stiff, flat, uninteresting style, this earnest but dull cartoon remains faithful to the plot of *Great Expectations* while draining all the life out of the story. Pip's growth from childhood to young manhood is traced in a dutiful but monotonous way, and all the melodramatic things that happen to him end up seeming pretty ordinary, if not downright boring. The unfortunate result of exposing young children to Dickens in this form is that it might well reinforce their notion that literary classics are dry, tedious, and moth-eaten works that no one would ever read for pleasure.

With so many mindless cartoons around, it's hard to be too disapproving of an animated movie as well-meaning and intelligent as this one. Clearly, this is the sort of cartoon that deserves high marks for its good intentions. But I'm afraid that it can't be wholeheartedly recommended. In the end, it might actually do a disservice to Dickens, since it's hard to believe that the experience of seeing this film would make any child eager to read his novels.

The other titles in this series are: *David Copperfield, Oliver Twist, A Tale of Two Cities, The Old Curiosity Shop, The Pickwick Papers, Nicholas Nickleby,* and *A Christmas Carol.*

GUMBY'S INCREDIBLE JOURNEY

FAMILY HOME ENTERTAINMENT (1956),
$29.95, 60 min.
Preschool–9, ★★★½

The title—*Gumby's Incredible Journey*—is misleading, since it suggests that this cassette is a single, continuous story. In reality, it is one of several video collections culled from the old "Gumby" television show. Although movie and TV special effects have come a long way since these charming little films were made in the late 1950s (Gumby was first introduced on the "Howdy Doody Show" in 1956 and later starred in his own Saturday-morning series), there is still something magical about the way Gumby, his horse Pokey, and the rest of the little clay figurines who make up the cast are brought to life. (The technique used to make them move is known as stop-motion animation or "pixillation," which consists of shooting the figures a few frames at a time, while changing their positions slightly between each exposure.)

Indeed, everything about these colorful, animated shorts—their sets, characters, and stories—is enchanting. Gumby inhabits a child's dream world—a land of living toys where the electric trains run by themselves, marionettes move without strings, and race cars zoom around a scale model track driven by teddy bears and a pair of bad-tempered alphabet blocks. When Gumby gets bored, he simply steps inside a book and enters an adventure. In the first episode, for example (there are ten altogether on this cassette), Gumby—fed up with being bossed around by his parents—escapes into a book called *Small Planets* and finds himself piloting a rocket ship to an asteroid belt. Other adventures take him to a medieval castle, a western farm, and an enchanted forest, where he learns a lesson about wildlife conservation from a wise old owl.

Unlike so many kiddie TV shows, the Gumby adventures are refreshingly nonformulaic. Though the story lines are simple, they are extremely varied. It's clear that the creators of this series were people with exceptionally fresh and fertile imaginations. Perhaps the most enchanting episode of all is "Too Loo," in which an adorable pair of musical notes escape from a record (they are tired of going round in circles) and go off in search of their original home, while a nasty Sour Note (who looks like a big green spider) pursues them on a flying LP. This cassette also contains two "Gumby Specials," starring a lovable hillbilly bear named Henry and his bird buddy, Roger.

Although they are thirty years old, these wonderfully crafted little films don't seem dated at all. On the contrary, at a time when so many video cassettes consist of superslick, prefabricated cartoons about battling robot-vehicles from outer space and cutesy-pie, greeting-card characters, the "Gumby" shorts seem more charming and truly magical than ever.

To date, Family Home Entertainment has released ten hour-long video anthologies of "Gumby" shorts. Available titles include: *A Gumby Summer, Gumby for President, Gumby's Holiday Special, Gumby Rides Again, A Gumby Celebration,* and *A Gumby Adventure,* Vols. 1–4.

HAMBONE & HILLIE

THORN/EMI (1984), $69.95, 97 min.
8 and up, ★★★

This well-made canine adventure film is like a *Benji* movie for slightly older children. The star is an adorable, shaggy, brown mutt named Hambone, who is the beloved companion of an elderly woman, Hillie Radcliffe (Lillian Gish). As the movie opens, Hillie and Hambone are at New York's Kennedy Airport, about to return to Los Angeles after a visit with Hillie's grandchildren. "Hammy" is placed in a pet carrier and Hillie boards the plane. When a little girl opens the door of Hammy's case, the pooch dashes after his mistress, but arrives at the gate just as the plane is taking off. The rest of the film concerns the adventures that befall the determined doggie as he makes the 3,300-mile odyssey back to his home.

The film is consistently well photographed. It is full of pretty—and occasionally gritty—American landscapes. (One of the admirable things about this movie is that it doesn't pretend that all Americans live in white clapboard houses on lovely, tree-lined streets. When Hammy travels through the inner cities, he actually comes upon derelicts, drunks, and even a garbage can full of rats. The film doesn't rub the audience's nose in squalor, but it does present a more realistic and varied picture of modern American society than most movies of its kind.) In terms of plot, however, the film is somewhat uneven. As Hammy travels across the country, he has a string of encounters, some dramatic, some touching, some suspenseful

—and a few that are totally pointless. For example, an early episode in which he is picked up by a trucker named Tucker (O.J. Simpson) falls completely flat. Nothing happens in it. Tucker talks to Hammy for a while, then the dog trots away. Even more surprising is a sequence in which Hammy is adopted by a crippled girl named Amy. This episode seems ripe with emotionally charged possibilities, but none of them are developed. Hammy simply hangs around for a few days, then moves on. (In general, the sequences that are meant to be heartwarming are the weakest in the film.)

On the other hand, many parts of the movie are very well done. The opening sequence in which Hammy is chased through the TWA terminal by a bunch of attendants is both funny and exciting, as is a sequence set in the Rocky Mountains, where the indomitable pooch is pursued by a pack of wolves and escapes by darting through the legs of a bear. A few episodes are genuinely moving, especially one in which a canine friend of Hammy's is run over by a car.

Parents should be advised that the film contains two extended, highly dramatic episodes that contain some potentially disturbing (and, in one case, very extreme) violence. In the first, Hammy is dognapped by a creep named Lester, who sells stolen animals to a vivisection lab. At one point, Lester administers a very brutal beating to a dog named Scrapper, who has come to Hammy's rescue. The second episode is the most tense and suspenseful in the movie, but it seems totally out of place. In it, Hammy is adopted by an Arizona sheriff with a very pregnant wife. When the sheriff is called away on an emergency, three escaped convicts, out for revenge, break into his house. One ends up skewered with a pitchfork, the second is killed by a guard dog, and the third is blasted by the wife, who whips out a .357 magnum from under her pillow just as she is going into labor. This sequence is exciting, all right, but it seems like a segment from *Sudden Impact* that accidentally got spliced into this film.

HANSEL AND GRETEL

CBS/FOX VIDEO (1982), $39.98, 60 min.
6 and up, ★★★½

Of all the classic fairy tales, "Hansel and Gretel" is the scariest. This tale of a young brother and sister who are abandoned in the woods and fall into the clutches of a cannibalistic witch is the first horror story most children are exposed to (in essence, "Hansel and Gretel" is simply the kindergarten equivalent of a movie like *Friday the 13th,* which is also about some youngsters who venture into the woods and meet up with a monstrous mother-figure.)

Unlike many other entries in the award-winning *Faerie Tale Theatre* series, this visually striking production plays it straight. In place of flip humor and broad comedy, we get a serious, straightforward dramatization of the tale. The results are a little uneven, but for the most part, this video retelling does an excellent job of capturing the magic—and terror—of the original tale. What makes this program work as well as it does are two terrific performances, both by Joan Collins, who appears as both the wicked stepmother and the child-devouring witch. As the former, she is the essence of manipulative, maternal treachery, using every weapon at her disposal—from guilt to sex—to persuade her weak-willed husband to dispose of his children. As the grotesque witch, she is a child's nightmare brought to life. With her hooked nose, warty chin, rotted yellow teeth, and cadaverous complexion, she is a truly terrifying vision. And her panting hunger for the flesh of young children is every bit as disquieting as her looks. (In one highly unsettling sequence, she cooks a plump little boy she's been fattening up for a few weeks, then mixes his heart into some batter and turns him into a life-size gingerbread cookie).

The other performances in this show don't begin to match Joan's. The kids (Ricky Schroeder and a newcomer named Bridgette Andersen) are sweet to look at but exceptionally wooden, and Paul Dooley turns in an uncharacteristically lifeless performance as the wishy-washy father. But the production—filmed in a park forest and featuring a terrific-looking gingerbread cottage—is a visual treat. All in all, this is an excellent adaptation of the classic tale, with a satisfyingly upbeat ending (the witch gets her just desserts and her previous victims are restored to life). Still, many children are (understandably) averse to scary-looking, cannibal witches under any circumstances. If yours is one of them, this probably isn't the best tape for him or her.

(See review of *Faerie Tale Theatre* for a description of this series as a whole.)

HEIDI

CBS/FOX VIDEO (1937), $59.95, 88 min.
Ages 6–9, ★★★½

Essentially, this first-rate production is a vehicle for filmdom's most famous child star, Shirley Temple (there's even an interpolated dream sequence in which the curly-haired little moppet gets to sing and dance in various adorable costumes). On the whole, however, it's a generally faithful adaptation of the classic story. Indeed, of all the available versions, this one comes closest to capturing the charm and emotional power of the original book.

A large part of its success has to do with the sweetness of its star. To grown-ups, Shirley Temple may seem a bit cloying, but young children are sure to find her as cute as a Care Bear. Adding to the film's effectiveness is a moving performance by Jean Hersholt as Heidi's brooding, reclusive grandfather, who is redeemed from his isolation and bitterness by the little girl's love. The technical qualities of the film also contribute significantly to its appeal. Though filmed in black-and-white, the movie is very handsomely produced, with lavish sets and beautifully painted backdrops that conjure up a completely enchanting, picturebook image of the Swiss Alps.

The most powerful part of the film comes at the very end. Heidi has been spirited away to Frankfurt to serve as the playmate of a wealthy young invalid. Unable to stand being separated from his grandchild any longer, Grandfather travels to the city to search for her. Arriving on Christmas night, he roams through the snow-covered streets, calling out Heidi's name. Heidi, meanwhile, has fallen into the clutches of the vicious governess, Fraulein Rottenmeier, who intends to sell the helpless girl to a sinister gypsy. Young viewers are sure to be in an agony of suspense throughout this sequence, particularly when Grandfather is thrown into jail by the police for disturbing the peace and things appear to be totally hopeless. This highly melodramatic episode has no basis in the original book, but it's completely irresistible.

When it comes to laying on the sentimentality, this classic film version of *Heidi* is completely shameless. It's a real junior-level tearjerker. But for that very reason it remains one of the most affecting—and popular—children's movies ever made.

HEIDI

PACIFIC ARTS (1975), $39.95, 90 min.
Ages 5–8, ★★★

Johanna Spyri's classic Swiss tale about a lovable little
orphan girl who goes to live in the mountains with her
reclusive grandfather has been adapted for the movies a
number of times. This feature-length cartoon is a sweet
but somewhat unimaginative version. It's faithful to the
story line, though it only hints at the charms of the
original book.

The first part of the movie concerns Heidi's happy
life on the mountaintop, where she quickly wins the
heart of her formidable grandfather (known to everyone as Uncle Alp) and establishes an idyllic friendship
with a young goatherd named Peter. When her Aunt
Detie takes her off to Frankfurt to be the companion of
a wealthy young invalid named Clara (whose governess
is an extremely nasty old battle-ax, aptly named Miss
Rottenmeier), Heidi begins to pine for home. Terribly
lonely, she is allowed to return to her beloved mountaintop. In the end, Clara comes for a visit and, with
the help of Heidi, Peter, and Uncle Alp, the invalid girl
makes a miraculous recovery.

This cartoon definitely has its charms: the animation
is simple but engaging (the Alpine scenery is particularly well done), and Heidi herself—a bouncy, round-
faced little cherub with a ready laugh and an irresistible
smile—is cute without being cloying. And the climax of
the story, in which Clara regains the use of her legs,
achieves real emotional power. True, the rest of the
cartoon falls a little flat. Still, this is a perfectly pleasant
and decently made cartoon. It isn't as entertaining as

the original book (or as the 1936 movie starring Shirley Temple, which is also available on video cassette). But for children too young to read *Heidi* for themselves, it makes a nice introduction.

HEIDI

VESTRON (1968), $69.95, 105 min.
Ages 7–10, ★★★

Produced for network television (the periodic blackouts for commercial breaks are still very much in evidence), this classy, live-action version of Johanna Spyri's classic has a great deal going for it. It features a script by Earl Hamner, Jr. (who later gained fame as the creator of "The Waltons"), spectacular scenery (much of the film was shot on location in the Swiss Alps), and a stellar cast, including Maximilian Schell, Jean Simmons, Walter Slezak, and—best of all—Sir Michael Redgrave in the key role of Heidi's stern, embittered grandfather. Given all these advantages, it's surprising that this movie isn't better than it is.

Heidi purists will undoubtedly object to the liberties that have been taken with the story. Perhaps the most glaring revision is the transformation of the heartless governess, Mrs. Rottenmeier, into a sensitive, loving, and glamorous woman, played by the beautiful Jean Simmons. This change is accompanied by a major (though largely uninteresting) addition to the story line—a burgeoning love affair between Miss Rottenmeier and her sensitive, loving, and glamorous employer, Herr Sesemann (father of the young invalid, Clara), played by Maximilian Schell. Besides robbing the story of much of its dramatic tension and pathos (without a mean Miss Rottenmeier to make her life miserable,

Heidi's unhappiness in Clara's home has much less impact), the added romantic subplot detracts from the true emotional center of the story: the redemption of Heidi's grandfather through the little girl's love. In this version, in fact, the scenes on the mountainside take a back seat to the goings-on in the Sesemann household. This is a particular pity since the single finest thing about this production is Michael Redgrave's moving and powerful performance as Heidi's imposing grandfather. Another weakness of this film is, unfortunately, the colorless acting of the little girl who plays the title role. She looks the part, but she seems utterly devoid of personality.

This *Heidi* is definitely a disappointment. Still, it has enough real virtues to make it a worthwhile video for slightly older viewers.

HEIDI'S SONG

WORLDVISION (1980), $49.95, 90 min.
5 and up, ★★★½

Heidi's Song represents an effort by William Hanna and Joseph Barbera (the kings of the cut-rate, Saturday-morning cartoon show) to produce a full-blown, Disney-style animated feature. Surprisingly, they end up doing a very creditable job. In terms of its technical qualities, this cartoon isn't on a par with even the weakest Disney feature, but its deficiencies seem less serious on the small screen.

In its broad outlines, *Heidi's Song* follows Johanna Spyri's classic tale about the lovable little orphan girl who wins the heart of her grouchy grandfather (whose voice is nicely performed by Lorne Greene), then is taken to Frankfurt to live in the home of the wealthy young invalid, Clara. This story line is filled out with lots of songs, comic skits, and a bunch of episodes inspired more by Disney films like *Snow White* and *Cinderella* than Spyri's original book. For example, after being cruelly mistreated by Clara's nasty governess, Heidi retreats to the basement, where she falls down weeping. Seeing her unhappiness, a cute little owl named Hooty flies off to tell Heidi's friend Peter, who gathers a bunch of animal friends together and zooms down the mountainside to her rescue. There's nothing remotely like this in the book, but it's a rollicking episode that kids are sure to enjoy.

Consistently entertaining and handsomely produced, *Heidi's Song* features richly detailed artwork, radiant colors, lively songs, vivid characters (including several Disney-style villainesses), lots of cute, funny animals, and several highly imaginative musical numbers, including an elaborate Las Vegas routine performed by a chorus of rats. (Sammy Davis, Jr. supplies the voice of their leader, Head Ratte). There's another way in which *Heidi's Song* resembles a Disney movie: it contains a number of scenes that might well be disturbing to younger viewers. The scariest is Heidi's dream of a midnight jamboree with a bunch of bizarre-looking forest spirits—a dream that turns into a nightmare when a mountain assumes the shape of a towering monster and begins to pursue her.

All in all, *Heidi's Song* is a surprisingly well-made and highly enjoyable cartoon that (in spite of its limited animation) really does simulate the look and feel of an old-fashioned Disney movie.

HE-MAN AND THE MASTERS OF THE UNIVERSE, Vols. 1–11

RCA/COLUMBIA (1982–84), $24.95 each, 50 min. each
Ages 4–9, ★★

In the good old days, one way that toy companies made money was by manufacturing dolls modeled after popular cartoon characters like Felix the Cat and Mickey Mouse. Nowadays, the process is reversed, with Hollywood animation factories cranking out cartoons based on hot-selling toys. Filmation's *He-Man* cartoons are probably the most notable example of this phenomenon. He-Man and the Masters of the Universe (for the information of adults who have spent the last couple of years vacationing in Siberia) are a bunch of brawny, mostly male "action figures" that are tremendously popular with young children, primarily with boys between the ages of four and eight. As of January, 1985, the Mattel Company had sold more than 60 million Masters of the Universe toys, which means you'd be hard pressed to find an American male under the age of nine who hasn't spent at least some of his time playing with one or more of these muscle-bound little dolls. The toys themselves have a lot to recommend them: they are colorful, sturdy, imaginative. They're perfect for the kind of elaborate, make-believe adventure games young children love to play.

The cartoons are another matter. Set in the mythical world of Eternia, they are kiddie versions of Conan the Barbarian, in which the mighty He-Man and his band of warrior comrades do endless battle with the minions of the evil lord, Skeletor. Though the He-Man cartoons make an honest effort to avoid gratuitous violence and to provide uplifting, moral messages (according to the closing credits, a Ph.D. named Donald F. Roberts serves as the series' "Educational and Psychological Consultant"), they are, for the most part, pretty unsatisfying fare. This is a pity, since *He-Man* is one of the highest-rated children's shows in the country, with an audience of around nine million young viewers.

One problem—endemic to made-for-TV cartoon shows—is simply the quality of the animation, which is crude, stilted, and highly repetitious. Every time He-Man (who looks less like a mythic hero than a pumped-up version of the kid on the "Dutch Boy" paint cans) throws a punch or holds aloft his power-sword and recites the magic incantation that is the source of his superhuman abilities, the exact same bits of animation are used. The fact that this kind of corner-cutting is the only economically feasible way of producing cartoons for TV (the kind of full-motion animation done, for example, by the Disney studio is enormously expensive and time-consuming) is irrelevant. What matters is that the resulting TV shows have a flat, mechanical, soulless quality. They look like badly drawn comic books, and the characters are about as lifelike as the cardboard dolls in a cut-out book.

The simple-minded way *He-Man* handles moral issues also leaves a lot to be desired. While many parents and educators approve of the uplifting messages tacked onto the end of each show, the fact is that these mini-sermons generally have so little to do with the stories themselves that it's hard to imagine that viewers really learn anything from them. For example, a show in which the evil Skeletor forces an army of kindly fire-breathing dragons to attack Castle Grayskull— and which consists of twenty-five typically mind-numbing minutes of nonstop action—concludes with a little speech about the importance of being kind to animals.

Each of these "volumes" of *He-Man* cartoons contains two TV episodes minus the commercials. Why parents would be interested in renting or purchasing these tapes when *He-Man* is broadcast every day (and in some places twice daily) virtually everywhere in the country is an interesting question. There isn't anything especially harmful about *He-Man* cartoons (though there is growing concern about the way such TV shows serve as half-hour commercials for the toys they are based on), but if you are going to the trouble to rent something for your kids, there are lots of better choices.

HE-MAN AND THE MASTERS OF THE UNIVERSE: THE GREATEST ADVENTURES OF THEM ALL

RCA/COLUMBIA (1983), $24.95, 60 min.
Ages 4–9, ★★

Don't be fooled by the cover blurb, which describes this cassette as an "action-packed, feature-length film." It's action-packed, all right, but it's really just a trio of episodes from the *He-Man* TV show, linked together with a little newly animated material in which the Sorceress takes the audience on a guided tour of the art gallery in Castle Grayskull. Each of her magical "living paintings" is a portrait of one of the Masters of the Universe—Skeletor and his evil minions, He-Man and his heroic friends. This rather lame device (copied, apparently, from *The Bugs Bunny/Road Runner Movie*) serves as a lead-in to the three recycled *He-Man* cartoons.

The subtitle of this cassette—"The Greatest Adventures of Them All"—is also misleading, since these cartoons are no better, worse, or in any way distinguishable from the adventures contained on the other *He-Man* volumes.

THE HOBBIT

SONY (1977), $34.95, 76 min.
6 and up, ★★★

J.R.R. Tolkien's famous fantasy books—his three-part epic, *The Lord of the Rings* and its slightly more whimsical prelude, *The Hobbit*—are among the most engrossing and richly imagined wonder-tales ever written. Several attempts have been made to turn them into animated features, but the results have been mixed. This handsome, made-for-TV cartoon lacks the power and charm of the original book. Still, it's an above-average production, full of engaging characters, magical settings, and heroic doings.

Set in Tolkien's colorful dream world, Middle-earth, the story is a traditional hero's quest. Its hero is Bilbo Baggins, a diminutive, roly-poly fellow with oversized, furry feet and a taste for domestic comfort. One day, Bilbo is visited by a white-bearded wizard named Gandalf and a company of dwarves, who invite him along on an adventurous journey to recover a legendary treasure from a fire-breathing dragon named Smaug. Along the way, the travelers must contend with bestial trolls, bloodthirsty goblins, giant spiders, and a hissing, repulsive being named Gollum. A number of these creatures—particularly Gollum, who has the cadaverous look of a dead, decaying frog—might give younger viewers a few serious chills.

Although the animation here is limited, the artwork

141

is richly detailed and quite elegant. There are also some good voice characterizations by John Huston, Orson Bean, Hans Conreid, Richard Boone, and others. This cartoon doesn't ignite the imagination the way the book does, but it's a lovingly made and generally faithful adaptation that children should enjoy watching repeatedly.

Hurray for Betty Boop

WARNER (1980), $39.98, 81 min.
Ages 5–8, ★½

Animation buffs who see this video cassette are sure to be outraged by it. Children are only likely to be totally baffled and bored to tears. This horrendously misconceived effort is a feature-length film patched together from snippets of vintage Betty Boop cartoons, which have been redubbed, recolored, and rescored with a bunch of inane rock songs.

Tommy Smothers—supplying the voice of Betty's dog, Pudgy—narrates this terribly contrived tale of Betty's attempts to become the first woman president. After her father laughs at her ambitions, she runs away from home and is soon embroiled in various adventures, which are strung together in the most strained and arbitrary way. One moment, Betty is washing dishes in a greasy spoon called "Ye Olde Quainte Coffee Potte." The next, she's at the beach, riding a rubber horse in the ocean. A minute later, she's performing a song-and-dance routine on Broadway, and so on.

Each of these episodes is recreated from scraps of the classic Max Fleischer cartoons of the 1930s, but new dialogue has been added to make the images conform to the updated story. At times, the difference between what's taking place on screen and what the characters are saying is so extreme that the viewer can only gape in astonishment. In one segment, for example, we see Betty peddling a concoction called Jippo from a wagon covered with satiric signs ("Makes Young Men Old!" "Removes Teeth, Grows Tonsils!" "Stops Breathing!"). In the meantime we hear Betty describing Jippo as mineral water! This transformation of snake-oil into Perrier is typical of the mindless way this movie has been assembled. At times, this patchwork production is so incoherent that it seems like a movie edited with a Cuisinart. Only one complete Betty Boop cartoon is reproduced in its entirety—Fleischer's classic 1933 version of "Snow White"—though even this surrealistic mini-masterpiece has been marred by the addition of sickly, pastel color.

Hurray for Betty Boop is a movie guaranteed to have cartoon fans grinding their teeth and children stifling yawns. If you're in the market for a good collection of Betty Boop cartoons, the best one available is *Betty Boop: Special Collector's Edition* (NTA, $39.95, 90 min.). Parents should be advised, however, that Betty Boop shorts aren't necessarily the best form of entertainment for children. Although they are among the most inventive cartoons ever made, they contain a high proportion of extremely unsettling, often nightmarish, images.

IMAGINE THAT! GREAT MOMENTS IN HISTORY, Vol. 1

KID TIME VIDEO (1983), $49.95, 60 min.
Ages 4–9, ★★

If children's shows were rated solely for their good intentions, this cassette would earn high marks. This educationally oriented program uses a cast of colorful animal puppets, plus a number of special guest comedians, to introduce young viewers to some of the great figures of history. It's certainly a more worthwhile cassette than many kiddie videos currently on the market. At the very least, your children should learn a few rudimentary facts about people like Benjamin Franklin and Wilbur Wright. The trouble with *Imagine That!* is that it's just not very well written. It's a nicely produced but often exasperatingly silly program.

Each of the three episodes on this cassette follows the same basic format. One of the puppets on the show is having a problem: Cromwell the Cat is bored, Oliver the Orangutan feels he can't do anything right. The "star" of the series—a sensible turtle named Toby (who might be Kermit the Frog's second cousin) —offers helpful advice that generally involves some lesson drawn from the history books. These introductory sketches then cut to brief comedy routines, featuring the historical characters themselves, who are played by the special guest stars. In the first, Shelley Berman appears as a very woebegone Columbus, who likes to spend his winters in Miami. The second episode features Jim Backus as a rather doddering Ben Franklin. In the last, Pat Morita (an Academy Award nominee in 1984 for his performance as the wise old martial-arts master in the movie *The Karate Kid*) stars as Wilbur Wright. In addition to the jokes that pass back and forth between the puppets and the comedians, there are a number of better-than-average songs in each episode.

The idea of teaching children history lessons in the form of short, musical comedy skits, starring a bunch of lovable puppets, isn't bad in theory. However, the actual results leave a lot to be desired. The main problem is that the scripts tend to be extremely lame. The humor is not particularly funny (a fact which is only reinforced by the heavy-handed use of a laugh track), and the dialogue, particularly in the historical segments, is terribly weak. At times, it's hard to make sense of what the characters are talking about. At one point, for example, Jim Backus, as Benjamin Franklin, is explaining to Toby that there is nothing wrong with "caring too much about something. Look at Thomas Jefferson," says Ben. "I won't sign his Declaration of Independence. He keeps hounding me about it. Just the other day, I found him in my root cellar, pen in hand."

"And?" asks Toby.

"You've got to see it from my point of view," Ben answers.

"What's that?"

"Well, that young Hancock is trying to make a name for himself in the insurance business."

Non sequiturs like this one (which are, unfortunately, all too common in the show) make the proceedings a bit hard to follow, even for an adult. Worse, they make the program seem both slipshod and a little simpleminded (not the most desirable qualities in a children's cassette, especially in one that aspires to teach). This is too bad, since in many ways, *Imagine That!* is a handsomely produced program, with appealing hand-puppets, colorful sets, good music, and amusing performances by the featured comedians. This is by no means a terrible cassette—just a disappointing one.

INSPECTOR GADGET, Vols. 1–4

FAMILY HOME ENTERTAINMENT (1983),
$39.95 each, 90 min. each
Ages 6–9, ★★★

Inspector Gadget is a funny, skillfully animated secret agent spoof—a kind of cartoon version of the old TV sitcom "Get Smart." Not coincidentally, the hero's voice is provided by none other than Agent 86 himself, Don Adams. Like Maxwell Smart, Gadget is a man of unbounded (and totally unfounded) self-confidence, who blunders amusingly through a variety of capers accompanied by his spunky niece, Penny, and loyal dog, Brain.

The basic comic premise of these entertaining cartoons is an extension of Maxwell Smart's old telephone-in-the-shoe gag (which was itself a parody of James Bond's booby-trapped attaché case and other state-of-the-art, concealed weaponry). Gadget's clothes—his standard-issue, secret agent trench coat, snap-brim hat, even his pants, gloves, and shoes—are packed with weird contraptions. At the push of a coat button or the tug of a thread, his coat inflates into a helium balloon, his shoes sprout wheels, his hat grows a propeller, and mechanical arms telescope out of his sleeves. Needless to say, these elaborate secret agent devices—designed to help Gadget get out of tight spots—generally end up creating incredible havoc when the hero sets them off.

Each of these *Inspector Gadget* cartoons (there are four per tape) follows the same basic formula. At the start of the episode Gadget is contacted by Chief Quimby, who hands him a self-destructing message that informs the agent of his latest mission. (These self-destructing messages are a running gag throughout the series; as soon as Gadget reads one, he simply crumples the paper up and tosses it away, leaving it to detonate under the nearest unlucky bystander.) Then, the steely-eyed superklutz is off to some exotic locale —the Swiss Alps, Hong Kong, a lost city of gold in the jungles of Peru—to combat the forces of the evil organization MAD, led by the criminal mastermind, Dr. Claw.

The stories themselves are nicely paced, interestingly plotted, and full of broad, pratfall humor. The violence

146

(what little there is of it) is about as savage as an exploding cigar. At one point, when Gadget is confronted by a crew of villainous sailors, he accidentally activates the roller skates hidden in his shoes and, in a vain effort to keep his balance, goes flailing through the crowd of baddies, knocking all of them unconscious. Kids love this kind of silliness and are sure to be amused by Gadget's endless, comical bungling.

The artwork here is very impressive; even when the humor falls flat (as it does from time to time), these cartoons are always a pleasure to look at. There are other good things about them as well. Every episode ends with a short but worthwhile safety lesson, drawn from the story. When Brain catches a cold during a mission in the Swiss Alps, for example, Gadget comes on and delivers a little speech about the sensible way to use medicine. The adventure in the Peruvian jungle concludes with useful travel tips ("Make sure you always dress warmly enough," "Take along a first aid kit, just in case.") An episode featuring a boat chase is followed by a list of water-safety rules, and so on.

Perhaps the best thing about these cartoons, however —at least from the point of view of parents (especially the parents of young girls)—is the character of Gadget's pretty blond niece, Penny. Because Gadget is so stupendously incompetent, it is left to Penny, working behind the scenes, to solve the cases. Gadget (who is never aware of Penny's help) always ends up getting the credit, but the audience knows who the real hero is. Though Penny looks a bit like Rainbow Brite, she is a much more unusual, refreshing, and nonsexist character—a little girl whom we admire, not solely for her sweetness and charm, but because she is smart, resourceful, and extremely capable.

IT'S FLASHBEAGLE, CHARLIE BROWN/SHE'S A GOOD SKATE, CHARLIE BROWN

MEDIA (1984/1980), $29.95, 55 min.
5 and up, ★★★

This cassette contains two half-hour cartoons with nicely contrasting moods. The first, *It's Flashbeagle, Charlie Brown,* finds the Peanuts gang celebrating the pleasures of working out and breakdancing. There's not much of a story here—just a string of lively musical numbers featuring different characters, with some comic filler in between. Peppermint Patty, in leg warmers and leotard, performs a dancercise number called "I'm in Shape," while conducting an aerobics class consisting of Lucy, Linus, Schroeder, Sally, and a huffing-and-puffing Charlie Brown. That night at a party, Lucy leads the gang in her own variation of Simple Simon (called "Listen to Lucy") performed to a disco beat. Then everyone joins in for a rousing (if dusty) square-dance number, "The Pigpen Hoedown." The high point of the cartoon comes toward the end, when Snoopy dolls himself up in his best Flashdance finery, heads off to a disco in the company of a breakdancing pal, and wows the crowd with a sensational John Travolta routine.

After the disco-boogie buoyancy of part one, the second half, *She's a Good Skate, Charlie Brown,* is a nice change of pace. The mood here is quiet, almost lyrical. This cartoon finds Peppermint Patty training for a regional ice-skating competition under the watchful eye of Coach Snoopy. Much of the action takes place on a lovely winter pond, where Patty comes each morning at dawn to practice. There is a tense moment toward the end of the cartoon, when the tape of Patty's accompanying music gets fouled up during the big contest. But Woodstock the bird comes to the rescue by whistling a hauntingly beautiful melody into the mike, and Patty walks (or rather skates) away with the trophy.

Considering how limited the animation is on these made-for-TV cartoons, the figure-skating sequences are surprisingly graceful. For all her tomboyishness, Peppermint Patty performs a truly elegant routine. Like Patty, this cassette is a winner.

IT'S MAGIC, CHARLIE BROWN/CHARLIE BROWN'S ALL STARS

MEDIA (1981/1968), $29.95, 55 min.
5 and up, ★★★

This cassette brings together two more half-hour Peanuts specials originally broadcast on network TV. It's not clear why these two particular shows have been collected on the same tape. They certainly don't share a common theme in the way that other cartoons in this series do (the two Charlie Brown Valentine stories, for instance–*It's Your First Kiss, Charlie Brown* and *Someday You'll Find Her, Charlie Brown*—make a much more logical package). Still, it's hard to complain about a video cassette with as much charm, warmth, and humor as this one.

The first cartoon, *It's Magic, Charlie Brown* (1981), finds America's favorite beagle up to some new tricks.

When Charlie Brown decides that it's time for his dog to do something besides eat and sleep, Snoopy marches off to the library, takes out a book called *How to Perform Magic,* and is soon billing himself as "The Great Houndini." His stage act (which occupies the first half of the cartoon) is pretty impressive, though not without its rough edges. Snoopy cuts Linus's security blanket into a hundred shreds, then forgets how to reassemble them. He levitates Lucy, then lets her crash to the stage floor. For his grand climax, he actually succeeds in making Charlie Brown invisible. Unfortunately, he doesn't know how to make him reappear.

For the rest of the cartoon, Charlie Brown wanders around like Claude Rains in the old science fiction movie. Snoopy finally learns a spell that brings his master back, but not before Charlie Brown discovers the one great advantage of invisibility. With Lucy unable to see him, he sneaks up on her while she is fooling around with a football and actually manages to place-kick it out of her hands.

The second cartoon on this cassette, *Charlie Brown's All Stars,* is of an earlier vintage (1968), and it's a real gem. There is never much plot in a Peanuts cartoon, and this one is no exception. But it is packed with classic Charles Schulz gags.

The cartoon deals with Charlie Brown's thankless efforts to manage the world's most incompetent (and unappreciative) baseball team. Frieda doesn't want to play in the outfield because no one will be able to see her naturally curly hair. Schroeder has to leave games in the middle so he can go home and practice Beethoven. When an opposing batter hits a high fly ball and Charlie Brown stands under it, waiting for it to fall into his outstretched glove, the rest of the team gathers around him making comments like, "If he drops it, let's all kick him." Needless to say, he drops it, causing the team's 1,000th consecutive loss. Things go from bad to worse, but Charlie Brown—though he blows every chance to be a little league hero—ultimately makes a sacrifice that wins the respect and gratitude of his team.

Older Peanuts fans will spot noticeable differences between this cartoon and *It's Magic, Charlie Brown:* the characters are drawn in a slightly different style, Snoopy (though he has a rich fantasy life) has not yet evolved into Superbeagle, and the jokes here are somewhat more sophisticated (and funnier). The two halves of this cassette don't really have much to do with each other, but they make an appealing package nevertheless—one that the whole family can, and will, enjoy.

IT'S YOUR FIRST KISS, CHARLIE BROWN/SOMEDAY YOU'LL FIND HER, CHARLIE BROWN

MEDIA (1977/1981), $29.95, 55 min.
5 and up, ★★★

Charlie Brown discovers the agony and ecstasy of love in two cartoons that (except for one surprising bit of thoughtlessness) are full of the usual easygoing Peanuts charm. *It's Your First Kiss, Charlie Brown* takes place on homecoming day, when Charlie Brown discovers that he has been picked to be the homecoming queen's escort at that night's big dance. Since the homecoming queen is none other than the Little Red-Haired Girl —Charlie Brown's unapproachable dream-lover—our round-headed hero is reduced to a state of quaking anxiety that is magnified a hundredfold when he is informed that his duties include giving her a kiss in front of the whole crowd. Before the dance, however, there is the big homecoming-day football game, in which Charlie Brown has several choice opportunities to prove himself a hero and ends up (naturally) being the goat. In this cartoon, however, things don't turn out too badly for good ol' Charlie Brown, who gets a first, intoxicating taste of true love.

Things don't go quite as well for Charlie Brown in the second cartoon, *Someday You'll Find Her, Charlie Brown*. This one is a Peanuts version of "The Courtship of Miles Standish," with Linus in the role of John Alden. After Charlie Brown spots "the world's most beautiful girl" sitting in the stands during a televised football game, he enlists Linus's help in tracking her down. When they finally do find her, Charlie Brown is too tongue-tied to approach her himself, so he asks Linus to serve as an intermediary. Unfortunately for Charlie, the girl in question not only is devastatingly adorable but also carries a pink security blanket. She and Linus instantly recognize that they are meant for each other, and Charlie Brown is left (literally) out in the cold. "For one brief moment, I thought I was winning in the game of life," a sadder-but-wiser Charlie Brown reflects. "But there was a flag on the play."

The Peanuts cartoons are so consistently sweet-natured that it comes as a shock to find a moment in *Someday You'll Find Her, Charlie Brown* that is extremely insensitive, almost cruel. At one point in Charlie Brown's quest, he and Linus arrive at the house they believe belongs to Charlie's dream girl. The little girl who answers the door, however, is extremely plain: frizzy-haired, buck-toothed. Linus calls out to Charlie Brown (who is hiding behind some bushes), "Is this the girl?" and Charlie Brown screams back, "No!!" The little girl, meanwhile, simply stands there, looking bewildered. This sequence strikes a very sour (and sexist) note, since it implies that physical attractiveness is the single most important quality in a girl. It suggests to young boys that only pretty girls need to be treated considerately, and might well make any young female viewer who doesn't conform to a stereotyped ideal (blond hair, big blue eyes, etc.) feel pretty bad about herself. All in all, it's a surprisingly off-key moment in what is otherwise a delightful cartoon.

JACK AND THE BEANSTALK

CBS/FOX VIDEO (1982), $39.98, 60 min.
6 and up, ★★★★

Excellent special effects and a pair of outstandingly funny performances by Jean Stapleton and Elliot Gould distinguish this splendid *Faerie Tale Theatre* production.

Dennis Christopher (the star of the hit movie, *Breaking Away*) plays Jack, a spirited, totally impractical lad whose head is, as his mother tells him, "always in the clouds." Jack's idea of a way to make money is to market dirt ("We've got plenty in the garden," he explains to his long-suffering mom.) On the way to the village to sell the family cow, Spot (amusingly played by a couple of actors in a vaudeville cow costume), Jack meets a strange, beak-nosed peddler. This character turns out to be a kind of guardian angel and later appears to Jack in the guise of the world's ugliest Southern belle (he resembles Corporal Klinger doing a Blanche DuBois imitation).

That night, Jack discovers a giant beanstalk growing outside his bedroom window, and (dressed in nothing but his red longjohns) makes the first of three journeys to the land of wonderment high in the clouds (in a production full of enchanted moments, one of the most magical is Jack's first glimpse of the giant beanstalk disappearing up into the moonlit sky). There, in the cloud kingdom, he discovers a fairy-tale castle inhabited by a huge, overworked housewife (Jean Stapleton, doing a coarse, funny variation of her Edith Bunker routine) and her cloddish hubby, an evil giant who comes home exhausted every evening after a hard day of ravaging the surrounding countryside. Elliot Gould (unrecognizable under his scraggly beard and heavy makeup) gives his best performance in years as the giant. He's a crude, dimwitted lug, who manages to be scary and funny at the same time. Jack makes three trips to the giant's castle altogether, stealing a sack of coins, a hen that lays golden eggs (this creature is portrayed by a comical chicken-puppet that kids are sure to adore), and a magical singing harp (Jerry Hall—Mick Jagger's inamorata—appears as the spirit of the harp).

This is one of those *Faerie Tale Theatre* productions that manages to be true to the traditional story while enlivening it with contemporary humor and real charm. It also boasts some of the best special effects in the series. Sophisticated trick photography makes it possible to show Jack and his mother living in a radiant, storybook landscape that is actually a colorful miniature set. The same technique is later used to show the tiny-sized Jack interacting with the two giants. This is an altogether outstanding cassette for parents and children alike.

(See review of *Faerie Tale Theatre* for a description of this series as a whole.)

JACK AND THE BEANSTALK

VCI HOME VIDEO (1952), $29.95, 87 min.
Ages 5–8, ★★

This low-budget Abbott and Costello vehicle is a rather anemic affair (even the colors are washed-out). If

Shelley Duvall's *Faerie Tale Theatre* often seems to aim its hip, sophisticated humor at grown-ups, this movie takes the opposite approach. It's hard to imagine anyone older than a first-grader being amused by Costello's juvenile mugging and even more childish jokes. (In a typical gag, he lifts a flagon of water to his mouth and ends up pouring the contents into his nose.) The songs achieve the same level of sophistication. When Costello (playing Jack) and a greedy butcher named Mr. Dinklepuss (Bud Abbott) ascend the beanstalk, the villagers break into a song, whose first verse goes like this:

> There goes Jack, that reckless fool
> Scooting up the beanstalk with another fool
> Maybe by tonight, the two'll
> Be bottled in alcohool.

Another weakness of this movie—one which even a five-year-old is bound to be bothered by—is that the ferocious giant is played by an actor who isn't any bigger than the average NFL halfback. (At her first glimpse of this less-than-awesome figure, one six-year-old member of my home audience turned to me and said, "Shouldn't that giant be bigger?")

This is by no means a terrible film, but to appreciate it, you have to be young enough to: a) not be put off by its cheap look, half-baked script, and sappy romantic subplot; and b) be amused by the silly shenanigans of Lou Costello (who seems a little weary of them himself in this generally lackluster production).

JACOB TWO-TWO MEETS THE HOODED FANG

CHILDREN'S VIDEO LIBRARY (1977), $39.95, 90 min.
7 and up, ★★★½

This live-action movie, based on Mordecai Richler's best-selling children's book, is wonderful fun for grown-ups and youngsters alike. Winner of a well-deserved gold medal at the Greater Miami International Film Festival, it is a delightful, modern-day fairy tale—a comic fantasy-adventure with echoes of such classics as *Alice in Wonderland* and *The Wizard of Oz*.

Its hero, Jacob Two-Two, is an angelic-looking little boy who has to say everything twice because no one ever pays attention to him the first time. When a policeman pretends that he's going to arrest Jacob for rudeness, the boy runs off into a park, where he falls asleep and has the thrilling dream that makes up most of the movie.

Charged with the heinous crime of insulting an adult, Jacob is sentenced to two years, two months, two weeks, two days, and two minutes in the dreaded Children's Prison. At his trial, however, a pair of young, costumed superheroes—Fearless O'Toole and The Intrepid Shapiro, agents for the group known as "Child Power"—make a dramatic appearance and slip Jacob a "supersonic bleeper" that will help them locate the secret whereabouts of the illegal prison. Accompanied by two nasty, cackling guards named Mistress Fowl and Master Fish, Jacob is taken on a perilous journey that leads through a sinister swamp, across an alligator-infested lake, and finally to the smog-enshrouded place known as Slimer's Island. Locked up in a medieval dungeon, Jacob and the other juvenile hardcases (one child has been thrown into the slammer for the crime of coming down with the measles on the very day his father's boss was invited to dinner) are forced to live on bread and water and to slave in the prison's Smog Workshop. They are kept from escaping by the creepy Slime Squad, who patrol the corridors and resemble a troop of evil, walking Brussels sprouts. Worst of all is the prison's warden, the evil, vicious (and extremely dimwitted) ex–pro wrestler, The Hooded Fang (hilariously played by Alex Karras), who insists that he's the meanest man alive, though he guards a dread secret (he really isn't very mean; in fact, he's a big baby who lives with his mommy). In the end, Jacob smuggles a note out to Child Power and, during the climactic battle, single-handedly saves the day by sabotaging the prison's Smog Machine.

Parents who are philosophically opposed to kiddie movies with anything remotely unsettling in them might find this film objectionable, since it does deal with children locked in a dungeon and mistreated by some pretty nasty characters. Mistress Fowl in particular —who is made up to look like a chicken and who resembles, in appearance, voice, and personality, the Wicked Witch from *The Wizard of Oz*—might indeed be upsetting to preschoolers. But this isn't a film for preschoolers anyway, and no child old enough to understand what's going on in the film is likely to be disturbed by it. For one thing, the villains are so comically exaggerated that most children will think they're amusing (which, in fact, they are). For another, there is no real violence or brutality here; the film is scary only in the funhouse way that a ride through the Haunted Mansion at Disneyland is. Most important, this film doesn't exploit or gratuitously play on children's fears. On the contrary, like the best fairy tales, it addresses one of the most common anxieties of childhood—the sense of being small and insignificant —and reassures children that, powerless as they may sometimes feel, they possess the inner resources to accomplish marvelous things. In short, this is one of those uncommon children's movies that conveys valuable meanings in the form of a witty, intelligent, and terrifically entertaining story.

JASON AND THE ARGONAUTS

RCA/COLUMBIA (1963), $59.95, 104 min.
8 and up, ★★★½

Ray Harryhausen is the greatest living practitioner of the art of stop-motion animation. In essence, this technique consists of taking a small, intricately sculpted model (generally of some awesome, nonexistent creature, either extinct or mythological) and making it come to life on screen by filming it one frame at a time, altering its position slightly between each exposure. A few years ago, Harryhausen's achievements were officially recognized when he was honored with a retrospective of his work at New York's Museum of Modern Art.

Jason and the Argonauts is generally regarded as Harryhausen's masterpiece. Like virtually all of his movies, it is characterized by mediocre acting and an extremely thin story line. But Harryhausen's contributions—four extended sequences involving his marvelously imaginative creations—send the film soaring into the realm of magic.

Based on the classical Greek legend of Jason and his quest for the Golden Fleece, the movie follows the crew of the *Argo* as they undergo various adventures and encounter a series of mythic monsters. The first (and possibly scariest) is Talos, an awesome bronze statue that comes to life and pursues the Argonauts in a slow-moving, terrifyingly inexorable way. Next, the adventurers come upon a pair of horrific bat-winged harpies—blue-skinned monstrosities that take joy in tormenting a blind man. The Golden Fleece itself is protected by a fierce, seven-headed hydra. Finally —in one of the most stunning special effects scenes in the realm of fantasy cinema—Jason and his crew are forced to do battle with an army of living skeletons.

Harryhausen's movies aren't suitable for younger children (besides *Jason,* his best works include *The Seventh Voyage of Sinbad, The Golden Voyage of Sinbad, Sinbad and the Eye of the Tiger,* and *Clash of the Titans*). His animated monsters are simply too nightmarish. But for slightly older viewers, his films are a very special treat. Lovers of "sword-and-sorcery" adventure films are guaranteed to have their dreams enriched and their imaginations fired by the wondrous visions that this brilliant effects artist—a genuine movie magician—is able to conjure up on screen.

JIM HENSON'S MUPPET VIDEO,
Seven volumes

PLAYHOUSE VIDEO (1985),
$59.95 each, 54–57 min. each
Preschool and up, ★★★½

"The Muppet Show"—the syndicated series that made international superstars out of a bunch of multicolored, polyurethane handpuppets—was one of the most wildly creative programs ever produced for TV. Every episode took the form of a lavishly produced (if totally lunatic) variety show, composed of hilarious skits, outrageous song-and-dance routines, and regular off-the-wall features such as "Pigs in Space," "Veterinarian's Hospital," and "Bear on Patrol." Presiding over all this zaniness was the long-suffering M.C., Kermit the Frog, who did his best to keep the proceedings from degenerating into utter anarchy—a difficult task when a typical production number might consist of having a strange, beak-nosed creature eat a tire to the accompaniment of "Flight of the Bumblebee."

Great moments from this memorable series are now available on seven hour-long volumes from Playhouse Video. Instead of simply rereleasing the original shows on video cassette, the producers have taken outstanding bits and pieces, arranged them according to various themes, and added some original material to link the various snippets together. In *Children's Songs and Stories with the Muppets,* for example, Scooter turns the pages of a book while recalling an assortment of highlights: Kermit's nephew Robin performing "Octopus's Garden," Julie Andrews, in full Swiss-miss regalia, trilling a song about a "Country Goatherd," Brooke Shields in an extended *Alice in Wonderland* sketch, and so on. *The Muppet Revue*—a miscellany of riotous routines and bouncy musical numbers featuring various big-name guests (Harry Belafonte, Rita Moreno, Linda Ronstadt, Paul Williams)—has Kermit and Fozzie reminiscing about favorite moments from "The Muppet Show" while cleaning out an attic full of old props. The wild-eyed keyboard wizard, Dr. Teeth, is the host of *Rock Music with the Muppets,* which features performances by an all-star lineup, including Alice Cooper, Debbie Harry, Paul Simon, and Linda Ronstadt. The other titles in this series are: *The Kermit and Miss Piggy Story* (with guest appearances by Cheryl Ladd, Tony Randall, Loretta Swit, and Raquel Welch), *Muppet Treasures* (featuring Loretta Lynn, Ethel Merman, Zero Mostel, Buddy Rich, Peter Sellers, and Paul Simon), *Gonzo Presents Muppet Weird Stuff* (featuring Julie Andrews, John Cleese, Dom DeLuise, Madeline Kahn, Vincent Price, and Jean Stapleton), and *Country Music with the Muppets* (with Johnny Cash, Roy Clark, Roger Miller and others).

There are so many comic and musical gems on these video cassettes that any Muppet fan can only be grateful for their existence. Still, in spite of the care that apparently went into their creation, they are awkwardly patched together. There's something unsatisfying about seeing the original shows (which were mini-masterpieces of organized hysteria) chopped up and reassembled in this fairly artificial way. The thematic connections among the assorted routines often seem strained and arbitrary. *The Kermit and Miss Piggy Story,* for example—in which the two characters wax nostalgic about their relationship over the course of a candlelit dinner (at which Miss Piggy does all the eating)—is a very mixed bag of songs and comedy skits, many of which have very little to do with the legendary (if completely one-sided) affair between the passionate pig and her reluctant lover. And including performers like Ben Vereen and Loretta Swit on a rock music video seems to be forcing things a bit.

Still, it's impossible to complain too much about these utterly endearing programs. Any videotapes that include Kermie's classic rendition of "Lydia the Tattooed Lady" and Dr. Benson Honeydew's demonstration of his Solid State Gorilla Detector ("At last your family can be protected from the heartbreak of gorilla invasion!") are to be cherished.

JOHNNY WOODCHUCK'S ADVENTURES

FAMILY HOME ENTERTAINMENT (1978),
$29.95, 60 min.
Preschool–6, ★★★

Little Johnny Woodchuck leaves home to explore the
Green Forest and learns some valuable lessons about
friendship and sharing in this animated adventure from
the appealing *Fables of the Green Forest* cartoon series.
(See review under *Fables of the Green Forest*.)

JON GNAGY LEARN TO DRAW,
Vols. 1 and 2

BEST FILM AND VIDEO (195?),
$39.95 each, 60 min. each
7 and up, ★★★½

When I was growing up in the 1950s, Jon Gnagy's
syndicated "Learn to Draw" TV program was one of
my favorite shows. Using a few simple tools—pencils,
charcoal, a kneaded eraser—Gnagy would transform a
blank sheet of paper into a richly detailed drawing
within minutes. The subjects were a little hokey—snow
scenes, mountain lakes, country landscapes—but, as an
art teacher, Gnagy was a natural. When you tried to
follow his step-by-step directions, you discovered that
they weren't nearly as simple as he made them seem.

But he could teach you basic lessons about depth, perspective, composition, and texture in a remarkably short time. And he made the act of artistic creation seem like tremendous fun.

Ten of Gnagy's brief TV art lessons have been collected on two video cassettes, and, in spite of their technical crudeness, they still hold up extremely well. The show looks unmistakably dated, even primitive —it's in black and white and the set consists of nothing but an easel. Gnagy himself, with his neatly trimmed goatee and plaid lumberjack shirt (which he wore on every show), looks very much like a tidied-up fifties hipster. And since these tapes simply string together segments of his TV show, they contain periodic fade-outs for commercial breaks. Every few minutes, Gnagy puts down his charcoal pencil, folds his hands, turns to the camera, and says, with obviously forced enthusiasm, "Now I'd like to have you take a look at something I think will be of interest to every one of you!"

In the end, however, it's the art lessons that are important, and they are just as much fun to watch —and follow—today as they were thirty years ago. Unlike another excellent how-to tape, *Draw and Color Your Very Own Cartoonys Right Along with Uncle Fred* (which is intended for very small viewers and stresses fun and imaginative play), these cassettes are aimed at somewhat older children. Gnagy's pictures are polished, professional, and comparatively sophisticated. Packaged in a box the size of a board game, each cassette comes complete with all the art materials a child needs—sketch chalks, drawing pencils, carbon pencils, a kneaded eraser, even several sheets of paper. Unless your children are exceptionally talented, they will probably find that their finished pictures don't look *quite* like Jon Gnagy's. But they are sure to come away from this tape with a basic grasp of some important artistic principles that they will be able to apply to their own, original drawings. And they'll have a good time watching Gnagy—a born teacher and extremely deft craftsman—turn out impressive works of art with the greatest of ease.

JOURNEY BACK TO OZ

FAMILY HOME ENTERTAINMENT (1974),
88 min., $49.95
Preschool and up, ★★★

The full-length animated sequel to the classic *Wizard of Oz* features Liza Minnelli (or in any case her voice) in the role originated by her mother, Judy Garland. Because of this casting, it's especially hard not to draw comparisons between the two films. And the fact is, there *is* no comparison. The cartoon simply doesn't hold a candle to the 1939 movie (which may well be the most enchanting film ever to come out of Hollywood). Still, judged strictly on its own merits, *Journey Back to Oz* is a very charming and entertaining cartoon that features a large cast of colorful characters—including a few old favorites—in an exciting, all-new adventure in the magical land of Oz.

Like the earlier movie, this one begins in Kansas. Once again, Dorothy and her dog Toto are swept over the rainbow by a cyclone and find themselves back in the lush, exotic fantasyland of Oz. The plot revolves around an evil witch named Mombi, who invades the Emerald City with an army of magical green elephants and captures Toto and Dorothy's old friend, the Scarecrow. Accompanied by a pair of new companions—a living jack-o'-lantern named Pumpkinhead and a former merry-go-round horse named Woodenhead—Dorothy seeks help from the Tin Man and the Cowardly Lion. Finally, Glinda, the Good Witch of the North, appears and gives Dorothy a small, silver box containing the only weapon powerful enough to defeat an army of magical elephants: namely, an army of magical white mice. In the end, Mombi gets what's coming to her, and Dorothy gets to return home to Uncle Henry and Aunt Em.

There are some very nice things about this cartoon (which was nominated by *Parent's Choice* magazine for its Best Children's Video award). Though the animation is limited, a great deal of care has gone into the artwork. The scenery in particular is richly detailed and beautifully rendered. (For the most part, the look of this film owes less to *The Wizard of Oz* than to Walt Disney's *Alice in Wonderland.*) And while there's no substitute for the unforgettable quartet who starred in the 1939 classic—Bert Lahr, Ray Bolger, Jack Haley, and, of course, Judy Garland—the voices in this cartoon are provided by a large and impressive cast that includes Milton Berle (the Cowardly Lion), Mickey Rooney (Scarecrow), Danny Thomas (the Tin Man), Herschel Bernardi (Woodenhead), Paul Lynde (Pumpkinhead), and Ethel Merman (Mombi). Merman's cackling performance as the wicked witch is especially effective. In fact, like the original witch (played by Margaret Hamilton, who makes a cameo appearance in this cartoon as the voice of Aunt Em), Mombi may be a bit frightening to younger viewers, particularly when she first appears on screen, looking like the green-skinned first cousin of the witch in Walt Disney's *Snow White.*

The only really weak part of this cartoon is the music. There are fourteen songs in this movie, written by the famous team of Sammy Cahn and Jimmy Van Heusen, and all of them are exceptionally mediocre. On the whole, however, this is a sweet and nicely done children's film, full of excitement, color, and charm.

JOURNEY TO THE CENTER OF THE EARTH

PLAYHOUSE VIDEO (1959), $59.98, 132 min.

8 and up, ★★★★

The dream of escaping from the mundane routines of everyday life into an exciting wonderland of action and adventure is at the heart of every fantasy film. Few movies have made that dream seem so delightfully real as this sumptuous, 1959 version of Jules Verne's *Journey to the Center of the Earth*, a true classic of children's cinema.

James Mason stars as Sir Oliver Lindenbrook, a professor of geology whose discovery of a mysterious plumb bob inside a chunk of Icelandic lava leads him from the lecture halls of Edinburgh University to the peril-filled depths of the underworld. Accompanying him on his incredible journey are his student, Alec McKuen (Pat Boone); Frau Carla Goetaborg (Arlene Dahl), the strong-willed widow of Lindenbrook's archrival; a Herculean Icelander named Hans; and the expedition's mascot, an uncommonly clever duck named Gertrude. Their trip is filled with breathtaking marvels and hairbreadth escapes, as they dodge giant, runaway boulders, cross narrow bridges over bottomless pits, discover a cave of priceless crystals, battle a horde of prehistoric monsters, and much more. In the end, after reaching their destination, they stumble upon the ruins of the lost city of Atlantis and are hurtled back to the surface in a spectacular volcanic eruption.

Graced with first-rate performances (particularly by Mason and Dahl, who make a very appealing couple), excellent special effects, and a splendid score by the great Bernard Hermann, *Journey to the Center of the Earth* is an extremely appealing fantasy film, one with real imaginative power. It's the kind of movie you'll have fun watching with your kids. Parts of it, however, are probably too intense for smaller viewers. The flesh-eating dinosaurs (real lizards made to look enormous by being filmed on miniature sets) are a pretty scary sight. Even more upsetting is the murder of Gertrude the Duck, who is eaten by the film's heartless villain, the satanic Count Saknussem. Most children regard this act as one of the most heinous crimes ever recorded on film, and more impressionable youngsters might be seriously upset by it.

THE KERMIT AND PIGGY STORY

PLAYHOUSE VIDEO (1985), $59.95, 57 min.
Preschool and up, ★★★½

Sipping champagne through straws, Kermit and Miss Piggy enjoy a romantic candlelit dinner while they reminisce about their legendary love affair in this hour-long collection of snippets from "The Muppet Show." (See review of *Jim Henson's Muppet Video*.)

KOOKY CLASSICS

MGM/UA (1984), $29.95, 54 min.
Ages 5–8, ★★★½

Popular kiddie entertainer Shari Lewis introduces young viewers to the pleasures of classical music in this charming program, one of several superior videos starring this extremely talented (and apparently ageless) performer.

A big concert is approaching and Shari's three irresistible handpuppets—Lamb Chop, Charley Horse, and Hush Puppy—are eager to be involved. Since none of them knows a thing about music, Shari offers them a few simple lessons. Each of these short segments combines Shari's special brand of comedy with a bit of basic music appreciation. In the first, Shari and Lamb Chop sing a tongue-twisting duet to the tune of Chopin's "Minute Waltz." (Besides being very amusing, this routine—like several others on this tape—is a tour de force of ventriloquism). A bit later, Shari plays Brahms's "Hungarian Dance No. 5" with a visiting kangaroo-puppet named Captain Person. (When Lamb Chop comments that it seems funny to name a kangaroo "Captain Person," Shari points out that it isn't any stranger than calling a person "Captain Kangaroo.")

One of the high points of the show is Shari's comic performance of Bizet's *Carmen*. The "characters" are elaborately costumed rag dolls, mounted on a black backdrop with holes cut out where their heads should appear. By sticking her own head through these openings, Shari is able to play the part of each character and sing a humorous synopsis of the story (Sample lyric: "I am Carmen, I'm soft as snow/ Men all want me to be their loving wife/ So I warn every Romeo/ Don't squeeze the Carmen or you'll be hooked for life.") In other segments Shari conducts an orchestra, sings the "William Tell Overture," and plays Ginger Rogers to a life-size Fred Astaire puppet.

Young children are sure to have a good time with this lively, engaging tape. And while they do, they'll be getting a small but tantalizing taste of some of the world's great music.

THE LAST UNICORN

PLAYHOUSE VIDEO (1982), $59.98, 95 min.
Five and up, ★★★½

Based on Peter Beagle's popular sword-and-sorcery
fantasy, *The Last Unicorn* is one of the best cartoon
features of recent years. It doesn't use Disney-style full
animation, but the artwork is very elegant—the landscapes have the richness and texture of medieval
tapestries—and the characters are imaginatively designed. They also seem completely alive, thanks to the
exceptional cast of actors who provide the voice characterizations: Alan Arkin, Jeff Bridges, Tammy Grimes,
Robert Klein, Angela Lansbury, Christopher Lee, and
Mia Farrow in the title role.

Like most movies in this genre, *The Last Unicorn* is a
tale of magic, heroism, and high adventure, in which
the protagonist—a brave and beautiful creature who
learns that the rest of her race has been driven off by a
monstrous Red Bull—sets out to find and free the
missing unicorns. Along the way, she faces various
ordeals, including capture by an evil witch named
Mommy Fortuna, who displays her in a grim "midnight
carnival." She also makes several bosom friends, who
accompany her on her journey and lend their support.
The most colorful (and endearing) is Shmendrick the
Magician (Alan Arkin), a novice wizard whose command over his powers is fitful at best, though he does
manage to come through in several emergencies. When
the travelers arrive at the dark, forbidding castle of
King Haggard, the fiery Red Bull suddenly materializes
from a tower and begins pursuing the helpless unicorn.

To save her, Shmendrick casts a spell that changes her into a beautiful young girl. There is a lyrical, romantic subplot, in which the king's son, Prince Lear, falls madly in love with the transformed heroine. In the end, however, the unicorn reverts to her animal form. In a stirring climax, she defeats the Red Bull and liberates the other unicorns.

This is one of those rare fantasy movies that really manage to evoke an atmosphere of magic and wonder. It does, however, have some scary and upsetting moments. Mommy Fortuna is an extremely grotesque-looking character (as is her helper, a hunchbacked dwarf named Rook). The scene in which Mommy is killed by one of her prizes—a nightmarish harpy with a white beard, a vulture's beak, and triple dugs—is very unsettling. Two inhabitants of Haggard's castle—a peg-legged, piratical cat and a living skeleton with an iron crown around its skull—are also a bit disconcerting. Most frightening of all, however, is the Red Bull, a gigantic monster with huge, flaming horns and a demon's eyes. Some children find this creature too scary to look at. Others, however, respond powerfully to the beauty and enchantment of this exceptionally well-done fantasy film.

THE LEATHERSTOCKING TALES,
Vols. 1 and 2

MASTERVISION (1979), $64.95 each, 60 min. each
8 and up, ★★★★

In his five "Leatherstocking" novels (published in the early nineteenth century), James Fenimore Cooper gave birth to the American Western hero. His character, Natty Bumppo—known variously as Deerslayer,

Pathfinder, Long-Rifle, Leather-Stocking, and Hawk-eye—is the direct ancestor of every rugged, gun-toting gallant from the Virginian to Shane, the Lone Ranger to Marshall Matt Dillon.

These superior adaptations of Cooper's famous adventure tales were originally produced as part of PBS's first-rate "Once Upon A Classic" series. Each tape consists of two half-hour shows. Volume One is a two-part adaptation of *The Deerslayer.* Set on a glorious wilderness lake in upstate New York during the French and Indian Wars, the story introduces us to the valiant frontiersman, Natty, a young man who has been raised by the Delaware Indians and whose bosom companion is the noble Mohican chief, Chingachgook. In the course of this adventure, Natty helps rescue the young chief's bride, Wah-ta-Wah, from the clutches of the treacherous Iroquois, earns his warrior's name, Hawkeye, by slaying an opponent in a gun duel, and is subjected to a fiendish ordeal—the nerve-racking Test of the Tomahawks—by his bloodthirsty foes. As in most of Cooper's tales, there are hairbreadth escapes, heroic exploits, and gunfights galore (though the violence is kept to a minimum; Natty, a legendary marksman, is naturally averse to killing and prefers, whenever possible, to shoot the weapons out of his enemies' hands.)

The two half-hour episodes in the second volume are loosely drawn from *The Last of the Mohicans* and *The Pathfinder.* In the first, Natty and Chingachgook help a pair of young women—Alice and Cora Munro, the daughters of the English commander—reach their father's fort. Along the way, they must fight off a band of hostile Indians, led by Natty's nemesis, Le Renard Subtil. In the second part, Natty finds himself attracted to a handsome young woman named Molly. The highlight of this show is a shooting match between Natty and his rival, Jeff Sweetwater. The target is a nail lightly hammered into a board. Jeff fires first, hits the nail squarely on the head, and drives it deep into the wood. Natty steps to the line, quickly raises his long-rifle to his shoulder, fires (without aiming)—and shoots his bullet directly into the hole made by his predecessor!

Beautifully photographed, splendidly acted (particularly by Cliff De Young in the key role of Natty), and full of exciting frontier action, these videotapes make a terrific introduction to the pleasures of Cooper's books. Young viewers will not only thrill to the exploits of America's first Western hero; they'll also discover that literary classics are not dry, lifeless tomes but some of the greatest stories ever told.

THE LION, THE WITCH, AND THE WARDROBE

VESTRON (1979), $69.95, 95 min.
5 and up, ★★★½

This animated adaptation of C.S. Lewis' fantasy classic, *The Lion, the Witch, and the Wardrobe* (the first novel in his "Chronicles of Narnia" series) has impressive credits. It was produced by the Children's Television Workshop and directed by Bill Melendez (the Emmy Award winning director of the animated "Peanuts" films and TV specials). And it comes with the recommendation of the National Education Association.

Hardcore fans of the Lewis book might feel (with some justification) that no cartoon can capture the richness and magic of the original tale. On the whole, however, this is a surprisingly effective production. The animation is simple but expressive, and the artwork is graceful and full of innocent charm. Most important of all, Lewis's dramatic parable about courage, sacrifice, forgiveness, and the eternal war between Good and Evil comes across with much of its power intact.

The story centers on four young siblings—two brothers and two sisters—who, while visiting a rambling house in the English countryside, climb into a wardrobe that turns out to be the doorway to a magical kingdom called Narnia. There they find themselves caught in a conflict between an evil witch, who has caused an endless winter to fall over the land, and the forces of Good, led by a magnificent golden lion named Aslan. The most riveting part of the tale comes near the end, when the wicked witch lays claim to the blood of youngest boy, Edmund (who has betrayed his brothers and sisters to her). To save the child's life, the noble Aslan offers himself in Edmund's stead, and is subjected to a horrifying ordeal. He is mocked, tormented, and then slain by the gloating witch and her nightmarish followers. In the end, however, Aslan undergoes a glorious resurrection and leads his army of righteous warriors in a triumphant battle against the powers of darkness.

Although Lewis's story has its share of terrors, this cartoon handles the more frightening aspects of the story with great sensitivity. The witch's evil minions, for example, are grotesque but not especially scary. The witch herself, though a threatening enough figure (her unvarying tone of voice is a crazed, infuriated shriek), is far less terrifying than the wicked witch in *The Wizard of Oz*. And the battle sequences—such as the climactic fight between the witch's army and Aslan's—are deliberately understated. There is far more graphic, gratuitous violence in any given episode of *He-Man and the Masters of the Universe*.

This is the kind of cartoon that children will enjoy seeing over and over. It is not only exciting and highly imaginative but also (and this makes it a real rarity in the realm of kiddie cartoons) genuinely uplifting.

LITTLE LULU

NTA (1944–49), $19.95, 48 min.
5 and up, ★★★

Of the seven vintage cartoons on this cassette, four of them feature the curly-headed moppet, Little Lulu, star of one of the best-loved comic books of all time. Actually, these cartoons (which were made in the 1940s) bear very little resemblance to the comic books. Tubby, Iggy, Annie and the rest of the neighborhood gang are nowhere to be found, and Lulu herself is a slightly different character here: taller, skinnier, and more of a troublemaker. Still, no one will come away from these cartoons disappointed. They are immeasurably better than almost anything being produced today. Grown-up fans of Little Lulu will find this cassette funny and engaging, and children raised on a steady diet of Saturday-morning schlock will discover just how well-made cartoons used to be.

One of the nicest things about these Little Lulu shorts is the heroine's impish personality (another is the high quality of the animation). At a time when the cartoon role models for little girls tend to be prefabricated bundles of sheer adorableness like Strawberry Shortcake, it's refreshing—and salutary—to see a heroine who is allowed to be as high-spirited and spunky as, say, Dennis the Menace. In the words of the theme song, this Little Lulu is "always in and out of trouble/ But mostly always in." Discovering a heartbroken little boy whose mutt has been ejected from a dog show, she helps smuggle the pooch back into the contest, completely disrupting the proceedings ("The Dog Show-Off," 1948). In "Lulu at the Zoo" (1944), she creates a similar state of havoc, feeding the lion his own tail on a hotdog bun, using a slingshot to feed the giraffes and, in general, making life miserable for her exasperated zoo guide. The most charming cartoon on this cassette is the 1944 "I'm Just Curious," in which a teary Little Lulu (who has just been spanked by her Dad) explains that she isn't bad, just highly inquisitive—and then recalls various occasions when her curiosity got her into trouble (such as the time she disassembled her parents' heirloom clock because she wanted to see how it worked). For all her mischievous behavior, however, Little Lulu remains a sweet, good-hearted, and thoroughly engaging character.

In addition to the "Little Lulu" cartoons, this cassette also contains a trio of animated musical shorts. There are two sing-along cartoons (also from the 1940s). In "Little Brown Jug," some beavers manufacture apple jack in an abandoned mill. The stuff overflows into the river, inebriating all the creatures who come down for a drink. This amusing little sketch leads into a follow-the-bouncing-ball performance of the title tune. The same technique is used in "The Big Drip" (here the sing-along number is "It Ain't Gonna Rain No More"). The best of the musical cartoons on this videotape is Max Fleischer's 1937 "A Car-Tune Portrait." Here, a very cultivated lion, dressed in white tie and tails, appears on the stage of a concert hall and announces that, with the help of his comrades, he intends to dispel the misapprehension that cartoon creatures are lacking in the "finer sensibilities." He then proceeds to conduct his orchestra of animal musicians in a stirring symphony, which quickly degenerates into a slapstick free-for-all.

All in all, this video cassette (which is part of NTA Home Entertainment's excellent "Cartoonies" series) offers a very pleasing collection of charming, beautifully crafted, old-fashioned cartoons—the kind that (unfortunately) they just don't make anymore.

LITTLE LULU

MEDIA (1978), $29.95, 48 min.
Ages 5–8, ★★★

The two made-for-TV cartoons on this video cassette do an excellent job of capturing the charm of the old Little Lulu comic books (which many parents will remember fondly from their own childhoods).

In the first, Lulu vows to be a little angel and sets out to find people in need. Unfortunately, everyone she helps ends up in worse shape than before. Tubby can't fit into his new suit jacket, so Lulu takes him for a weight-reducing run, with frequent rest stops for corn dogs and banana snacks. By the time they return, Tubby has put on so much weight that his jacket rips at the seams when he buttons it. Lulu, however, has already gone skipping merrily down the street in search of her next victim. She helps Alvin climb a tree, then leaves him stuck in a high branch. She teaches Iggy and Annie how to resolve their arguments by a method that has them rolling on the ground, trying to strangle each other. Throughout it all, Lulu remains cheerfully oblivious to the catastrophic effects of her philanthropy.

The second cartoon finds Lulu baby-sitting for Tubby —a situation so humiliating to Tubby that he tries every means at his disposal to get Lulu out of the house. The ensuing battle of wits between the two characters is the comical crux of this amiable cartoon.

In terms of style and content, these Little Lulu shorts are similar to the made-for-TV Peanuts specials. The animation is simple but engaging. The characters' voices are provided by real kids, not professional actors (except in the case of Lulu herself). There is a pleasant, jazz-flavored score. Most important, these good-natured cartoons manage to be funny and entertaining without resorting to violence or low comedy. Their humor grows entirely out of the personalities of the characters and the amusing situations Lulu finds herself in. This is a nice video cassette.

Other episodes from this charming cartoon series are available from Family Home Entertainment under the title *The Adventures of Little Lulu and Tubby*, Volumes 1 and 2.

THE LITTLE MERMAID

CBS/FOX VIDEO (1984), $39.98, 60 min.
6 and up, ★★★★

Of all the shows in the *Faerie Tale Theatre* series, this lovely adaptation of Hans Christian Andersen's "The Little Mermaid" is unquestionably the most moving. By the end of it, several six-year-old members of my home audience were crying uncontrollably.

Pam Dawber stars as Pearl, a beautiful young mermaid who is burning with curiosity about the world above the ocean. On her first visit to the surface, she catches a glimpse of a handsome young sailor (Treat Williams), who turns out to be a prince named Andrew. Smitten with love, Pearl implores the Sea Witch (Karen Black) to make her into a human being. The witch agrees, but there are two provisos: Pearl will lose the power of speech, and if she cannot win Andrew's love before he marries another woman, she will be turned into a speck of sea foam and disappear forever.

Unfortunately, while Pearl is visiting the Sea Witch, Andrew is washed ashore during a shipwreck and ends up in the kingdom of a neighboring princess named

Emilia (Helen Mirren). By the time Pearl arrives on the scene, Andrew and Emilia are on their way to becoming engaged. Andrew is touched by Pearl's innocence and beauty, but he is committed to Emilia. In the end, Pearl is given a chance to become a mermaid again and return to her beloved father and sisters—but only at the cost of Andrew's life. Naturally, she refuses. For her generosity, she is spared from destruction, but the climax is bittersweet: Pearl is transformed into a spirit of the air, whose duty is to watch over and protect the royal lovers until the end of their days.

This is a radiant and romantic story—a touching fable about self-sacrificing love.

(See review of *Faerie Tale Theatre* for a description of this series as a whole.)

THE LITTLE PRINCE: NEXT STOP, PLANET EARTH

CHILDREN'S HOME VIDEO (1983), $39.95, 60 min.
Ages 5–8, ★★★

The opening credits for this above-average cartoon series (which has been endorsed by the National Education Association) admit that it is not based directly on Antoine de Saint-Exupéry's 1943 children's classic. That's for sure. Except for the title character—a blond, wide-eyed cherub who is the ruler (and sole inhabitant) of the tiny world known as Asteroid B-612—these cartoons have virtually nothing to do with the original story. Still, this is an endearing cassette. In each of its two half-hour episodes, the angelic hero hitches a ride down to earth on a comet, meets some troubled people, and helps them achieve some peace of mind.

In "Higher Than Eagles Fly," the Little Prince sets

down in the Andean mountains and becomes involved with an unhappy, headstrong little boy named Carlos, who is determined to conquer the mountain his father died on. When Carlos becomes stranded on a high ledge, the Little Prince and the boy's Uncle Pedro take off in a hot air balloon to rescue him. At first, Carlos refuses to be carried to the summit in a balloon, but ultimately he learns that (as the Little Prince tells him), "You can get to the top of different things in many ways, and one of the best ways is to do it with others."

In the second cartoon, "The Chimney Sweep," the Little Prince lands in London and is befriended by a cheerful chimney sweep named Harvey, whose fierce sense of pride ("I'm higher than the other blokes!") conceals deep-seated feelings of inferiority. Harvey, it turns out, is the father of a celebrated ballerina named Marta, from whom he's been separated since her infancy. How the Little Prince brings this pair together is the crux of this warmhearted tale.

Although the animation on this program is minimal, the characters are nicely drawn and its background scenery—from its colorful South American landscapes to its windswept city streets—is impressively rendered. And the stories, though simple enough for young viewers to follow, are unusually dramatic for a made-for-TV cartoon. Best of all is the character of the Little Prince. He may be a little less interesting than his literary prototype, but he still manages to convey the unaffected innocence and purity of spirit embodied in Saint-Exupéry's original. And it's very refreshing to find a contemporary cartoon character who derives from a classic children's book instead of from the market research department of a toy corporation.

The other available titles in this series are: *The Adventures of the Little Prince* and *The Little Prince: Tales of the Sea.*

THE LITTLE RASCALS CHRISTMAS SPECIAL

FAMILY HOME ENTERTAINMENT (1979), $29.95, 60 min.

Ages 5–8, ★★★

The first half-hour of this cassette consists of an animated Christmas story starring cartoon versions of the popular Our Gang characters. All the familiar faces are here—Alfalfa, Darla, Spanky, Stymie, Porky, even Pete, the pooch with a black ring around one eye. The story, set during the Depression, centers on Spanky, who is yearning for a deluxe electric train called a Blue Comet. When Spanky's hard-working Mom sees how much his heart is set on this gift, she returns her new winter coat, even though she desperately needs it, and uses the money to buy him the train. Soon afterwards, she is bedridden with a cold—so Spanky, after enlisting the help of his gang, sets out to buy her a new coat. The heart of the cartoon concerns the gang's comical efforts to make enough money for the purchase. When a sudden hot spell spoils their snow-shoveling plans, Alfalfa hits on the idea of dumping chicken feathers onto a neighbor's driveway and offering to remove them instead. An attempt to make and market plum pudding is equally unsuccessful, since none of the gang can cook (Stymie's idea of separating and beating eggs is to divide them into two piles and smash them on the table). The story ends happily, though, thanks to a disgruntled street-corner Santa, whose own cheerless attitude toward the holidays is transformed by the sight of Spanky's selflessness and devotion.

This is a nice cartoon, though it's not without faults. The original Our Gang shorts had an impudent, raucous quality, which made them cruder but funnier than this program. In fact, the humor here is sometimes pretty strained. Alfalfa spouts endless silly malapropisms ("necessity is the brother of invention," "divided we're stranded but united we're tall"), and a few of the supposed comic high points, such as the episode with the chicken feathers, fall pretty flat. The characters in this cartoon are also much blander than the real Little Rascals. Still, this is an above-average Christmas program. It's handsomely animated, and its story offers a sweet holiday message about love and unselfishness.

Following the main feature is a program of four beautifully animated cartoons from the 1930s, with appropriately seasonal themes. The first is the 1934 "Jack Frost" by master animator Ub Iwerks (Walt Disney's famous collaborator and the real inventor of Mickey Mouse). This cartoon is about a brash little grizzly who decides to sneak out of his house while his parents are hibernating. It's a wonderfully imaginative cartoon, but there are a number of things in it —including a very scary version of Old Man Winter, who chases after the little bear like a blue-skinned bogey-man—that might easily terrify young children. The remaining three cartoons, all from Max Fleischer, are extremely charming. The first is the story of "Rudolph the Red-Nosed Reindeer." Then there is the delightful "Christmas Comes But Once a Year," starring the lovable inventor Grampy, who sneaks into an orphanage on Christmas morning and tinkers together a pile of toys out of household utensils. Finally, there is "Somewhere in Dreamland," a gorgeously animated fantasy about two waifs who fall asleep and find themselves in a land where the plants sprout ice cream cones and gumdrops grow on trees.

Note: The original Little Rascals comedies, made by Hal Roach in the 1930s, have been released by Blackhawk Films on nineteen separate cassettes. Each cassette contains three episodes, runs approximately 45-60 minutes, and costs $29.95.

LITTLE RED RIDING HOOD

CBS/FOX VIDEO (1983), $39.98, 60 min.
6 and up, ★★★

Malcolm McDowell is outstanding as Reginald the Wolf in this typically handsome (if slightly uneven) *Faerie Tale Theatre* production. Reggie—who has been kicked out of his pack "just because I ate that little boy all by myself"—is an inspired creation, a thoroughly seedy character whose crude charm masks the soul of a bloodthirsty killer. Whenever McDowell is on the screen, the story springs to life.

At other times, however, this production seems slow-paced and slightly spiritless. Mary Steenburgen (in real life, McDowell's wife) is sweet but colorless as the title character, a young lady poised on the brink of maturity, whose confusion about various adult matters (including sex) makes her vulnerable to the approaches of the treacherous wolf. (She also seems a bit old for the role.) The scenes in which Reggie eats Riding Hood's grandma and then lures the heroine herself into bed may strike some parents as unduly disturbing (especially since the sexual overtones of this episode are accentuated. After Reggie rolls on top of Riding Hood, there is a quick fadeout, followed by a shot of him in bed, sighing, "Oh that was good. About the best I ever had. So young and tender and juicy").

Still, "Little Red Riding Hood" is *meant* to be disturbing, and young viewers who watch this well-made version are sure to take its message—beware of sweet-talking strangers—to heart.

(See review of *Faerie Tale Theatre* for a description of this series as a whole.)

LITTLE WOMEN

CHILDREN'S VIDEO LIBRARY (1983), $29.95, 60 mins.
Ages 6–9, ★★

All the things that have made Louisa May Alcott's famous Civil War story beloved by generations of readers—the drama, excitement, laughter, and pathos —are completely missing from this slick but soulless cartoon. Like so many animated adaptations of literary classics, it dutifully runs through the highlights of the book while draining all the life out of them. It's less like an animated version of the original book than a cartoon adaptation of the Cliff Notes.

There is some decent artwork here—the cartoon does a creditable job of evoking the nineteenth-century New England setting. It also does a fairly good job of capturing the personality of the central character, Jo, the spunky, high spirited, ambitious sister who struggles to succeed as a writer. But the three other March sisters are ciphers, and the film as a whole is flat and mechanical. It is devoid of emotion (the only scene that even comes close to being affecting is the famous one in which Jo has her beautiful blond hair cut off to sell to a wigmaker). A particularly moving (if sentimental) episode in the original book is the death of the sweet sister, Beth, from scarlet fever. Here, the character simply lies in bed for a few days, then makes a complete recovery. This change is obviously intended to make the story less upsetting to young viewers, but its only effect is to water down this insipid movie even more. If you're looking for a good video cassette version of *Little Women*, rent the 1933 George Cukor movie starring Katharine Hepburn.

THE LOONEY TUNES VIDEO SHOW, Vols. 1–7

WARNER (1940s–1960s), $39.98 each, 38–51 min.
5 and up, ★★★

Each of these volumes brings together seven vintage Warner Brothers cartoons featuring Bugs Bunny, Daffy Duck, Tweety and Sylvester, Wile E. Coyote, Pepe LePew, and other animated superstars. Since these packages present unedited cartoons without adding any new material to tie them together, animation buffs prefer them to the longer anthologies (like *The Bugs Bunny/Road Runner Movie*), which contain a fair amount of filler. Young viewers, on the other hand, might appreciate the greater sense of continuity and coherence that the feature-length movies have. (See review of *The Bugs Bunny/Road Runner Movie*.)

THE MAGIC OF DR. SNUGGLES

EMBASSY (1979), $29.95, 60 min.
Preschool–7, ★★★

Dr. Snuggles—a sweet, white-haired inventor who looks like a cross between Ben Franklin and a leprechaun—lives in a colorful fairy-tale land where everything, from his pocket watch to a rainbow, is alive and endowed with a human personality. This appealing Dutch-produced cartoon, which consists of three Dr. Snuggles adventures, is several cuts above the average made-for-TV kiddie show. Although the animation is very limited, the graphics are bright and imaginative. And the characters (including a mischievous mouse named Knobby, Dennis the Badger, and a pair of zany rabbits called Benjy and Freddy, who wear scarves and stocking caps) are just off-beat enough to seem cute without being saccharine.

In the first episode, Dr. Snuggles and his animal helpers tinker together a robot housemaid they name Mathilda Junkbottom. Like L. Frank Baum's Tin Woodman, Mathilda is despondent because she lacks a heart, so the good doctor persuades his alarm clock (who spends most of his time snoozing anyway) to take up residence inside Mathilda and serve as her ticker. The second cartoon on the cassette is closest in spirit to a traditional fairy tale. In order to win $1,000, which he intends to donate to Granny Toots's cat hospital, Dr. Snuggles and his friends enter a balloon race. Their opponents are a couple of foul-playing critters, Willy the Terrible Fox and Charlie Rat. Snuggles and his crew undergo a bunch of delightful adventures along the way, taking time to assist some ants, a family of octopi, and a witch named Winnie Vinegarbottle, all of whom repay the good doctor by helping him win the contest. In the final episode, Snuggles must invent a special diamond-making machine in order to restore the color to a washed-out, miserable rainbow.

The three "Dr. Snuggles" stories on this cassette vary in quality—the second cartoon is unquestionably the best of the lot. But all of them are likable, entertaining, and sweet to the core. And the values embodied by their kindly main character—goodness, caring, a readiness to lend others a helping hand —make him a truly commendable cartoon hero.

THE MANY ADVENTURES OF WINNIE THE POOH

WALT DISNEY HOME VIDEO (1976), $34.95, 74 min.
Preschool–7, ★★★½

If your children are already fans of A.A. Milne's beloved Winnie-the-Pooh stories, they'll be enchanted by this video cassette. If they have not yet discovered the pleasures of Pooh, this animated adaptation will serve as a delightful introduction.

There's no central story line here—just a string of episodes involving the adorable (if none-too-bright) teddy bear and the other inhabitants of the Hundred Acre Wood. The characters—from the incurably gloomy Eeyore to the irrepressibly bouncy Tigger—are a completely irresistible crew, and their adventures are full of charming, childlike absurdity. In one "chapter" (the cartoon is cast in the form of a storybook whose pages come to life before our eyes), Pooh attempts to steal honey from a beehive by passing himself off as a little black rain cloud. In another, he invites himself to lunch at Rabbit's house and eats so much honey that he becomes wedged in the front door and has to remain there until he loses some weight. There are sequences in which Pooh and Piglet go hunting for a Woozle, Owl's house is blown down during a blustery day, Tigger gets himself stuck up a tree, and much more.

Full of funny little songs and first-rate voice characterizations (especially by Paul Winchell as the mischievous, manic Tigger), *The Many Adventures of Winnie the Pooh* is an intensely sweet and winsome cartoon that does an excellent job of capturing the special innocence and charm of the original stories.

MARY POPPINS

WALT DISNEY HOME VIDEO (1964), $84.95, 140 min.
5 and up, ★★★★

Mary Poppins was the Disney studio's biggest commercial success—and for good reason. It's a glowing, joyful, and continuously entertaining movie, one of the best family films ever to come out of the Hollywood dream factory.

Based on P.L. Travers' popular books about a magical English nanny, *Mary Poppins* is set in a postcard-pretty version of Edwardian London. The story is about a pair of irresistibly cute, though "incorrigible," children, Michael and Jane Banks, who have gone through six nannies in the past four months. Their father, a stiff, humorless, and supremely self-satisfied man, determines to find a strict, no-nonsense governess who will keep a tight rein on his children. Jane and Michael, however, want a different sort of nanny altogether, and their prayers are answered when Mary Poppins (Julie Andrews, looking radiantly pretty) floats down from the clouds, clutching a carpetbag and a parasol. What Mary brings to the Banks household is not only the discipline that Mr. Banks desires, but also something much more important—she brings magic into the dreary, routine lives of Jane and Michael. The enchantment begins immediately, when Mary tidies up the children's nursery by casting a spell that causes the room to clean itself up. Rumpled pajamas fold themselves neatly and fly into a bureau drawer, the bed makes itself, toys march obediently back to their shelves. A bit later, Mary and the children leap inside a sidewalk drawing done by the pavement artist/street musician/chimney cleaner Bert (charmingly played by Dick Van Dyke) and find themselves in a cartoon wonderland, where they frolic and dance with a host of animated creatures. This "Jolly Holiday" sequence is one of the most dazzling and exuberant pieces of cinemagic ever performed by Disney's corps of effects wizards. It's a high point of the film. Another is a stunningly choreographed sequence in which Bert and his fellow chimney sweeps do a rousing dance routine on the rooftops of London. By the end of the film, Mary has managed to pull off the most magical feat of all, turning Mr. Banks from a cold, aloof businessman who can think of nothing but money into a warm and loving father.

At two hours and twenty minutes, *Mary Poppins* may be too much of a good thing. Given their notoriously short attention spans, many small viewers are bound to get fidgety before the movie is over. Still, it's hard to wish that this film were shorter—from beginning to end it's an absolute delight.

MIGHTY JOE YOUNG

NOSTALGIA MERCHANT (1949), $29.95, 94 mins.
8 and up, ★★★

This first-rate fantasy adventure was made by the same people who created the original (1933) *King Kong*. As a work of cinematic art, *Mighty Joe Young* does not begin to match the brilliance of the earlier film, which is an undisputed masterpiece. But it's probably a better movie for children. *Kong* can be very frightening to kids, and its climax—in which the doomed, giant ape is gunned down from the top of the Empire State Building—upsets many young viewers. *Mighty Joe Young,* on the other hand, is occasionally tense but never especially scary, and it has a happy ending that older viewers might find extremely sentimental but which is guaranteed to send the little ones away with a smile.

The story is a rehash of the successful *Kong* formula. A brash, fast-talking impresario named Max O'Hara (played by Robert Armstrong, who performed the identical role in *Kong*) comes to Africa to capture wild animals for his posh New York City nightclub, the Golden Safari. Instead of bringing hunters to bag the game, however, he is accompanied by a bunch of cowboys, a wildly improbable situation that seems perfectly logical when you're eight years old. O'Hara and his cowhands come upon a king-size gorilla who seems to be a monster but turns out to be the pet of a sweet young woman named Jill (Terry Moore). Though this giant ape—whose name is Joe—is ferocious enough to wipe out a pack of lions, he turns into a teddy bear when Jill is around. (All she has to do is sing a few bars of "Beautiful Dreamer" to him and he grows weak in the knees.) O'Hara convinces Jill to take Joe to New York, where he is forced to appear in a series of humiliating nightclub routines. Eventually, after being fed a few bottles of whiskey by some obnoxious drunks, Joe goes berserk and demolishes the club. He becomes a fugitive from justice, but redeems himself by risking his life to save a little girl from a burning orphanage.

There are marvelous things in this film. The special effects are among the most dazzling ever put on screen. Like Kong, Joe is basically a highly sophisticated puppet, made to seem uncannily alive through the magic of stop-motion animation. Every scene in which he appears is spectacular, and a few (his early confrontation with the lasso-swinging cowboys, a nightclub act in which he plays tug-of-war with a bunch of beefy musclemen, his rescue of the orphan from the blazing building) are truly unforgettable. *Mighty Joe Young* lacks the depth and tragic dimension of *King Kong;* it's a smaller scale movie in every way (instead of an awesome ape with a screaming woman clutched in his paw, we get a pretty girl with an oversized gorilla wrapped around her little finger). But, for that very reason, it's more suitable for young viewers. *Mighty Joe Young* might not be the epic adventure its creators intended, but it is certainly one of the most entertaining and highly polished kiddie films ever made.

MOUSERCISE

WALT DISNEY HOME VIDEO (1985), $39.95, 55 min.
Ages 6–10, ★★★★

Although it comes in a box featuring scenes from the Disney Channel's daily "Mousercise" show, this cassette is, in fact, an original, made-for-video production. In spite of its whimsical name (and a brief opening appearance by Mickey Mouse, who welcomes all the Mouseketeers in the audience to the Mickey Mouse Health Club), this program doesn't kid around. On the contrary, it's a polished, professional, no-nonsense workout tape designed to get school-age children onto their feet and into the best physical condition possible.

A pretty, perky, enormously energetic young woman named Kellyn leads a group of preteen boys and girls through a series of routines, beginning with warm-ups and stretches and moving through arm strengtheners, "belly burners," fast-paced aerobics, and leg exercises. In between each segment, Kellyn offers a brief discussion of some issue relating to fitness and nutrition.

Besides conveying important information, these "Health Breaks" give kids a chance to catch their breath. After a final cool-down period, there is a special "bonus" segment, in which Kellyn teaches viewers how to perform a rather elaborately choreographed dance routine to disco music.

If you're looking for a tape that will help your preteen children discover the benefits—and pleasures —of regular, vigorous exercise, *Mousercise* is as good as they come.

THE MUPPET REVUE

PLAYHOUSE VIDEO (1985), $59.95, 56 min.
Preschool and up, ★★★½

An hour-long compilation of songs and sketches from TV's "The Muppet Show," with a bit of new material to link the different segments together. (See review of *Jim Henson's Muppet Video*.)

MUPPET TREASURES

PLAYHOUSE VIDEO (1985), $59.95, 56 min.
Preschool and up, ★★★½

Zero Mostel, Loretta Lynn, Ethel Merman, Buddy Rich, Peter Sellers, and Paul Simon are the special guest stars on this collection of classic bits from "The Muppet Show." (See review of *Jim Henson's Muppet Video*.)

MY LITTLE PONY

CHILDREN'S VIDEO LIBRARY (1984), $19.95, 30 min.
Ages 5–9, ★★

If you are the parent of a young girl, then you are probably already familiar with Hasbro's "My Little Pony" play figures—those plastic, pastel-colored horses with oversized eyes, brushable tails, and identifying symbols on their haunches. They're extremely hot-selling toys, and this made-for-TV cartoon exists for no other purpose than to sell a few million more of them. It's a marketing tool disguised as a fairy tale—a crudely animated, garishly colored, empty-headed contrivance with all the heart and soul of a half-hour TV commercial.

The story itself is a weird hybrid, a mixture of saccharine "Care Bears" sentimentality and "Dungeons & Dragons" action-fantasy. The villain is a giant horned centaur named Tirac, the Master of Midnight Castle, who intends to use his Rainbow of Darkness to spread eternal night throughout the world. To accomplish this fiendish plan, he sends his bestial henchman, Skorpan (actually a handsome young prince, transformed into a monster by Tirac's evil magic), to kidnap four of the ponies. Tirac intends to change the little critters into flying dragon-steeds to pull his skyborne chariot. Enlisting the aid of a spunky girl named Megan, the rest of the ponies set off on a quest to rescue their friends from the clutches of Tirac and destroy his evil power before it's too late.

Tony Randall and Sandy Duncan lend their voice talents to this insipid collection of cartoon clichés. It's interesting (and disheartening) to see how consistently cartoons of this type deny any real power to their female heroes. True, the ponies, with Megan's assistance, do defeat the bad guy. But (like the Care Bears, the Charmkins, and other fantasy characters aimed at small girls) the only weapons they're permitted to wield are rainbows, songs, and disarming gentleness (whereas the Transformers, G.I. Joe, He-Man, and other boy-oriented figures are equipped with complex, futuristic weaponry). Associating girls strictly with nature and tenderness and boys with high technology and aggression can only reinforce the most retrogressive kinds of sexual stereotypes.

In short, virtually everything in this cartoon is objectionable. Young girls will undoubtedly eat it up, but that doesn't make it any less offensive.

NATIONAL VELVET

MGM/UA (1944), $24.95, 124 min.
8 and up, ★★★★

Twelve-year-old Elizabeth Taylor lights up the screen in this deservedly famous family movie. Dreamy-eyed, radiant, and thoroughly enchanting, Taylor plays Velvet Brown, a butcher's daughter living in a picturesque English village in the late 1920s. Like many girls her age, Velvet is infatuated, almost obsessed, with horses —she spends most of her waking hours daydreaming about having a racehorse of her own and becoming "the best rider in England." Two things happen to make her dreams come true. First, a troubled but good-hearted young drifter and ex-jockey named Mi Taylor (Mickey Rooney) is taken in by Velvet's family. Soon afterward, Velvet wins a high-spirited sorrel gelding (named The Pie) in a village raffle. Determined to enter her horse in the Grand National, the "greatest race in the world," Velvet persuades Mi to help her train The Pie. The race itself serves as the exciting climax of the film. When Mi and Velvet fail to find a suitable jockey, the spunky young girl disguises herself as a man and—in a sequence packed with thrills, spills, and suspense—wins the big race. When Velvet's ruse is discovered, she is disqualified. But her amazing feat turns her into an international celebrity.

Everything about this movie—from the consistently fine acting to the stunning views of the lush English countryside—is a pleasure. Especially appealing is the portrayal of Velvet's family. The many scenes inside the Brown cottage are full of warmth, charm, and humor. Angela Lansbury is delightful as Velvet's boy-crazy older sister, Edwina, and Donald Crisp is equally outstanding as Velvet's stern, frequently exasperated, but always loving father. Best of all is Anne Revere as the mother, a woman of tremendous wisdom, strength, and dignity—the real heart and soul of the family (Revere's performance won the Oscar for Best Supporting Actress). As a young girl, Velvet's mother had pursued (and realized) her own impossible dream, becoming the first woman ever to swim the English Channel. Seeing the same fires burning in her daughter, she offers the girl all the support and encouragement she can.

All in all, *National Velvet* is a heartwarming, inspiring, and immensely entertaining film for everyone in the family.

NELVANAMATION

WARNER (1980), $49.95, 100 min.
6 and up, ★★★★

This cassette brings together four 25-minute animated fantasies from Canada's celebrated Nelvana studio.

Unlike Disney cartoons, which have a very glossy, lifelike quality, the Nelvana style is more loose-limbed and whimsical. But Nelvana shares with Disney a commitment to high-quality, full animation. You won't find any mass-produced, cookie cutter artwork here. And you won't find the sort of low humor and mind-numbing action that characterizes most Saturday morning kiddie cartoons, either. In addition to splendid, highly imaginative animation, these cartoons offer strong, compelling stories, vivid characters, excellent music (supplied by the likes of John Sebastian, the leader of the great sixties folk-rock group The Lovin' Spoonful, and Sylvia Tyson, formerly one-half of the splendid Canadian folk duo, Ian and Sylvia), and morals that are uplifting without ever being corny.

The first cartoon, "A Cosmic Christmas," involves three extraterrestrial wise men who arrive on earth on the evening of December 24th. They have come to investigate the "transitory celestial phenomenon" which occurred two thousand earth years ago. The hero of the tale is a young boy named Peter, who realizes that they are talking about the Star of Bethlehem and offers to show them the true meaning of Christmas. He has a bit of trouble finding any evidence of the holiday spirit at first, but, in an exciting, dramatic, and ultimately heartwarming climax, the wise old aliens get a firsthand demonstration of the qualities that Christmas is meant to celebrate: peace, love, and caring for others.

The second cartoon is a witty retelling of the classic American legend, "The Devil and Daniel Webster." Here, a young girl-mouse named Jan, one half of a folk team called Dan and Jan, sells her soul to the devil for rock superstardom. Trading her jeans for bangled dresses and her dulcimer for an ultracool backup band, she becomes an overnight sensation, lead singer for the platinum-selling supergroup, Funky Jan and the Animal Kingdom. When the devil comes to claim her soul, her old friend Dan intervenes and manages to save her from eternal damnation with a heartfelt folktune. (Moral: A song from the heart can beat the devil every time.) There *is* a potentially disturbing element in this cartoon (the only one, really, on the cassette). The devil here is no stereotyped Satan with horns and a pitchfork, but a bloated, repellent pink lizard. He's an amusing creation: with his white suit, gold chains, and ruffled shirt unbuttoned to the belly, he's a witty caricature of a sleazy Hollywood agent. But young children might well find him unsettling, particularly in one sequence where he chases Jan while assuming a variety of bizarre animal shapes.

The third cartoon, "Romie-0 and Julie-8," is a futuristic version of the famous love story—an imaginative blending of Shakespeare and *Blade Runner*. Two attractive robots from rival cybernetics companies meet, fall in love, and run away to a junkyard planet, where the pretty Julie-8 is pursued by a mechanical monster named Spare Partski. Unlike Shakespeare's tragedy, this story has a happy ending, whose moral paraphrases the title of another Shakespeare play: Oil's well that ends well.

The last cartoon on this tape, "Please Don't Eat the Planet," is the weirdest—and also the best—of the bunch. It concerns a family of space farmers who look like nineteenth-century pioneers and sail through the heavens in an interstellar Conestoga wagon. Landing on a planet called Laffalot, they meet a community of extraterrestrial zanies who resemble Dr. Seuss characters and whose ruler is a king named Goochi (son of Eric the Whoopeecushion). Goochi's voice characterization is supplied by the immortal Sid Caesar in his funniest performance in recent years. The story tells how the farmers save the aliens from their own subterranean food-making machine, which is eating up the

196

planet from the inside. There's not much of a moral here—just plenty of sweetness, charm, and fun.

Also available: *Nelvanamation II*—two more 25-minute cartoons ("Take Me Out to the Ball Game" and "The Jack Rabbit Story"), featuring music by Rick Danko (of The Band) and John Sebastian and voice characterizations by Phil Silvers and Garrett Morris.

THE NEVERENDING STORY

WARNER (1984), $79.95, 94 min.
7 and up, ★★★

Based on a best-selling novel by Michael Ende, *The NeverEnding Story* is a handsomely produced but slightly simple-minded fantasy movie. The opening of the film introduces us to a lonely young boy named Bastian, whose life seems empty and sad. His mother has recently died, his father has very little time for him, and Bastian himself is a sweet but "wimpy" little fellow who is shaken down each day for his lunch money by a trio of neighborhood bullies.

To escape his troubles, Bastian immerses himself in adventure novels. One day, he ducks into a musty old bookshop and discovers a strange, leather-bound volume called *The NeverEnding Story*. Carrying it to the attic of his school, Bastian spends the rest of the day reading it. This story—a mythical tale of magic and adventure—forms the main part of the movie. Set in the imaginary world of Fantasia, it involves a heroic young warrior named Atreya, who is sent on a long and dangerous quest to find a cure for the dying empress and save the world from a mysterious annihilating power called The Nothing. Atreya's quest is full of wonders and perils. Along the way, he encounters a variety of mythical creatures, ranging from a rock-eating giant to a flying, white-furred "luck-dragon," with the body of a serpent and the face of a lovable pooch. In the end, the kingdom of Fantasia is restored to wholeness, thanks to the last-minute intervention of Bastian, who gradually becomes drawn into the fantasy world that has taken shape inside his mind.

The NeverEnding Story is a slick, high-budget production with some first-rate special effects. The imaginary landscapes of Fantasia—luminous mountains, crystalline towers, parched wastelands, and lush forests —are genuinely dreamlike. Even more impressive are the mythical creatures Atreya meets on his odyssey: Falko the luck-dragon, a malevolent wolf-monster, a giant, wise old turtle who looks like the great grandfather of E.T.

Still, there are problems with this film. Parts of it seem much too upsetting for a children's movie. There's a very disturbing scene in which Atreya's beautiful, loyal pony sinks to his death in a sinister swamp. At another point, the young warrior walks past the body of a slain knight, whose visor suddenly blows open, revealing a rotted corpse's face that looks like an image out of *Poltergeist*. And some of the inhabitants of Fantasia—bird men, triple-faced females, and creatures with grotesquely oversized heads—seem like nightmares out of a painting by Hieronymus Bosch.

The climax of the film is also problematic. Though many children will find the ending deeply satisfying (Bastian is allowed to take a very fitting revenge on his three youthful tormentors), the film's message is a little ambiguous. The movie seems intended as a celebration of the human imagination, but it comes across as an apology for escapism.

Still, this movie has definite pleasures. If your children are fans of sword-and-sorcery fantasy films, then

The NeverEnding Story will provide them with real rewards.

THE NEW THREE STOOGES, Vols. 1–7

EMBASSY (1965), $24.95 each, 30 min. each
6 and up, ★

Some parents have always deplored the Three Stooges, regarding the group's crude physical comedy as the lowest form of humor. On the other hand, many of today's grown-ups grew up watching old Three Stooges shorts on TV and find the trio's infantile antics absolutely hilarious. Only the most rabid Stooge fan, however, is likely to find *The New Three Stooges*—a shamelessly cheap, made-for-TV cartoon show—even remotely entertaining. For the most part, these video cassettes are without redeeming value of any kind.

Each cartoon (there are four per cassette) is framed by a live-action segment featuring the real Stooges —Moe Howard, Larry Fine, and a blubbery character, Curly Joe (not the original Curly, but a later, less manic replacement, Joe De Rita). These live-action sketches offer slightly toned-down bits of vintage Stooge humor. There's lots of head-bopping, ear-cuffing, and smacking people in the face with wet paint brushes, though some of the more vicious gags have been eliminated (Moe doesn't jab anyone in the eyes, for example). Diehard Stooge fans should find these routines amusing enough, and kids will probably think they're hilarious (whether or not you *want* your children to watch this stuff is another question).

Interestingly, the cartoons themselves contain no violence at all. The probable explanation for this fact, given the overall quality of the cartoons, is that the producers couldn't afford the cost of animating a smack in the face. There is very little movement of any kind in these crudely made, static cartoons. There is also no logic, intelligence, or wit. Here's an example of *New Three Stooges* humor: At the start of one cartoon, set in the trenches during World War I, a soldier says to his commanding officer, "If we don't get a phone to the front line, we'll be in trouble, Captain." Replies the officer, "It's taken me thirty years to become a general. If you don't remember that I'm a general, *you're* in trouble." That's about as funny as these cartoons get.

If you think the *old* Three Stooges are terrible, you certainly won't want to rent this cassette for your children. And if you think the old Three Stooges are terrific, you still won't want to rent this tape for your children.

THE NEW ZOO REVUE, Vols. 1–3

FAMILY HOME ENTERTAINMENT (1972–75),
$29.95 each, 60 min. each
Preschool–7, ★★★

The New Zoo Revue has its heart in the right place. This determinedly bouncy TV show, syndicated nation-wide in the early 1970s, uses songs, skits, and an amusing trio of animal characters (Charlie the Owl, Freddie the Frog, and Henrietta Hippo) to impart valuable lessons about a variety of important issues. Each cassette contains two half-hour episodes. In one, Charlie—a brainy bird with a weakness for crackpot inventions and corny jokes—concocts a happiness pill.

This situation serves as the basis for a lesson on drug abuse. In another episode, Freddie learns that trying too hard to gain attention is a good way to alienate people. A third show, in which Henrietta gets furious with Freddie for helping himself to one of her pastries, deals with the destructive effects of anger. And so on.

Unlike some other made-for-TV kiddie shows, there's nothing tacky about the look of *The New Zoo Revue*. The sets (especially Henrietta's home, which resembles a full-size Victorian dollhouse) are bright and appealing, as are the elaborate costumes worn by the three animal players. Unfortunately, though the show doesn't look cheap, it does seem extremely dated. Its two human stars—a somewhat goofy-looking guy named Doug and his intensely perky "helper," Emmy Jo—look as though they've stepped out of a time capsule buried in San Francisco in 1969. Both dress in a sixties "mod" style that seems very quaint (if not downright silly) nowadays. Doug favors paisley shirts and polyester bell-bottoms, while Emmy Jo wears white boots and miniskirts that barely cover her behind. The songs—about love, friends, and feelings —also sound very old-fashioned, like music from a kindergarten version of *Hair*. It doesn't help matters that no one in the cast can carry a tune. In fact, the song-and-dance routines (of which there are about a half-dozen per episode) are far and away the most grating thing about this show.

The New Zoo Revue is a program that teaches while it entertains, and it comes complete with a recommendation by the National Education Association. Still, there is something distinctly recycled about these cassettes. They have the look of material that someone has dug out of a vault and dusted off in order to cash in on the booming market in children's video.

Nicholas Nickleby

VESTRON (1978), $59.95, 72 min.
8 and up, ★★½

See review of *Great Expectations*.

The Nightingale

CBS/FOX VIDEO (1983), $39.98, 60 min.
6 and up, ★★★

Faerie Tale Theatre often gets very impressive performances from its guest stars by casting them against type. (Joan Collins' surprisingly effective portrayal of the hideously ugly hag in *Hansel and Gretel* is a good example.) Mick Jagger's starring role in *The Nightingale* is not quite as successful. As the Emperor of Cathay, Jagger plays (with mixed results) a part that is the complete opposite of the fast-living, high-voltage image he usually projects. This king may be as privileged as any rock superstar, but he is shy, lonely, and listless to the point of immobility.

Surrounded by fawning ministers and servants, the emperor does nothing but sit around all day watching dull performances by jugglers and mimes and sampling a range of exotic delicacies (paté made of yak meat and hummingbird tongues, peacock stuffed with goose stuffed with pigeon stuffed with quail). Though he is waited on hand and foot, he lacks the only things that make life worth living: true love and friendship. Hearing about a magical nightingale whose whereabouts are known only to a little kitchen maid (Barbara Hershey), he commands that it be brought to court—and instantly becomes enamored of its singing. Soon afterward, however, the Emperor of Japan sends him a gift of a gold, clockwork bird who trills with mechanical perfection. At the advice of his counselors, the emperor chooses the artificial bird over the nightingale, which flies back to its forest. No sooner has the bird departed, however, than the emperor becomes terminally ill. Hastening to the forest, the kitchen maid finds the nightingale and persuades it to return to the court. In the end, the bird's singing heals the emperor, who finds in the nightingale and the little kitchen maid the real friends he has so desperately craved.

There are some very nice things about this production. Its lavish sets and exquisite costumes make it a visual feast, and its score is genuinely lovely. At moments, the production has an authentically magical quality. Best of all is the dark, dreamlike forest, where the talking nightingale lives among dancing fairies and frogs that wear golden crowns. (Parents should note, however, that this program also contains several exceptionally nightmarish scenes in which the ailing king is visited by the angel of death—a grotesque, demonic dwarf who torments him with terrifying visions.)

The trouble with this production is simply that it is extremely slow-moving and lackluster. Jagger brings some surprising sweetness to his role, but his performance is as drooping as the long, Fu Manchu mustache glued to his upper lip. Older viewers may well appreciate the understated pleasures of this beautifully mounted fairy tale, but younger children are likely to be bored silly by it.

(See review of *Faerie Tale Theatre* for a description of the series as a whole.)

THE NUTCRACKER FANTASY

RCA/COLUMBIA (1979), $39.95, 80 min.
6 and up, ★★½

E.T.A. Hoffmann's "The Nutcracker and the Mouse-king," which served as the inspiration for Tchaikovsky's *The Nutcracker Suite*, is also the basis for this above-average musical fantasy, which uses puppet animation to bring the story to life. The characters are elaborately sculpted and costumed dolls, filmed one frame at a time on exquisitely crafted miniature sets. Visually, this is a very polished and handsome production. There's a nice score, combining snatches of Tchaikovsky with some bouncy folk tunes by a duo called Bishop and Gwinn, several graceful, live-action ballet interludes, and effective voice characterizations by a cast that includes Melissa Gilbert, Christopher Lee, Jo Anne Worley, Dick Van Patten, Roddy McDowell, and Eva Gabor.

The story is about a pretty young girl named Clara who, in a dream, climbs inside her uncle's big grandfather clock and finds herself in a colorful wonderland, a magical Kingdom of Dolls. The king's daughter, Princess Marie, has been turned into a sleeping mouse by the evil, two-headed mouse queen, Morphia. Visiting the mysterious gypsy fortune teller known as the Queen of Time, Clara learns that the only way to save the princess is to use a magical, pearl-handled sword to crack the evil Shell of Darkness in the land of the mice. A handsome soldier named Franz leads an army of windup toy soldiers in an epic battle with the nasty rodents. Franz manages to shatter the magical shell, but not before Queen Morphia casts a spell on him that changes him into a wooden nutcracker. The last section of the film concerns Clara's quest to restore Franz to human form.

This film actually sounds more interesting than it is. Parts of it go on for far too long (in fact the whole film seems to drag after a while). Although the dolls move with reasonably expressive gestures, they don't have very much personality; they remain (so to speak) wooden. The plot is occasionally very convoluted (there are dreams within dreams within dreams) and the action is sometimes unclear and—particularly in the battle sequence—pretty chaotic. It would be hard for younger viewers to follow the story without an adult present to explain what is going on. In fact, you might not want small children to see this film at all, since it contains a number of very (even gratuitously) scary elements. The movie opens with a prologue in which a menacing character called The Ragman—a bogeyman who preys on naughty children—sneaks up on a young boy who has stayed up past his bedtime and transforms him into a mouse. This sequence, which would be as terrifying to a young child as anything in *Poltergeist* or *Gremlins,* has nothing at all to do with the main story. Other bits, such as Clara's first, nightmarish encounter with the two-headed mouse queen, are equally chilling.

Still, this is, on the whole, a well-made and enjoyable film, one which does a respectable job of combining the dark, weird fantasy of Hoffmann's original tale with the more familiar enchantments of the famous ballet.

THE OLD CURIOSITY SHOP

VESTRON (1978), $59.95, 72 min.
8 and up, ★★½

An earnest but slow-moving animated adaptation from Vestron Video's *Charles Dickens Collection*. See review of *Great Expectations*.

OLIVER TWIST

VESTRON (1978), $59.95, 72 min.
8 and up, ★★½

See review of *Great Expectations*.

ON VACATION WITH MICKEY MOUSE AND FRIENDS

WALT DISNEY HOME VIDEO (1956), $49.95, 47 min.
Preschool–8, ★★★½

This animated anthology is actually an old Disneyland TV show from the 1950s with the commercials removed. With "the Boss" away on business, Jiminy Cricket is handed the assignment of putting together the weekly show. This is the device used to string together a half-dozen vintage cartoons. Jiminy calls on his celebrity buddies for help, only to find that each is away on vacation—Mickey is out playing golf, Goofy's gone fishing, Donald is at a dude ranch, and so on.

The cartoons themselves range from a run-of-the-mill Donald, "Dude Duck" (1951), to a certified Mickey Mouse masterpiece, "Mickey's Trailer" (1938), which features some of the most luscious animation and rollicking physical comedy ever created by the studio. Another gem is "Goofy and Wilbur" (1938), a landmark cartoon which marks "the Goof's" debut as a solo performer.

There are (as is often true of Disney cartoons) a few potentially disturbing moments. In "Hawaiian Holiday" (1937), Disney's penchant for posterior humor is displayed when Donald gets his rear-end scorched in a campfire; in another scene, Pluto has his nose mauled by a belligerent crab. Some young viewers find these bits of physical cruelty upsetting. Another disquieting moment occurs midway through "Goofy and Wilbur," when the Goof's grasshopper pal (an early prototype of Jiminy Cricket) is swallowed by a hungry frog that is devoured in turn by a voracious stork that flies away before Goofy can reach it. The climax of this cartoon, however, features a joyful resurrection as magical as anything in the brothers Grimm.

On the whole, this video cassette will enchant not only young viewers but those baby-boom parents with fond memories of sitting around watching the old Walt Disney TV show on weekend nights.

THE OWL AND THE PUSSYCAT

AVG (1985), $19.95, 30 min.
Preschool–7, ★★★

See review of *Read-Along Magic Videos*.

PETER COTTONTAIL'S ADVENTURES

FAMILY HOME ENTERTAINMENT (1978), $39.95, 70 min.
Preschool–6, ★★

This "full-length feature film" has actually been stitched together (clumsily) from bits and pieces of the cartoon show *Fables of the Green Forest* (see review). The *Green Forest* cartoons are nice for younger viewers. Based on the children's stories of author Thornton Burgess, they are animated in a simple but charming style and feature a sizable cast of amusing, believable creatures (Peter Cottontail, Reddy Fox, Buster Bear, Sammy Jay, Chatterer the Squirrel, Johnny Chuck and others) in gently paced, sweet-natured stories.

The problem with *Peter Cottontail's Adventures* is that—because it tries to patch together a feature-length movie out of parts of various cartoons—it doesn't have much coherence. There *is* a common thread that runs throughout the film—Reddy Fox's efforts to trap Peter. But the film has been put together so awkwardly that it's hard to follow in places. One moment, Johnny Chuck is lying on the ground in a faint after saving

too, but because you'll help them get more out of it. (The language of Browning's poem is very sophisticated at times. And because "Cinderella" uses no language at all, there are places where a small child might not completely understand the pantomimed action without an older person there to explain what's going on.)

THE PIED PIPER OF HAMELIN

CBS/FOX VIDEO (1985), $39.98, 60 min.
6 and up, ★★★★

Based on Robert Browning's haunting poem, this *Faerie Tale Theatre* version of *The Pied Piper of Hamelin* is not only one of the best shows in the series but also one of the most unusual.

The program opens in an English country house in 1834, where Browning himself is entertaining a young visitor, Master William, with the bedtime tale of the legendary Piper. As Browning begins to recite his poem, we move back in time to the medieval town of Hamelin. All the outstanding qualities associated with *Faerie Tale Theatre* are very much in evidence here —marvelous sets and costumes, first-rate acting, fine direction. What makes this particular program different from all the others in the series is that it is written entirely in rhymed couplets. Its dialogue and narration combine the language of Browning's original poem with additional verse provided by the show's multi-talented writer/director, Nicholas Meyer (author of the bestselling novel *The Seven Percent Solution,* as well as the director of such films as *Time After Time, Star Trek III,* and *The Day After*). Because the script draws so heavily on Browning's original (which employs a fairly sophisticated vocabulary), some of the language may well go over the heads of young children. Still, the audience of six-year-old viewers with whom I watched this video had no trouble following the story, and they were utterly entranced by the *sound* of the rhymed dialogue, even when (as occasionally happened) they had difficulty grasping its meaning.

Eric Idle (of "Monty Python" fame) plays two roles in this splendid production, appearing as both Browning and the Piper. As the latter, he is convincingly unearthly—a pallid, lank-haired, totally mysterious figure who seems to have stepped straight out of the land of Faerie.

Needless to say, this tape shouldn't be shown to any child who is squeamish about rats, since it is full of close-up shots of the creatures. But to everyone else, this lovely, lyrical program can be recommended without reservation.

(See review of *Faerie Tale Theatre* for a description of the series as a whole.)

The Pied Piper of Hamelin

MEDIA (1957), $59.95, 90 min.
Ages 6–9, ★★★

Originally broadcast as a prime-time TV special in the late 1950s, this generally enjoyable production has all the ingredients of an old-fashioned Hollywood family musical: lavish costumes and sets, genial (if forgettable) songs, a handful of lively production numbers, a bit of comic relief, and a gooey romantic subplot. It seems a little dated (its star, Van Johnson, looks distinctly like a matinee idol of an earlier era). But on the whole, this is a handsome, briskly paced, and entertaining show, enhanced by some excellent special effects and a couple of outstanding performances.

As the villain of the piece—the delightfully hateful, glory-seeking mayor of Hamelin—Claude Rains is (as always) outstanding. In his hunger to win the king's banner in a clock-building competition, this mayor is willing to sacrifice the health, wealth, and happiness of his entire community. The only person willing to stand up to him is the schoolteacher—and the mayor's prospective son-in-law—Trueson (Van Johnson), who is ultimately thrown into jail for his defiance. Meanwhile, a flash flood in a neighboring village creates an infestation of rats in Hamelin. Soon afterwards, the mysterious title character appears. Johnson, wearing a cape, feathered cap, and trim little goatee, also plays the Piper, whose signature tune is Edvard Grieg's haunting "The Hall of the Mountain King."

The Piper agrees to rid the town of its vermin for a specified fee. When the mayor and his fawning council renege on their promise, the uncanny musician retaliates by leading the children into a magical Candyland hidden deep inside a granite mountain. There is a comic interlude in which the mayor tries to arrange a match between his daughter and a foppish royal emissary (Jim Backus, doing his patented pompous fool routine). In the end the children are returned to their parents, the mayor repents, and Trueson and his love are reunited.

This production is at its best when it sticks close to the original story. The scenes of the uncanny musician, weaving his magical spell, first on the rodent population, then on the children of the town, have real power to them. Another element that works surprisingly well is the dialogue, which consists entirely of simple rhymed couplets.

All in all, this is a slick, heartwarming production —the kind of old-fashioned family entertainment they just don't make anymore.

PINOCCHIO

WALT DISNEY HOME VIDEO (1940), $79.95, 87 min.
6 and up, ★★★★

Pinocchio is the greatest feature-length cartoon ever made—which is not to say that it is necessarily the best film for children. To watch this animated masterpiece as a grown-up is to be awed by its beauty and technical brilliance. Every viewing reveals new wonders, from the exquisite renderings of the carved clocks and musical toys in Gepetto's woodshop to the way the puddles ripple around Jiminy's shoes as he walks through a rainswept street. Every image in this movie is as stunningly detailed as the finest nineteenth-century book illustration. In fact, the only difference between classic book illustrators like N. C. Wyeth and Arthur Rackham and the makers of *Pinocchio* is that, through an innovative combination of high art and high technology, the latter were able to create paintings that have the power to move, laugh, and sing—in short, pictures that are completely alive.

Children, however, are less likely to be impressed by the visual and technical genius of this cartoon than to be caught in the grip of its powerful story—and therein lies the problem. For *Pinocchio* is not only the most lavish, spectacular, and exciting Disney movie—it is also the most terrifying. Again and again on his quest to prove himself brave, truthful, and unselfish, the hero finds himself in situations straight out of a child's nightmare—caged by a bearded giant who turns from a jolly father figure into an axe-wielding ogre within minutes; swimming desperately from the jaws of an implacable monster whale; threatened with a grotesque transformation. (The scene in which the juvenile delinquent, Lampwick, is changed into a donkey is not only the single scariest scene in this movie; as film critic William K. Everson puts it, it is one of the "supreme moments of horror" in the history of motion pictures.)

This is not to say, of course, that *Pinocchio* is the kiddie equivalent of a horror movie—on the contrary, it is packed with joy and sweetness and pervaded by the reassuring presence of the wise and loving Jiminy Cricket. Still, if it is the richest of all Disney films, it is also the darkest.

For animation buffs, fantasy fans, or anyone interested in movies, the availability of Disney's masterpiece on video cassette is unequivocally a cause for rejoicing. For parents of small children, things are a bit more complex. In trying to decide whether or not to show this film to your kids, you might keep in mind that the greatest children's stories and films always contain elements of terror (just think of "Hansel and Gretel," "Little Red Riding Hood," and *The Wizard of Oz*) precisely because it is one of the functions of such art to articulate the unspoken fears of childhood and, in doing so, to help children come to terms with them. My own feeling is that a single viewing of *Pinocchio* is a more rewarding and meaningful experience for most children than exposure to a hundred Care Bears movies.

PINOCCHIO

UNICORN VIDEO (1968), $39.95, 74 min.
Preschool–8, ★

This live-action version of Collodi's classic children's story is depressingly bad (especially if you rent it in the mistaken belief that you are getting Disney's animated masterpiece). Everything about this low-grade Czechoslovakian import is so tacky that the movie is actively unpleasant to watch. The dubbing is awful, the sets seem to be made out of cardboard, the color makes your heart sink (the whole film is tinted a sickly green), and the story moves along at a glacial pace.

Pinocchio himself—the little puppet boy who can move without strings—is portrayed by an actual marionette from the Prague Marionette Theater. His movements *are* convincing (they're the best thing about the film), though his strings are glaringly visible in every frame he's in. Strangely, one of the key elements in the Pinocchio story is entirely missing from this version: this Pinocchio tells lies, but his nose never grows longer. Perhaps this isn't so strange after all. Judging from the overall quality of this film, the producers probably couldn't afford to invest in an extra nose.

The Disney version of *Pinocchio* is the best animated feature ever made. When you go to rent (or buy) it, just make sure you don't get stuck with this turkey by mistake.

PINOCCHIO

CBS/FOX VIDEO (1983), $39.98, 60 min.
6 and up, ★★★★

Though it lacks the grandeur and sheer technical brilliance of Disney's *Pinocchio*, this live-action adaptation of Collodi's story is one of the best entries in the *Faerie Tale Theatre* series. Paul Reubens—aka Pee-wee Herman—is perfectly cast as the gawky title character, an overgrown child who is constantly getting into mischief. With his perpetually wide-eyed expression and weirdly infantile mannerisms, Reubens seems born for the role. The other actors are equally outstanding: Carl Reiner as the slightly doddering woodcarver, Gepetto; Lainie Kazan as the hot-blooded fairy, Sophia, who just loves little boys; James Belushi as the juvenile delinquent, Mario, who lures Pinocchio into trouble; and James Coburn as a supremely sinister gypsy who runs a crooked puppet show and possesses a magical amulet that can change bad little boys into donkeys. There is even a cameo appearance of sorts by Father Guido Sarducci (Don Novello), who provides the offscreen narration.

Though some of the actors—particularly Kazan —have lots of fun with their roles, the story is essentially played straight. After Gepetto carves him out of a chunk of enchanted wood, Pinocchio is brought to life by the Blue Fairy, who warns him that he must prove himself kind, truthful, and loving before he can become a real boy. Sent out into the big world for the first time, Pinocchio instantly goes astray, ending up caged and transformed by the villainous gypsy. In the end, he redeems himself by rescuing his father from the belly of a monster whale, and is rewarded by being turned into a flesh-and-blood boy.

Besides the first-rate performances, this program features the high-quality production values characteristic of the whole *Faerie Tale Theatre* series. The story never lags and is, by turns, comical, dramatic, and genuinely tense. Coburn's gypsy is an extremely threatening figure, and there are parts of this production that are every bit as dark and potentially disturbing as the scarier bits in the Disney version. (The most nightmarish scene—as in the cartoon—is the one in which Pinocchio is turned into a donkey-boy.) The only real letdown is the segment involving the monster whale, which looks like a plastic bathtub toy. On the whole, however, this is an excellent dramatization that will appeal to young children and grown-ups alike.

(See review of *Faerie Tale Theatre* for a description of this series as a whole.)

PINOCCHIO IN OUTER SPACE

RCA/COLUMBIA (1964), $49.95, 71 min.
Ages 6–9, ★★½

As its title suggests, this cartoon is an updated, sci-fi version of *Pinocchio*. Thanks to some above-average animation, it's not quite as atrocious as it sounds. Still, it's pretty mediocre.

This Pinocchio is a blond little puppet with a nose that resembles a wine cork. Because he has reverted to his rebellious ways, Pinocchio has been turned back into wood and has been given only one more chance to redeem himself. (We learn all this from the Blue Fairy, whom we first see sitting up in the clouds, dodging assorted rocket ships, space capsules, and weather satellites.) To prove his bravery and selflessness, Pinocchio decides to capture a giant extraterrestrial whale named Astro, which has been demolishing rocket ships. Setting out for school one morning, he runs into two familiar scoundrels, Mr. Sharp—a fast-talking fox— and his dimwitted sidekick, Mr. Groovy, a beatnik cat with a beret, goatee, and a debilitating (supposedly comical) stutter. Mr. Sharp cons Pinocchio into spending his school money on a book called *Hypnotism Made Easy,* and the gullible little marionette decides that he'll capture Astro by mesmerizing him. His chance comes when an extraterrestrial turtle named Nertle picks up Pinocchio and takes him on a journey to Mars, where they find an abandoned city full of mutant animals. In the end (after being swallowed by Astro) Pinocchio and Nertle manage to capture the great flying whale and bring him safely back to earth.

The artwork here is actually quite charming. The problem with this cartoon is that the story is exceptionally weak and the characters are completely uninteresting. Nertle (whose voice is performed by Arnold Stang) is the most vivid individual in the cartoon, but even he is pretty colorless. The only mildly exciting part of the film is a scene in which Pinocchio and Nertle make a last-minute escape from a bunch of giant mutant sand crabs. (These great, drooling monsters might be scary to some small viewers.) For the most part, however, this space-age retelling of Collodi's classic falls very flat. And there is one seriously objectionable element: the attempts of the filmmakers to milk laughs out of Mr. Groovy's stutter. Children who suffer from this speech impediment will not be amused. Nor will their parents.

PINOCCHIO'S STORYBOOK ADVENTURES

VCI HOME VIDEO (1976), $39.95, 80 min.
Ages 6–8, ★

Everything about this videotape smacks of shoddiness. According to the package, its title is *Pinocchio's Storybook Adventures*. When you begin watching it, however, you discover that its title is actually *Pinocchio and His Magic Show*. You also discover that this film has very little to do with Pinocchio and nothing at all to do with a magic show.

What this tape really consists of are three little stories done with puppet animation (the "actors" are miniature wooden figures photographed one frame at a time to create the illusion of movement). These stories are strung together with a weak plot involving Pinocchio (who is portrayed by a clumsily handled marionette). When Maestro Eisenbeiss, the owner of the local puppet theater, comes down with a cold and can't put on his Saturday matinee performance, Pinocchio and the rest of the marionettes decide to do the show by themselves. This device serves as a way of introducing the three animated segments, which are the heart of the movie: whenever Pinocchio pulls the curtain, one of the animated stories appears. Of the three, the best is a straightforward version of *Sleeping Beauty*, featuring some handsome costumes and nicely detailed miniature sets. The other two stories are completely pointless. The first involves a little dog who gets stuck on an ice floe and has to be rescued by a passing boat. The second is a charmless fairy tale about three goofy carpenters who squander the wishes that a grateful elf grants them. Even the most mediocre examples of puppet animation usually have a modicum of interest, since there's something inherently magical about the sight of little wooden dolls that seem to be alive. But these three animated stories are as mediocre as they come.

As for the parts of the movie involving Pinocchio, they are nothing short of atrocious. Everything about them is tacky, beginning with the glaringly visible strings used to make Pinocchio move. The scenes in which Pinocchio appears with live actors (such as the ridiculously made-up individual who plays Gepetto) are poorly acted, poorly lighted, and shot on depressingly ugly sets. Collodi's famous creation is the source of one of the great kiddie films of all time—Disney's animated masterpiece. It has also inspired some of the worst children's films around—and this substandard video-tape is one of them.

PIPPI LONGSTOCKING

VIDEO GEMS (1969), $34.95, 99 min.
Ages 6–9 ★★★

It's easy to see why this movie—in spite of its shortcomings—appeals so strongly to young viewers (especially girls). For polite, well-bred little children living in a world of rules, regulations, and restrictions (all imposed by adults), Pippi Longstocking is a wish-fulfillment fantasy come to life—a high-spirited girl who is totally free of parental supervision, who can do, eat, and say exactly what she likes, and who is strong enough to toss a grown man up a tree.

Based on Astrid Lundgren's highly popular children's book, *Pippi Longstocking* (with a couple of episodes added from the book's two sequels, *Pippi Goes on Board* and *Pippi in the South Seas*), this German-Swedish production is clearly a low-budget affair, and the dubbing leaves a lot to be desired. For children, however, these technical details are largely irrelevant. All that matters to them is that the film is lots of fun and the character of Pippi completely irresistible. With her carrot-red braids, mismatched stockings, and shoes two sizes too big, Pippi looks exactly as she's described in the book. She is a child without parents (her mother is "in heaven" and her adventurer-father is a cannibal king in the South Seas), living in a ramshackle home called the Villa Villekulla with her horse and pet monkey. Part trickster, part supergirl, Pippi introduces her young neighbors, Tommy and Annika, to a life of freedom, independence, and fun. The movie is fast-paced and episodic.

Pippi makes fools of two policemen, beats up a bully, disrupts a genteel coffee klatch, buys eighty pounds of candy for herself and her friends, goes on a balloon flight, defeats a pair of comical burglars, and more. In the end, Pippi's footloose father comes to take her back with him to the South Seas, but Pippi decides to remain with her two friends.

At a time when so many kiddie heroines (like Rainbow Brite and Strawberry Shortcake) are nothing more than prepackaged bundles of sweetness and light, it's refreshing to see a female character like Pippi —independent, self-confident, and (in spite of her tiny stature) possessed of enormous physical strength. Technically, this movie is undistinguished, but children love it all the same. Pippi embodies a fantasy of freedom and power that—for quite valid and understandable reasons—children find tremendously exhilarating.

Also available from Video Gems: *Pippi in the South Seas, Pippi Goes on Board,* and *Pippi on the Run.*

POGO FOR PRESIDENT—"I GO POGO!"

WALT DISNEY HOME VIDEO (1979), $49.95, 82 min.
5 and up, ★★★★

Walt Kelly's newspaper strip *Pogo*—which was discontinued in the mid-1970s, a few years after its creator's death—remains dear to the hearts of millions of devotees. Packed with hilarious slapstick comedy, terrific dialogue, brilliant political satire, and a large cast of pricelessly funny swamp critters, it is regarded by many as the greatest comic strip of all time. It would be impossible for any mere film to match the genius of Kelly's work. But this full-length animated feature comes amazingly close. Everyone, from diehard fans of the original strips to children too young to remember them, will find *Pogo for President* an absolute delight from beginning to end.

One of the best things about this movie is the way it is animated. This isn't a cartoon. Rather, the characters are beautifully detailed figurines, sculpted in a claylike substance and brought to life by means of stop-motion photography (the same method used to make Gumby move; basically, it consists of filming a small, flexible figure one frame at a time, while changing its position slightly between each exposure). Technically, the film is a marvel. Pogo and his pals seem completely alive. They are full of personality, their gestures are subtle and expressive, and they act more convincingly than most soap opera stars. The scenery is also a treat. The painted backgrounds of most made-for-TV cartoons are pure hackwork: flat, crudely colored, and devoid of detail. By contrast, the setting of this film—a fairy tale version of Okefenokee Swamp—is a gorgeously crafted miniature that is lush, glowing with color, and amazingly three-dimensional (you almost feel at times as though you're watching this movie through a Viewmaster).

Pogo himself is a modest, gentle, childlike possum. When his friends Albert the alligator, Howland Owl, and Churchy La Femme (a turtle who speaks with the voice of Arnold Stang) decide that he should run for president of the "U.S. and A.," Pogo decides to go fishing. His pals pay him no heed, however, and proceed to mount the most inept campaign in the annals of American politics. Among its highlights are a fund-raising carnival run by the smooth-talking huckster bear, P.T. Bridgeport, and the convention itself, which Pogo refuses to have any part of. Needless to say, he wins the nomination on the first ballot.

This is one of those rare children's movies that work on enough levels to satisfy viewers of all ages. Some of the comedy—especially the political satire—will undoubtedly go over the heads of younger viewers. On the other hand, though this film is sweet and nonviolent to the core, it is full of the kind of good-natured slapstick and pratfall humor little kids love. And every single character, from the cigar-chomping Albert to the gun-toting baddie, Wiley Catt, is infinitely more charming and amusing than all the Care Bears combined. Most endearing of all is Porky the porcupine, whose voice characterization is supplied by the inimitable Jonathan Winters. At one point, after a spectacularly unsuccessful fishing trip that ends in a humiliating defeat (the fish get together and laugh at him), Porky shakes his head sadly and utters one of those bayou-country folk sayings that contain so much profound wisdom and truth: "When the fish talk back to you, it's time to go home."

POOCHIE

CHILDREN'S VIDEO LIBRARY (1985), $39.95, 45 min.
Ages 5–8, ★½

This cartoon, based on another toy popular with young girls, tosses together scraps of story elements lifted from various sources: *Star Wars, Superman, Raiders of the Lost Ark,* assorted mummy movies. The result (unsurprisingly) is the animated equivalent of a junk-pile.

Poochie herself is a very weird little mutt. With her pretty face, red hairdo, sunglasses worn on top of her head, and gold jewelry, she looks like some unnatural cross between a schnauzer and a high fashion model. The adventure story which the filmmakers have devised for her in this cartoon is breathtakingly idiotic. Poochie (who is apparently owned by a latter-day Citizen Kane named Edward Gregory Price) works for a great metropolitan newspaper in New York City called *World Now*. Every morning, she arrives at work in a limousine and takes a private elevator up to her penthouse office, where she sits at a futuristic console and dictates her popular advice column ("Dear Poochie") to a robot named Hermes. This robot—a fussy, British, gold-plated android who has the ability to translate any language (including Canine)—is a brazen rip-off of *Star Wars'* C3PO. As the movie opens, a young boy named Danny, who is being chased through a Middle Eastern bazaar, manages to send a letter off to Poochie, asking for help. When the stylish mutt and her faithful robot companion receive it, they immediately set off by rocket ship on a journey that leads them into a forbidden pyramid and down to a subterranean city inhabited by a tribe of ancient Egyptian priests who attempt to turn our heroes into mummies. Nothing in this exceptionally lame cartoon is even remotely amusing, charming, or diverting. This cassette makes *Strawberry Shortcake's Pets on Parade* look like *Gone With the Wind*.

Since the Poochie adventure is (mercifully) only thirty minutes long, this cassette is padded out with three cartoons about a cute young boy named Tim and his toy winged horse, Luno. When Tim recites a magic incantation, Luno comes to life and carries his owner off on exciting adventures. There are three short Luno cartoons on this cassette: In the first, Tim flies back to the Stone Age, meets a caveman, fights a dinosaur, and helps invent the wheel. The second finds him in the court of King Rounder of the Square Table. In the last, he helps Captain Ahab (who talks exactly like Mr.

Magoo—a physical detail Melville somehow forgot to mention) battle the awesome Moby Dick. These Luno cartoons are far from great—the story lines and animation are pretty rudimentary—but they have a simple charm that the feature attraction entirely lacks.

POPEYE—TRAVELIN' ON ABOUT TRAVEL

MEDIA (1984), $29.95, 60 min.
Ages 5–8, ★

The black-and-white Popeye shorts of the 1930s, produced by the Max Fleischer studio, are among the best cartoons ever made. Unfortunately, they are not available on videotape. Instead, Media Home Entertainment has released several collections of later, made-for-TV cartoons featuring the famous, spinach-eating sailor. These newer cartoons are unrelievedly awful —atrociously animated, numbingly repetitious, and completely unfunny.

Five of the eleven cartoons on this tape find Popeye and his pals involved in silly adventures in various exotic locales. In one, Olive becomes the high priestess of a group of ancient Egyptians. In another, Popeye and Wimpy tangle with a man-eating tiger in "darkest Injia." A third finds Popeye and Olive in the jungles of South America, where they have a run-in with Popeye's bearded nemesis, Brutus. Supposedly, all the cartoons in this collection are connected by a common theme —travel. However, it is a sign of the overall shoddiness of this tape that more than half the selections have nothing at all to do with travel. In fact, five of them have nothing at all to do with Popeye—they are crudely made, asinine cartoons starring other comic strip characters from the King Features lineup: Snuffy Smith, Barney Google, and Beetle Bailey. The only halfway decent cartoon on this program is a mildly amusing Krazy Kat episode, which captures something of the style and charm of George Herriman's celebrated strip. But a single comparatively enjoyable cartoon is not nearly enough to redeem an otherwise hopelessly terrible videotape.

The other titles in this tacky series are: *Popeye and Friends in Outer Space* and *Popeye and Friends in the Wild West*.

(Note: The only classic "Popeye" cartoons currently available on video cassette are three Technicolor shorts made by Max Fleischer between 1936 and 1939: "Popeye the Sailor Meets Sinbad the Sailor," "Popeye Meets Ali Baba and His 40 Thieves," and "Popeye Meets Aladdin and His Wonderful Lamp." They are marketed by various distributors under different titles, including *Popeye Festival* from Budget Video and *Popeye the Sailor* from Video Yesteryear.

There are a number of potentially frightening things in these Fleischer cartoons. In "Popeye the Sailor Meets Sinbad the Sailor," for example, the evil Sinbad —played by Popeye's beefy nemesis, Bluto—lives on an isle populated by fire-breathing serpents, a monstrous condor, and a giant two-headed ogre. Some parents might also object to all the knock-down-and-drag-out brawls between Popeye and his foes. Still, these are beautifully made, highly imaginative, and thoroughly charming cartoons, superior in every way to the made-for-TV trash contained on cassettes like *Popeye—Travelin' On About Travel*.)

THE PREMIERE ADVENTURES OF SUPERTED

WALT DISNEY HOME VIDEO (1982), $49.95, 49 min.
6 and up, ★★★

The Superman fantasy never fails to appeal, no matter what form it appears in. This delightful British cartoon series—produced by the Siriol Animation Studio of Cardiff, Wales and distributed here by the Disney organization—stars an ordinary teddy bear who, through a rather unusual set of circumstances, becomes a mighty superhero. As a brief prologue informs us, Superted began life as a defective stuffed toy who was removed from the assembly line and consigned to an old storage room. By chance, he was discovered by a "spotty man" from outer space who brought him to life with cosmic dust and carried him to a magic cloud where Mother Nature gave him a potion that endowed him with special powers. All he has to do is say a secret word and—Shazam!—he is transformed into a Teddy Bear of Steel, complete with official superhero costume, cape and all.

Because this collection strings together a half-dozen Superted adventures, there is, inevitably, a certain amount of repetition. Charming as it is, the brief explanation of Superted's origins, which appears at the start of each cartoon, gets a little tiresome the third or fourth time around. And the story lines are all essentially the same. On the whole, however, these six short, briskly paced cartoons are terrific fun.

In each of them, Superted and his polka-dotted sidekick, Spotty (who, in spite of his Mr. T hairdo, is easily reduced to a state of quivering cowardice) do battle with a trio of the most oddball bad guys in the annals of crime. The ringleader is a scowling, mustachioed, and totally incompetent villain named Texas Pete, who looks like Captain Hook in a cowboy suit. His two accomplices (who are, if possible, even more inept) are a tubby, bumbling bird-brain named Bulk and—strangest of the lot—a prim, fussy, living skeleton, aptly named Skeleton, who does very little but complain about the hardships he has to endure and who has a habit of going to pieces (literally) whenever he's scared. While some parents may well find Skeleton's appearance a little unsettling, children, for the most part, won't be bothered a bit (on the contrary, he's likely to be their favorite character).

The humor throughout these cartoons is unforced and genuinely funny (the voices are supplied by some of Britain's best comic character actors, including Victor Spinetti and Roy Kinnear). Much of the comedy derives from the personalities of the bad guys, especially the dimwitted Bulk (who, when told that a treasure is located only a "short pony ride" away, becomes confused because he hasn't brought along a short pony) and the prissy Skeleton (whose voice and temperament closely resemble those of *Star Wars*' C3PO). The cartoons are full of the kind of good-natured slapstick that children find irresistible. And while the action is both fast paced and nonstop, the violence is kept to a minimum. Texas Pete gets tossed around a lot by the stalwart super teddy bear (who is given to saying things like, "Don't toy with me"). But with bad guys who can't even manage to steal oysters from a pearl-diver without capsizing their boat and ending up in the arms of an amorous octopus, Superted doesn't have to rely very heavily on physical force.

A final word about the artwork: While the animation is limited (in the style of TV cartoons everywhere), it is also fresh, imaginative, and (considering the restricted range of movement) surprisingly dynamic. Each of the cartoons takes place in a different exotic setting—the Amazon jungle, the Swiss Alps, a South Pacific isle, etc.—and these backgrounds are rendered in detail, depth, and rich, vibrant color. All in all, these cartoons are extremely sweet and appealing. And you'll look long and hard before finding another superhero whose favorite exclamations are "Bubbling blancmange!" and "Pulsating prunes!"

Also available: *The Further Adventures of Superted* and *Superted III: The Adventures Continue.*

THE PRINCESS AND THE PEA

CBS/FOX VIDEO (1983), $39.98, 60 min.
6 and up, ★★★

This *Faerie Tale Theatre* production stars the incomparable Tom Conti as the spoiled, none-too-bright Prince Richard, who yearns for something gentle, soft, and loving to make his otherwise perfect life complete. He thinks the solution might be to get a hamster, though his fool (Tim Kazurinsky) suggests that a wife might be a better choice.

Soon afterward, Liza Minnelli—doing her usual turn as a brash, earthy hoyden—shows up at the castle and wins the heart of the pampered but lonely prince (in many ways, this show is like a Grimm Brothers version of the hit movie, *Arthur*). To prove she is a true princess, she must pass the ultimate test: detect a single pea hidden under a pile of twenty soft mattresses.

There's a good deal of charm but very little drama in this story. Most of its appeal comes from its sophisticated dialogue and witty characterizations (including

Pat McCormick as the fatuous King Frederico, who loves to sit around issuing solemn proclamations—such as his decree that all men named Richard shall henceforth be known as Buddy). As a result, parents are likely to enjoy this tape more than children (though Tim Kazurinsky's hilarious tomfoolery is sure to delight youngsters).

(See review of *Faerie Tale Theatre* for a description of this series as a whole.)

THE PRINCESS WHO HAD NEVER LAUGHED

CBS/FOX VIDEO (1984), $39.98, 60 min.
6 and up, ★★★★

This delightful *Faerie Tale Theatre* production is like a Grimm Brothers' version of "Girls Just Want to Have Fun."

Howard Hesseman is very amusing as a strict, unsmiling king known to his subjects as "Your Seriousness." Years ago, his wife had been killed (indirectly) by happiness. (He had told her a joke that caused her to laugh so hard that her corset burst. When the royal corsetmaker came to repair it, he left a thimble behind. The queen ran after him in a thunderstorm, waving the metal thimble high in the air, and was hit by lightning.) As a result, the king has banished laughter and joy from his realm. The peasants' lives consist entirely of three activities: getting up early, slaving all day, and going straight to bed. Even more oppressed is the king's only child, Princess Henrietta (engagingly played by Ellen Barkin), who is forced to spend her days studying the "Three S's" of courtly leadership

—Solemnity, Severity, and Sitting Up Straight. Her only recreation is an occasional game of "Purposeful Pursuit," which she plays with her joyless father and her equally grim governess and tutor (sample question: "What is the proper punishment for a subject who falls asleep while bowing to the king?").

After twenty-one years of incessant hard work and sobriety, the princess goes a little berserk, tossing her schoolbooks out the window and locking herself in her room. She refuses to leave unless her father finds her someone who will make her laugh. Relenting, the king hits on the idea of holding a contest. All the funnymen from the surrounding kingdoms will be invited to perform at a big Royal Laugh-Off. The one who can make the princess laugh will win her hand. Runners-up get ten years in the dungeon.

The Royal Laugh-Off—in which a string of medieval comedians perform their stand-up routines—is the comic high point of this show. The contest is finally won by a local yokel named Wienerhead Waldo (Howie Mandel), a village idiot-type whose idea of a good joke is to put spaghetti on his head and make funny faces at himself in the mirror. Waldo turns out to be just what the princess needed, and as the tale ends, the kingdom is once again filled with the sounds of slapstick, pratfalls, practical jokes, and the occasional bad pun.

This is a very charming program—one that parents can enjoy along with their children.

(See review of *Faerie Tale Theatre* for a description of this series as a whole.)

PUFF THE MAGIC DRAGON

CHILDREN'S VIDEO LIBRARY (1978), $39.98, 45 min.
Preschool–8, ★★★

The first half-hour of this video cassette is a delightfully animated version of the famous Peter, Paul and Mary song. The hero is a troubled little boy named Jackie Draper who refuses to communicate with anyone. One day, an affable green dragon in a bow tie appears at his window. Inviting himself in, he opens a suitcase full of fairy tale items (Cinderella's glass slipper, Alice's mushroom, Peter Pan's shadow, gold spun from straw, a piece of the Yellow Brick Road), removes a sheet of paper and an enchanted crayon, and draws a picture of Jackie, which he brings to life with a puff of his breath. Then the magical dragon and his new friend, "Jackie Paper," take off on a marvelous quest to the land of Honna-Lee.

Along the way, Jackie learns to overcome his fears and self-doubts as he and Puff undergo various adventures. First, they are kidnapped by a giant, peg-legged pirate named Long John (whose real ambition is to be a cook). Then, they must pass through the angry Sea of Starless Skies. When they finally make it to Honna-Lee, they discover that this glorious fantasyland has been overrun and ravaged by an invading tribe of Living Sneezes. In an amusing climax, Jackie sails off and brings back Long John (now dressed in a cook's outfit), who restores the land to happiness with a shower of chicken soup from a gargantuan kettle.

Featuring highly imaginative artwork, a number of extremely charming songs (composed and sung by Peter Yarrow), an excellent performance by Burgess

Meredith as the voice of Puff, and a story that is by turns whimsical, adventurous, and touching, this cartoon is a delight from beginning to end.

The remainder of this videotape consists of three old "Hector Heathcote" cartoons. Hector—an uninspired character from the Paul Terry studio—is a Colonial American nebbish who (for some reason) pops up in all kinds of unlikely places (Columbus' boat, the Wild West). The best that can be said about these cartoons is that they are inoffensive.

Also available: *Puff and the Incredible Mr. Nobody*, ($39.95. 45 min.).

PUSS IN BOOTS

CBS/FOX VIDEO (1984), $39.98, 60 min.
6 and up, ★★★

This *Faerie Tale Theatre* show is far from bad, but, considering the lineup of talent involved in its production, it's a disappointment. With two sparkling performers—Ben Vereen and Gregory Hines—in the starring roles, and a script written by Jules Feiffer, it should have been a lot brighter and more amusing than it is. Still, it's worth a look.

In most respects, the program follows Perrault's fairy tale quite closely. A poor miller's son (Hines) inherits a preternaturally clever cat (Ben Vereen, dressed in a terrific feline outfit), who promises to catapult his master to wealth and station beyond his wildest dreams. After convincing his master to buy him some finery—a hat, cape, and dashing pair of boots—the cat proceeds to pass off his master as the noble Marquis of Carabas. By the end of the tale, the cat has managed to acquire both a princess and a castle for his sweet (if incompetent) owner.

Although this program drags in spots, kids will undoubtedly find Vereen's suave, smooth-tongued Puss extremely entertaining. They'll also be enthralled by the exciting, climactic encounter between the wily cat and a fearsome ogre (Brock Peters), whose vanity leads to his downfall. (Puss challenges the monster to prove his power by turning himself into a mouse, then pounces on the rodent and gobbles him up.) This *Puss in Boots* may not be the best show in the *Faerie Tale Theatre* series, but even the weaker productions are better than most of the kiddie tapes around.

(See review of *Faerie Tale Theatre* for a description of this series as a whole.)

PUSS 'N BOOTS TRAVELS AROUND THE WORLD

RCA/COLUMBIA (1983), $39.95, 60 min.
Ages 5–8, ★★

This slickly animated kiddie version of *Around the World in Eighty Days* contains some pretty (even striking) scenery. But on the whole, it's a flat and uninteresting film.

The story (such as it is) concerns a heroic feline named Pussty, who is challenged by the swinish Sir Rumblehog to complete a trip across the globe in eighty days. Throughout their journey, Pussty and his hippo pal, Tumbo, are pursued by both the villainous Dr. Mysterioso—a sinister character hired by Rumblehog to stymie the heroes—and a trio of caped, sword-waving assassins who are out to get Pussty because he has violated one of the sacred codes of cathood: he likes mice. The film is composed of short sequences, each set in a different exotic locale: Spain, Venice, Egypt, Morocco, Baghdad, Tibet, Athens, etc. These settings are rendered in lovely detail, but they are simply used as backdrops for endless (and witless) chase sequences. The film is like a Tom & Jerry cartoon produced by the National Geographic Society (though it lacks the vitality and visual wit of the best Tom & Jerry shorts). The characters have no personality, there is no humor or suspense. Even as an animated travelogue, it's not very satisfactory, since it doesn't attempt to convey any information about the places Pussty travels to. It's not a terrible cartoon (as far as the artwork goes, it's actually quite a polished and tasteful one). But it's surprisingly lifeless and dull.

RACE FOR YOUR LIFE, CHARLIE BROWN

PARAMOUNT (1977), $29.98, 76 min.
5 and up, ★★★

Charlie Brown, Linus, Snoopy, and the rest of the gang spend a fun-filled summer at Camp Remote in this entertaining full-length feature, the third Peanuts movie made for theatrical release. (See review of *A Boy Named Charlie Brown*.)

RAINBOW BRITE IN "PERIL IN THE PITS"

CHILDREN'S VIDEO LIBRARY (1983), $29.95, 45 min.
Preschool–8, ★★

Like the Care Bears, Strawberry Shortcake, My Little
Pony, He-Man, and many others yet to come, Rainbow
Brite is a wildly successful corporate "tie-in character"
whose licensed image can be found on everything from
lunch boxes and bedsheets to breakfast cereals and
birthday cards. Many parents (as well as groups like
Action for Children's Television) object to the cartoons
based on these characters, regarding them as nothing
more than extended commercials for the merchandise.
This is a legitimate complaint. But even apart from
their coldblooded commercialism, these cartoons leave
a lot to be desired.

What makes them so depressing in the end is how
formulaic and hackneyed they are. The same elements
appear again and again (and again) in all these cartoons. There is a colorful, fantasy world, Rainbowland.
Just as in *The Care Bears in the Land Without Feeling*,
this cartoon begins with a despondent young boy who
must be saved from his depression by the bright,
adorable star. There is a lovable meanie (in this case
named Murky Dismal) who lives in a gloomy land and
seeks to fill the world with sadness. There are the
obligatory flying horse, a few perfunctory perils the
hero must undergo, and rainbows galore. (It's interesting that in cartoons oriented toward young boys, such
as He-Man and Voltron, the characters wield extremely
nasty-looking swords and guns, whereas in cartoons
intended for girls, the characters, when they fight at all,

almost always use magical rainbows as their main weapons. In short, these cartoons associate boys with power and aggression and girls with sweetness and light.) And there's the usual slick, made-for-TV animation.

Because the Rainbow Brite cartoon is only a half-hour long, this cassette is filled out with three Terrytoons from the 1950s—"The Clockmaker's Dog" (about a tiny pooch who longs to be a St. Bernard), "The First Flying Fish" (an "Aesop's Fable" about a fish who earns his wings), and "Happy Valley" (a morality tale about the evils of greed). In the old days Terrytoons had the reputation of being the Woolworth's of the cartoon business (whereas Disney was regarded as the Tiffany's). It's a commentary on the overall quality of the Rainbow Brite cartoon that, in comparison to it, the three tacked-on Terrytoons seem extremely imaginative (though "Happy Valley" does contain one potentially disturbing element—a spooky figure who represents the spirit of greed and is a dead ringer for the wicked witch in Disney's *Snow White and the Seven Dwarfs*).

Also available: *Rainbow Brite in "The Mighty Monstromurk Menace."*

RAPUNZEL

PLAYHOUSE VIDEO (1982), $39.98, 60 min.
6 and up, ★★★½

Although it's spiced with a bit of humor, this *Faerie Tale Theatre* production is basically a serious and very lovely dramatization of the classic Grimm Brothers story.

Shelley Duvall (the creator and executive producer of the series) and Jeff Bridges play dual roles. In the first half, they appear as Rapunzel's parents, Marie and Claude. When the pregnant Marie develops a craving for the mysterious, blue-leaved radishes that grow in the garden of her neighbor—a formidable and quite glamorous witch, played by Gena Rowlands—her husband sneaks onto the sorceress's property to steal some of the vegetables. The witch catches him on his second trip and threatens to kill him unless he promises to turn over his new daughter to her. Several months after the child is born, the enchantress appears at Claude and Marie's home, freezes them with a look, and takes the child off to a distant land where she imprisons her in a high tower in the midst of an enchanted forest.

The second half of the show—which deals with Rapunzel's life in the witch's tower—is truly magical. In fact, this production gets better and more haunting as it goes along. Shelley Duvall makes an appealing (if not especially beautiful) Rapunzel, and Jeff Bridges is quite dashing as the handsome young prince who visits her in her tower by climbing her long braid of blond hair. The closing scenes, in which the blinded prince gropes his way to the desert and is reunited with Rapunzel (whose tears restore his sight) are genuinely moving. Visually, the second part of the show is very striking, with costumes and sets inspired by the artwork of Austrian painter Gustav Klimt.

Parents should note that a few things in this production may well be upsetting to younger children. The early scenes in the witch's garden are quite spooky, and there is one moment in particular—when the witch springs from her hiding place and paralyzes Claude with a magical glance—that gave the smaller members of my home audience a serious start. Even more disturbing is the scene in which the enchantress blinds the prince. We see a close-up of Jeff Bridges's face. Suddenly, a stream of blood pours from his eyes and flows down his cheeks. It's a very effective image, but it seems unnecessarily graphic. In all other ways, however, this is a lyrical and affecting dramatization.

(See review of *Faerie Tale Theatre* for a description of this series as a whole.)

READ-ALONG MAGIC VIDEOS

AVG (1985), $19.95 each, 30 min. each
Preschool–7, ★★★

How do you teach a love of reading in our increasingly nonliterate video age? One answer (proposed by Jim Trelease, author of *The Read-Aloud Handbook*) is to impose strict limits on the amount of time children are allowed to spend in front of the television set and to encourage them to pursue other interests—especially reading—instead. Another method is to accept the central role that TV plays in most American households and to use the electronic medium itself as a way of teaching kids to appreciate books. This is the approach taken by the creators of the *Read-Along Magic Videos*, a collection of half-hour cassettes priced at $29.95 apiece that are currently being sold across the country in big bookstore chains like B. Dalton and Waldenbooks.

These programs are not cartoons. Rather, they use colorful, computer-created images that seem to "draw themselves" onto the screen while a narrator recites the accompanying story. At the same time, certain key words and phrases appear at the bottom of the screen. The idea is to use video technology to create a kind of "read-aloud experience." The cassette called *All About Teddy Bears,* for example, begins with a number of toy bears introducing themselves to the viewer. As a computer-generated picture of a teddy is sketched onto the screen a cute, offscreen voice says, "My name is Little and I am a small brown bear." Simultaneously, the words "small, brown bear" are spelled out in white letters at the bottom of the picture. In theory, children watching the tape begin to associate the words with the sounds.

These cassettes have definite limitations. First, the quality of the stories varies a good deal. The best of the lot are the three cassettes based on children's classics —*Becoming Real Forever* (a version of Margery Williams's *The Velveteen Rabbit*), *The Beatrix Potter Collection* (featuring the tales of Peter Rabbit, Benjamin Bunny, and the Flopsy Bunnies), and *The Owl and the Pussycat* (a musical adaptation of the Edward Lear poem). The cassettes based on original material—*All About Teddy Bears, Bearobics,* and *Who's Afraid of the Dark?*—are much weaker. Another problem is the quality of the artwork. Though the graphics are advertised as "state-of-the-art," they are actually pretty uninteresting and completely without character. They look like what they are—pictures drawn by a machine. They are certainly no match for good book illustrations. If anything, they resemble highly sophisticated, full-color Etch-A-Sketch drawings. Finally, although the producer of these tapes insists that they enhance reading skills and provide children with an active video experience, it's hard to determine just how true these claims are. My own impression (from observing young viewers watching a few of these cassettes) is that children quickly forget about the printed-out words and simply imbibe the pictures and stories as passively as they would a Saturday-morning cartoon. It's particularly hard for a very young child (even one with rudimentary reading skills) to associate the printed text with the spoken narration, partly because only a few words of each sentence are projected at a time and partly because the words don't remain onscreen for very long.

One way of getting around this last problem is to watch the program along with your children. Each cassette comes with a one-sheet "Parent's Guide," which offers concrete suggestions for getting the most out of the cassette. For all their limitations, these videotapes represent an admirable, innovative attempt to use advanced technology to foster an appreciation for the printed word. These cassettes may not be perfect, but they offer an interesting and worthwhile alternative to much of the video junk being peddled these days.

There are six *Read-Along Magic Videos* currently on the market (with more on the way). The available titles are: *All About Teddy Bears, Bearobics, The Beatrix Potter Collection, Becoming Real Forever, The Owl and the Pussycat,* and *Who's Afraid of the Dark?*

RICHIE RICH

WORLDVISION (1981), $39.95, 60 min.
Ages 5–9, ★

Richie Rich is one of the most atrocious cartoon shows I've ever seen. Even by the pitiful standards of Saturday-morning TV, this is a truly awful program. The animation is insultingly crude, the story lines idiotic, the humor nonexistent. Do not—repeat, do not—subject your children to this cassette.

There are seven cartoons on this videotape. They vary in quality, ranging from the depressingly dumb to the hopelessly moronic. The hero of each is Richie Rich, the world's wealthiest little boy, who lives in an immense mansion where everything, from the living room carpet to his dog's coat, is decorated with dollar signs. One of the more nauseating things about this cassette is its undisguised worship of money. Another is simply the inanity of the stories. In one, Richie travels back in a time machine and meets his ancient Egyptian relatives, the Rich Tuts. In another, he travels back in time and meets his medieval relative, King Richly of Richalot. There is a lamebrained science fiction episode in which Richie uses his gold to trap a space pirate, and another in which he uses an antigravity ring (one of the many useless gadgets he is given to squandering his fortune on) to perform in a school variety show. There are also a number of equally dimwitted episodes starring his dog, Dollar, who is like a flea-bitten version of Snoopy. In one, Dollar imagines himself as a cadet going through basic training at West Point. This cartoon might almost be a canine spoof of *An Officer and a Gentleman,* were it not for the fact that (like every other cartoon on this cassette) it lacks the two key ingredients of parody: intelligence and humor.

The case that this tape comes packaged in describes the final episode as a cartoon in which "Dollar uses his just-cleaned teeth to 'shine' out some burglars." Since the final episode has nothing to do with Dollar and his teeth (it involves Richie's encounter with a Caribbean witchdoctor), it would seem that the people who produced this tape don't know what's on it. Apparently even *they* couldn't stand to watch it all the way through.

Rip Van Winkle

CBS/FOX VIDEO (1985), $39.98, 60 min.
6 and up, ★★★

Since this *Faerie Tale Theatre* production was directed by Francis Ford Coppola, it's not surprising that it is one of the most visually inventive shows in the series. It can't really be said, however, that it is one of the most enjoyable. In spite of its striking, often breathtaking imagery, it is a rather slow-moving and somber affair. This is a pity, since Washington Irving's "Rip Van Winkle" is one of the most delightfully fanciful tales in our literature. It certainly has a serious side to it, but its tone is anything but heavy.

While this production sticks relatively closely to the original storyline, it entirely fails to capture the special charm of Irving's story. For example, though the setting is supposed to be the lush, pastoral countryside of New York's Catskill Mountains, Coppola places Rip's farm in a bleak, ashen landscape that looks more like Iceland. At other points, Coppola resorts to highly stylized images that, while impressive in themselves, don't add anything to the story. When Rip goes fishing, for instance, his quarry is represented (for no apparent reason) by a giant marionette. Other scenes have a weird, surrealistic quality that is at odds with the whimsical nature of the material. The mountain range that forms the backdrop in a number of scenes has the disconcerting habit of sinking and rising at unexpected moments. Again, there's no good reason for this to keep happening. It's a completely gratuitous bit of visual razzle-dazzle that seems very self-indulgent.

There *are* a few authentically enchanting moments here. When Rip begins his fateful journey into the mountains, he sets out at the village tavern, whose front wall suddenly splits in half, becoming a magical pathway into the forest. The scenes involving Hendrik Hudson's spectral crew have real power, though some children may well find this gang of ghostly ten-pin players somewhat unsettling. The single best sequence in the program is the one in which we watch the seasons pass while Rip sleeps for twenty years. By the time he awakens, he seems to have merged with the forest floor—he is covered with moss and dead leaves, and his long white hair and beard have spread across the ground like tendrils.

As is often the case with Coppola's recent work, it is easier to admire this highly unconventional *Faerie Tale Theatre* production—for its daring and technical virtuosity—than it is to like it. If you're a fan of Coppola's movies, you may well find this program engrossing, but it will probably leave most children cold.

(See review of *Faerie Tale Theatre* for a description of this series as a whole.)

ROBIN HOOD

WALT DISNEY HOME VIDEO (1973), $79.95, 83 min.
Preschool–9, ★★★

Disney aficionados regard this feature-length cartoon as a major letdown. It certainly isn't one of the studio's more inspired efforts. It's pretty enough to look at, and the characters are beautifully animated. But there's something flat and spiritless about the film. It lacks the depth, drive, and emotional power of features like *Pinocchio* and *Snow White*.

Children, however, are less likely to be disappointed. In spite of its flaws, *Robin Hood* is a perfectly amiable cartoon, containing more than enough pleasures to keep young viewers happy. In this Disneyfied version of the famous legend, the characters are all played by animals. Little John is a bear, the Sheriff of Nottingham is a wolf, Friar Tuck is a badger, and Robin himself a fox. The voices are provided by a strong cast of performers, including Peter Ustinov, Terry Thomas, Andy Devine, Pat Buttram, and Roger Miller, who also supplies a number of laid-back, country-flavored tunes.

The story as a whole contains a significant number of dead spots, but individual episodes—particularly the famous archery tournament (which Robin wins by splitting his opponent's arrow in half) and the hero's thrilling, climactic escape from the tower of a burning castle—play very well. There is also a good deal of genuinely amusing slapstick, most of it provided by the film's comical villains, the whining, infantile Prince John and his fawning, reptilian henchman, Lord Hiss.

In comparison to the classic Disney features, *Robin Hood* is decidedly second-rate. It's a well-worn story, handled without real freshness or flair. Still, it's a polished, pleasant, and generally entertaining cartoon that kids will enjoy.

ROCK MUSIC WITH THE MUPPETS

PLAYHOUSE VIDEO (1985), $59.95, 54 min.
Preschool and up, ★★★½

Alice Cooper, Debbie Harry, Paul Simon, Linda Ronstadt, and others are featured on this hour-long anthology of songs and sketches from "The Muppet Show." (See review of *Jim Henson's Muppet Video*.)

ROMIE-0 AND JULIE-8

WARNER (1979), $29.98, 25 min.
6 and up, ★★★★

This delightful animated love story—a whimsical, science fiction version of *Romeo and Juliet* (but with a happy ending)—comes from Canada's superb Nelvana animation studio. It is one of the four cartoons on the outstanding collection, *Nelvanamation*, and is also available separately on this 25-minute cassette. (See review of *Nelvanamation*.)

ROMPER ROOM AND FRIENDS: GO TO THE ZOO

PLAYHOUSE VIDEO (1984), $19.98, 31 min.
Preschool–6, ★★★

ROMPER ROOM AND FRIENDS: NUMBERS, LETTERS, AND WORDS

PLAYHOUSE VIDEO (1984), $19.98, 40 min.
Preschool–5, ★★★

ROMPER ROOM AND FRIENDS: MOVEMENT AND RHYTHM

PLAYHOUSE VIDEO (1984), $19.98, 35 min.
Preschool–6, ★★★

ROMPER ROOM AND FRIENDS: PLAYFUL PROJECTS

PLAYHOUSE VIDEO (1984), $19.98, 40 min.
Preschool–6, ★★★

Produced in cooperation with the National Education Association, this well-made series features the cast of TV's long-lived nursery-school show, "Romper Room," in four half-hour programs, each devoted to a different topic. Clearly, a great deal of care, even love, has gone into the creation of this series, which has been designed with both preschoolers and parents in mind. It's hard to think of another videotape that achieves such a successful combination of entertainment and instruction for the three-to-five-year-old crowd.

While "Romper Room" lacks the slickness and wit of "Sesame Street," it offers the closest approximation of a nursery school environment you're likely to find on video. Presided over by the estimable Miss Molly—a bright, attractive young woman of enormous energy, enthusiasm, and patience—each of the programs mixes play, creative activity, and learning in just the right proportions. "Go to the Zoo," for example, alternates between scenes shot at the San Diego Zoo—in which the clown puppet UpUp tells viewers interesting facts about the animals—and segments back in Romper Room in which Miss Molly and the lovable shaggy brown monster, Kimble, lead a group of children in various activities: songs, games, and arts-and-crafts projects.

One of the best things about these programs is the way they get viewers (not only children but parents as well) to participate. The common complaint about TV watching—that it is a purely passive experience —definitely does not apply to these tapes. Whether she is demonstrating how to make a lion mask out of a paper plate and construction paper, showing kids the safe way to do somersaults, or leading the class in a rhyming song, Miss Molly, like any good teacher, makes sure to get everyone (the home audience included) involved. And since some of the activities require a little help from grown-ups, parents are invited to take an active part in the proceedings, too. Moreover, each tape concludes with additional "Tips for

Grown-ups": suggestions for simple projects and activities that are interesting, educational, and fun.

Another important ingredient in the success of these tapes is their pacing, which is fast but never frenetic. Each program consists of lots of little segments that are brief and varied enough to hold the interest of young viewers. Obviously the creators of these tapes have a clear understanding of the average preschool attention span. At the same time, there is no danger here of hyperstimulation or sensory overload: kids are not overwhelmed with video flash and dazzle. If Miss Molly is leading her onscreen class and "friends at home" in a lively session of "Quick-draw" (in which everyone kneels on the floor and sketches with crayons on a big sheet of brown paper), the kids are given plenty of time to sit there and create while Miss Molly sings her catchy Quick-draw song. After a few minutes of this activity, the program will cut to something new: a performance by a troupe of Chinese acrobats, a demonstration by a professional mime, a rhyming song, a counting game, or a round of kiddie calisthenics.

As commendable as these programs are, parents should note that—though the cassettes are very reasonably priced ($19.98 each) and apparently meant to be purchased rather than rented—they are not necessarily the kind of tapes that children will want to watch repeatedly. Once you've seen Miss Molly demonstrate how to make finger puppets three or four times, there is not much point in watching her do it again, even if you are one of her most devoted five-year-old fans. As rental tapes, however, the Romper Room series can be recommended without reservation to any parent with preschoolers at home.

RUMPELSTILTSKIN

CBS/FOX VIDEO (1983), $39.98, 60 min.
6 and up, ★★★★

Shelley Duvall—the creator and executive producer of *Faerie Tale Theatre*—stars as the miller's daughter in this first-rate dramatization of the classic fairy tale.

When her slightly slack-witted father (Paul Dooley) spins a yarn about his daughter's ability to spin gold from straw, the girl is brought to court and ordered to prove her talent or die. Hervé Villechaize is convincingly uncanny (and creepy) as the magical dwarf who, in return for performing the impossible task, demands her first-born child. When he comes to claim his payment, however, the miller's daughter—now the queen—becomes so hysterical that the little man offers to free her from her promise if she can guess his name in three days. In a dramatic climax, the young woman journeys into an enchanted forest, where, kneeling outside the dwarf's home, she overhears the name "Rumpelstiltskin."

Everything about this production is beautifully done, from its handsome production design (inspired by the artwork of renowned illustrator N. C. Wyeth) to the engaging performances by Duvall, Villechaize, and Ned Beatty as the self-centered king who is humanized by his love for his new queen and their infant child. This is a fairy tale that parents and children can watch and enjoy together.

(See review of *Faerie Tale Theatre* for a description of this series as a whole.)

SAMMY BLUEJAY

FAMILY HOME ENTERTAINMENT (1983),
$29.95, 60 min.
Preschool–6, ★★★

This video cassette contains a pair of cartoons (plus a "bonus episode") from the engaging *Fables of the Green Forest* series. (See review under *Fables of the Green Forest*.)

THE SECRET OF NIMH

MGM/UA (1982), $79.95, 83 min.
6 and up, ★★★★

In 1979, master animator Don Bluth quit the Disney studio to create the kind of cartoon Disney itself wasn't making anymore. Though the result was a box-office failure, it is—in terms of Bluth's artistic goals—a resounding success. This full-length, animated feature is a return to the glory days of *Snow White* and *Pinocchio*, a cartoon with all the qualities of the Disney classics: marvelously lifelike animation, stunning backgrounds, vivid characters, poignancy, comedy, suspense—and a few intensely scary and unsettling scenes that some young children may well find upsetting.

Based on Robert C. O'Brien's prize-winning novel, *Mrs. Frisby and the Rats of NIMH*, the story concerns a gentle, courageous mouse (named Mrs. Brisby in the movie) whose youngest child is bedridden with pneumonia and who must find a way to move her home—a hollow block in a farmer's field—before it is destroyed by tractors. Her quest leads her to a community of superintelligent rats, experimental animals who have managed to break out of the National Institute of Mental Health. The movie is packed with exciting moments: a hairbreadth escape from a housecat aptly named Dragon; a swashbuckling swordfight as tense and rousing as anything in an Errol Flynn movie. Parents might object to some of the violence in the film (the leader of the rats, for example—a wise, noble rodent named Nicodemus—is crushed to death in a phony accident engineered by his villainous opponent), and at least one of the characters—a terrifying owl with glowing eyes, a taste for spiders, and the doomsday voice of John Carradine—could easily induce a few nightmares.

All in all, however, this is a first-rate fantasy movie, with a genuinely inspiring climax and memorable voice characterizations by Elizabeth Hartman, Derek Jacobi, Hermione Baddely, Peter Strauss, and—most delightful of all—Dom DeLuise as an adorably klutzy crow named Jeremy.

SHERLOCK HOLMES AND THE SIGN OF THE FOUR

PACIFIC ARTS (1983), $59.95, 48 min.
8 and up, ★★★

This Australian-made cartoon, "starring" Peter O'Toole as the voice of the legendary sleuth, is a faithful, if somewhat slow-moving, adaptation of the early Conan Doyle story, "The Sign of the Four."

The adventure begins with a classic display of Holmes's astonishing deductive powers, as the great detective manages to recreate the life story of Dr. Watson's deceased brother simply by examining the scratches and dents on the dead man's pocket watch. Moments later, the friends are interrupted by the appearance of a young woman named Mary Morstan, whose father has been missing for a decade. During that time, she has been sent, once each year, a box containing a single, priceless pearl from an anonymous benefactor. His interest piqued, Holmes agrees to help Miss Morstan solve the mystery of her father's disappearance. The ensuing adventure is a corking tale of treachery and greed, involving a stolen treasure, a peg-legged convict, and a vicious aborigine named Tonga, who is highly proficient with a blowpipe and poison darts.

In spite of its terrific plot and top-notch star, this cassette is far from great. The animation is very mediocre and—though there are a few moments of action (including a climactic boat chase on the Thames)—it's a pretty static film. Much of it consists of talking, as Holmes patiently explains his deductions to his slightly plodding sidekick ("Really, Watson, it is simplicity itself!"). These explanations are not always easy to follow, and younger viewers will have trouble figuring out what is going on. On the other hand, there are some very admirable things about this cassette. Holmes's world—from his comfortable Baker Street lodgings to the foggy streets of Victorian London—is conjured up with a great deal of care. And the master sleuth himself—dressed in his deerstalker hat and Inverness cape and rubbing his hands hungrily at the prospect of a juicy case—looks, acts, and (thanks to O'Toole's fine performance) sounds just the way he should.

This cassette only hints at the pleasures to be had from the original Sherlock Holmes stories. But for children who aren't old enough yet to read Conan Doyle, it provides a nice introduction to one of the world's great fictional characters.

Also available in this series: *Sherlock Holmes and the Baskerville Curse*.

SLEEPING BEAUTY

CBS/FOX VIDEO (1983), $39.98, 60 min.
6 and up, ★★★

This *Faerie Tale Theatre* production is funny, wonderfully acted, beautifully designed—and far too sophisticated for most children. Its comedy relies heavily on lighthearted sexual joking and double entendres. Christopher Reeve brings his engaging mixture of dashing good looks and self-deprecating charm to the role of the handsome prince who is searching for the woman of his dreams. At one point, he encounters a conniving sexpot who tries to seduce him by having him pluck the pearls off the bosom of her harem-girl outfit with his mouth. As the title character, Bernadette Peters comes across (as usual) as the world's sexiest kewpie doll. The exceptionally strong supporting cast includes René Auberjonois and Sally Kellerman as the king and queen (who, in spite of their rather advanced years, need a bubbly little pixie—a kind of pocket-sized Dr. Ruth—to teach them how to make a baby), Carole King as a helpful fairy with a cutesy-pie voice, and Beverly D'Angelo as her malevolent sister, Henbane, who casts the wicked spell on Sleeping Beauty.

The production design—inspired by the artwork of renowned fantasy illustrator Kay Nielson—is strikingly pretty, and there are some nifty effects (including a scary, climactic battle between the prince and a horrific female giant with silver scales, long fangs, and a Medusa hairdo). This is an undeniably classy production, but it seems designed for grown-ups, not kids.

(See review of *Faerie Tale Theatre* for a description of this series as a whole.)

SMILE FOR AUNTIE AND OTHER STORIES

WESTON WOODS/CC STUDIOS (1985), $29.95, 40 min.
Preschool–8, ★★★★

Diane Paterson, Robert McCloskey, Ezra Jack Keats, and Barbara Cooney are the artists whose work is featured on this splendidly animated cassette from the incomparable Weston Woods studio. See review of *The Children's Circle*.

SNOOPY, COME HOME

CBS/FOX VIDEO (1972), $39.95, 80 min.
5 and up, ★★★

Fed up with "No Dogs Allowed" signs, Snoopy leaves home (in the company of his little pal Woodstock) and sets off to find his former owner, Lila. This full-length movie—the second Peanuts film made for theatrical release—features lots of vintage Charles Schulz humor and a number of charming songs by the Sherman brothers (best known for having composed the songs for *Mary Poppins*).

For the other Peanuts features available on cassette, see review of *A Boy Named Charlie Brown*.

THE SNOWMAN

SONY (1982), $24.95, 26 min.
Preschool and up, ★★★★

If I were asked to choose the single best children's video on the market today, I would unhesitatingly pick this beautiful adaptation of Raymond Briggs's well-known picture book, *The Snowman*. Nominated for an Academy Award as Best Animated Short Film, this absolutely magical movie is so good that, if you and your children haven't seen it already, you are hereby advised to put down this book, proceed to the nearest video store, and rent a copy. Better yet, invest the $25.00 and buy your own. Like the best children's books, it will provide pleasure for years to come. Parents will be as enchanted by it as their children. It is also guaranteed to bring joy to the lives of fantasy fans and lovers of animation. In short, it's a treasure.

The story, told without words (except for a brief, voice-over introduction), is about a young boy who builds a snowman that comes to life one magical midnight. Invited inside the house, the snowman (after politely doffing his hat) goes exploring with his new-found friend. In the kitchen, he removes the orange from the center of his face and tries on an assortment of nose-styles: cherry, pineapple, pear. In the bedroom of the boy's parents, he primps before a mirror and dresses up in funny clothes.

When he spots a motorcycle outside the window, he

takes the boy for a ride through the wintry woods. In a film full of stunning animation, this sequence—which cuts between the viewpoint of the riders, as they zoom through the trees, and that of the forest animals, startled by the approaching headlights—is one of the most breathtaking. Another glorious sequence comes shortly afterward, when the snowman takes the boy's hand and flies northward through the snow-filled skies. Accompanied by a hauntingly beautiful background song, this portion of the movie is pure enchantment, combining the exhilaration of the flying scenes in Disney's *Peter Pan,* the dreamlike magic of Maurice Sendak's *In the Night Kitchen,* and a special poetry all its own.

Arriving at the land of the Northern Lights, they discover a holiday party in progress, attended by a festive crowd of snowmen and presided over by none other than Santa Claus. After much merrymaking, Santa presents the boy with a gift—a lovely blue scarf. Then the boy and the snowman fly home. The next morning, the boy awakens to find a melted snowman on his lawn. Was it all a dream? Reaching into his bathrobe pocket, he finds a blue scarf. In any event, he has had an experience he will remember for the rest of his life.

For viewers young and old, seeing *The Snowman* is sure to be a memorable experience. This touching, lyrical, immensely entertaining film reminds you that, for a parent, one of the best things about owning a VCR is the chance it provides to expose your children to films they wouldn't otherwise be able to see—films infinitely superior to the usual low-grade TV fare. This animated jewel of a film bears about as much resemblance to most TV cartoons (like *He-Man*) as Vivaldi's "Four Seasons" does to "He Was a One-Eyed, One-Horned, Flying Purple People Eater."

THE SNOW QUEEN

CBS/FOX VIDEO (1983), $39.98, 60 min.
6 and up, ★★★

One of Hans Christian Andersen's finest stories, "The Snow Queen," is about the friendship between a young boy and girl named Kay (Lance Kerwin) and Gerda (Melissa Gilbert). The tale opens with a shot of a strange-looking goblin who zooms through space in a kind of intergalactic science lab, concocting ways to spread mischief. When he shatters a fiendish mirror into a thousand sparkling shards, they float down over Denmark like a sinister snow flurry. One tiny piece of glass lodges in young Kay's eye, transforming him into a bitter and coldhearted person, incapable of caring about his friends. Soon afterwards, Kay is carried off to the North Pole by the majestic Snow Queen (Lee Remick). The bulk of the story concerns Gerda's heroic quest to rescue Kay from the frigid domain of the Snow Queen before he turns entirely into a creature of ice.

In many ways, this *Faerie Tale Theatre* production is one of the loveliest in the series. It is stunningly designed and has a very moving climax (in which Gerda, having finally found Kay, embraces her beloved friend and thaws his cold heart with her tears). Unfortunately, it is also pretty slow-moving. Gerda's journey to find her abducted friend should be fraught with adventure, but it's actually rather boring. She spends a bit of time living in the garden of the Lady of Summer (Lauren Hutton), then meets a not-very-interesting Robber Girl (Linda Manz), then flies off to the Snow

Queen's palace. The scenes of Kay's life inside the palace are equally uninvolving. And in spite of Lee Remick's genuinely dazzling presence, there are no really shining performances here to bring the production to life.

As a result, it's unlikely that most younger viewers will find this program especially compelling. There are a few things they are sure to enjoy—the wicked goblin, a talking tree, and a magic reindeer—but not enough to make for a particularly absorbing hour. All in all, this is a decent but somewhat dull entry in the *Faerie Tale Theatre* series.

(See review of *Faerie Tale Theatre* for a description of the series as a whole.)

SNOW WHITE AND THE SEVEN DWARFS

CBS/FOX VIDEO (1983), $39.98, 60 min.
6 and up, ★★★★

Unlike many of the shows in the *Faerie Tale Theatre* series—which take a lighthearted, irreverent approach to their material—this elegant dramatization of *Snow White and the Seven Dwarfs* plays it absolutely straight. It's not totally somber—the seven dwarfs (a lovable crew named Barnaby, Boniface, Bruno, Baldwin, Bertram, Bernard, and Bubba) provide a bit of comic relief, and Rex Smith brings some easygoing charm to his role as the handsome prince. But on the whole, this production treats the famous fairy tale very seriously. The result is one of the most haunting, richly textured, and powerful productions in this generally first-rate series.

Vanessa Redgrave is intensely disquieting as the villainous queen who spends her days in a rapture of self-absorption before her magic talking mirror (Vincent Price) and who will stop at nothing to rid herself of her nemesis, Snow White. When her huntsman cannot bring himself to slay the girl, the evil queen undertakes to do the job herself. First, she transforms herself into a repulsive peddler and attempts to strangle Snow White with a handful of ribbons. Next, she becomes an equally loathsome fruit-seller and tricks the girl into biting a poisoned apple. In all three incarnations, Redgrave seems the very essence of evil and perversity. As an actress, Elizabeth McGovern is not in the same league with Redgrave, but she brings a sweet, fresh-faced innocence to the part of Snow White.

The sets—including a number of cleverly designed miniatures—are uniformly beautiful. And, although there are some disturbing scenes in the program (which is inevitable, given the number of deeply terrifying elements the story contains), the horror is played down as much as possible. Redgrave's evil apple-peddler, for instance, is not nearly as scary as the wicked witch in Walt Disney's famous animated version of this fairy tale (which as of this writing is not available on video cassette).

Like all the really good shows in the *Faerie Tale Theatre* series, this splendid *Snow White* manages to take a familiar, well-worn story and bring it completely to life again, in all its wonder, magic, and mystery.

(See review of *Faerie Tale Theatre* for a description of this series as a whole.)

SPACE ANGEL, Vol. 1

FAMILY HOME ENTERTAINMENT (1964),
$29.95, 50 min.
6 and up, ★

Some parents might remember *Space Angel* from their own TV-watching days, not because it's particularly good (in fact, it's pretty bad), but because it utilizes one of the weirdest animation techniques in cartoon history. Hardly anything moves in this show except the characters' lips, which look uncannily real. This is because they *are* real—not drawings, but actual human mouths superimposed onto the cartoon faces of the characters. This technique is novel enough to be mildly entertaining at first, but the charm wears off quickly, especially since the cartoon as a whole is so crudely made.

There are three *Space Angel* episodes on this cassette, and they are all pretty dreary. The hero is the dashing Scott McCloud, an eyepatch-wearing astronaut who zooms around in his spaceship, "Starduster," getting embroiled in various unlikely and repetitive interplanetary adventures. In the first, a fiendish extraterrestrial villainess, decked out in a Nefertiti costume, tries to hijack a "cosmic mirror" so she can take control of the universe. In the second (unforgettably titled, "Incident of the Loud Planet"), the same evil princess tries to gain control of a certain dangerous element so she can take control of the universe. The third episode offers a dramatic change of pace: here, Space Angel has to battle a whole community of extraterrestrials who dress in ancient Roman costumes (instead of ancient Egyptian ones) and want to take control of the universe.

Space Angel is actually drawn in a pretty interesting style (it was designed by a first-rate comic book artist named Alex Toth). But it must be one of the most static cartoons ever. The animation isn't limited—it's barely existent. This is one of the few cassettes I can think of that make an assembly-line cartoon show like *He-Man* look good. In our Lucas-Spielberg age of sci-fi pyrotechnics, *Space Angel* would almost seem quaint if it weren't so boring. Since it was made in the pre–Women's Movement days of the early 1960s, it also takes a very condescending attitude toward its female characters. Space Angel is accompanied on his adventures by a woman named Crystal, whose main function is to act helpless and squeal with pleasure whenever the hero compliments her on her looks. About to blast off in search of the hijacked cosmic mirror, Scott tells Crystal to get ready for departure. "You mean I'm going too?" Crystal chirps. "Of course," the hero replies. "Who could find a mirror better than a pretty girl?"

Like a number of other outer-space cartoons currently available on videotape, Volume 1 of *Space Angel* ends abruptly, midway through Scott's adventures with the space gladiators. This is a cheap device to get you to rent Volume Two. However, you can easily frustrate this ploy by simply not renting either of these flat and lifeless cassettes.

SPACE GHOST AND DINO BOY

WORLDVISION (1966), $39.95, 53 min.
Ages 6–9, ★

If you're wondering what a futuristic superhero has in common with a little boy trapped in the Stone Age, the answer is: nothing. *Space Ghost and Dino Boy*—a product of the Hanna-Barbera TV-animation mill —lumps together two totally different and unrelated cartoon characters in a show that first aired in the late 1960s. This video cassette contains five *Space Ghost* episodes and a pair of *Dino Boys*. On the whole, *Dino Boy* is the better cartoon, though that's not saying very much. In general these are contrived, mechanical, empty-headed fantasies.

Dino Boy at least has a nifty premise. Stories about modern-day people who stumble onto a mysteriously preserved, prehistoric world have tremendous appeal. It's the fantasy behind such pop masterpieces as Arthur Conan Doyle's *The Lost World* and the original *King Kong*. Unfortunately, *Dino Boy* treats this terrific idea in the most simple-minded way. The hero—a freckle-faced, all-American kid who has accidentally para-chuted into a lost, prehistoric valley—finds himself in various predicaments from which he has to be rescued by his Neanderthal buddy, Ugh, and pet brontosaurus "pup," Bronty. No matter what dangers Dino Boy faces—abduction by Tree People, imprisonment by Worm People—he never loses his cool. In fact, he is so blasé about his adventures that life in this prehistoric wonderland seems about as exciting to him as a trip through the housewares aisle at K-Mart. It's hard to imagine a more trivial version of the "lost world" theme than this cartoon.

Space Ghost is even worse. The hero is a kind of intergalactic Batman, complete with cape, cowl, and an adolescent sidekick named Jace. To make the show appealing to little girls, there is also a female sidekick —Jace's blond, pony-tailed, twin sister, Jan. Rounding out the team is the obligatory Cute Animal, "Blip"—a baby chimp in a Lone Ranger mask. Every one of these cartoons has the exact same plot. Jace and Jan are threatened by some bizarre, science-fiction creature (a lava monster, a mantis man, a "giant scaly ape"), and

Space Ghost has to zoom to their rescue. Essentially, *Space Ghost* is the TV equivalent of a superhero comic book. The only difference is that, in terms of plot, characterization, and artwork, the average comic book is far superior to these uninventive, highly repetitious cartoons.

SPACEKETEERS, Vols. 1–3

FAMILY HOME ENTERTAINMENT (1980),
$29.95 each, 46 min. each
Ages 6–9, ★½

Spaceketeers—a futuristic fantasy cartoon animated in Japan—has the structure of an old-fashioned, Saturday-afternoon movie serial. The three tapes together tell a single story (about a beautiful extraterrestrial princess named Aurora, who, with the help of a gallant cyborg warrior named Jesse Dart, undertakes a perilous mission to save the galaxy from an army of mutant invaders). There are two episodes on each cassette. Each episode picks up where the last one left off and ends at some exciting, cliff-hanging moment, which isn't resolved until the start of the next episode. For videotape renters, this situation poses a problem, since it means that there is no way to make sense out of one of these cassettes without renting all three. Actually the solution to this dilemma is very simple: Don't rent any of them. Your children won't miss a thing. For all its color, action, and exotic, interstellar scenery, *Spaceketeers* is a dull and unimaginative cartoon.

There are a few redeeming features to *Spaceketeers*, but every good point is more than offset by some irritating flaw. As with most Japanese cartoons, the animation here is slick and stylish (especially in comparison to such crude American counterparts as Hanna-Barbera's *Space Ghost*). On the other hand, the dubbing is atrocious, and the characters are distinctly weird looking. (You can tell when a cartoon comes from Japan by the grotesquely exaggerated size of the characters' eyes. Princess Aurora, for example, has the body of a high fashion model and the face of one of Walter Keene's street urchins—a very disconcerting combination.) The action is smoothly handled—Jesse Dart, for instance, is a kind of cosmic kung fu expert who fights like Bruce Lee in a space suit. On the other hand, the plot that holds the action together is more or less incoherent, particularly in the format in which these tapes have been released. Volume One, for example, opens up after the story has already begun. And it ends, two episodes later, right in the middle of a pitched battle.

In short, these are noisy, violent, empty-headed tapes, with little to recommend them except some above-average animation.

SPECTREMAN VERSUS HEDRON

KING OF VIDEO (196?), $39.95, 60 min.
8 and up, ⋆

If you're a fan of low-grade Japanese monster movies like *Godzilla Versus the Smog Monster*, you'll probably love this unbelievably schlocky science fiction show about a young Japanese fellow named George who has the ability to transform himself into the mighty Spectreman, a flying, superpowered robot dressed in a gold lamé jumpsuit.

In this horrendously dubbed adventure (the dialogue

bears no relation whatsoever to the movement of the actors' lips), a fiendish extraterrestrial apeman named Dr. Gori—played by an actor in a gorilla suit and a blond wig—plots to take over the earth by unleashing a hideous mound of living industrial waste called Hedron. Hedron resembles a giant tuber with a ring of rotating tentacles on its head. Gori is assisted by another actor in a gorilla suit, who, at one point, beats up a couple of Japanese technicians and cleverly disguises himself in a lab coat and sunglasses so that he can wander around an oil refinery unnoticed. This is the kind of movie in which people don't notice oversized extraterrestrial gorillas dressed in lab coats and sunglasses. It is also the kind of movie in which the wires on the flying saucers are always completely visible and guys in ridiculously phony monster outfits wreak spectacular destruction on cities obviously constructed of plastic and papier-mâché.

Shows like this are so breathtakingly awful that they have an appeal all their own, but unless you are interested in raising your child to be a schlock-movie aficionado, I wouldn't inflict this cassette—or any of the thirty-one (!) available episodes of *Spectreman*—on youngsters.

STORYBOOK CLASSICS

WALT DISNEY HOME VIDEO (1934–55), $49.95, 41 min.
Preschool–9, ★★★½

The four animated shorts on this compilation tape vary in quality, but they are all products of the Disney Studio's Golden Age—which means that they are infinitely better than any cartoons being created today.

The lead-off cartoon is a delightful adaptation of Hardie Gramatky's "Little Toot." The story (charmingly sung by the Andrews Sisters) is about a mischievous little tugboat whose high jinks cause an ocean liner to run aground. Banished from the harbor, Little Toot wanders alone in the open sea until he redeems himself by saving a stranded passenger ship during a violent squall. This tale of an underrated little fellow who proves himself a hero (and does his father proud) is a guaranteed child-pleaser.

The second cartoon is a tongue-in-cheek retelling of "Chicken Little." The humor here is more pointed than in most Disney cartoons. In fact, this 1943 short seems to be a satire about political manipulation and the gullibility of the masses. (To trap his prey, the fox follows the advice of a book on the psychology of propaganda.) There are some amusing bits in the cartoon, but the humor seems aimed at adults rather than children. And the ending (in which the fox kills all the chickens and uses their wishbones as grave markers) might be upsetting to some small viewers.

"The Grasshopper and the Ants," the third selection on this anthology tape, is one of Disney's classic "Silly Symphonies," and it's a gem. This 1934 fable of a carefree, fiddle-playing grasshopper who learns a lesson in prudence from a colony of hard-working ants features wonderful artwork, a catchy theme song ("The World Owes Me a Living"), and, of course, a valuable lesson about the rewards of delayed gratification.

Finally, there is Disney's engaging version of "Peter and the Wolf," set to Prokofiev's music. It's a colorful child's adventure story in which a fearless Russian boy named Peter—armed only with a popgun and accompanied by a cat, a duck, and a little bird—sets out to capture a ferocious, ravening wolf. The latter is one of the scariest creatures in any Disney cartoon (my youngest daughter kept her hands over her eyes the whole time the wolf was on the screen). And the scene in which Sonya the Duck is (apparently) gobbled up by this monster is a real shocker. (It turns out that Sonya isn't really dead, but the viewer doesn't discover that until the cartoon is almost over).

Still, this is an outstanding cartoon anthology that children, parents, and animation buffs of all ages will derive lots of pleasure from.

STRAWBERRY SHORTCAKE: PETS ON PARADE

FAMILY HOME ENTERTAINMENT (1982),
$29.95, 60 min.
Preschool–9, ★★

Unlike old-time cartoon characters (Mickey Mouse, Felix the Cat, Bugs Bunny), who were the inventions of individual artists, animated characters like Strawberry Shortcake and the Care Bears are the creations of market researchers and corporate committees with a canny understanding of the tastes of young (in this case female) children. As a result, there is something distinctly prefabricated and premeditated about these characters—a slick, mechanical quality. The films they appear in seem less like traditional cartoons than like lavish TV commercials. For all her apparent innocence, Strawberry Shortcake is one shrewd little cookie.

This cartoon does have its good points. The animation is quite pretty. The colors are bright but not garish (in fact, they're surprisingly delicate), and the Strawberryland setting—with its luxuriant landscape, smiling sunflowers, and cloudless sky—is cheery and appealing. There are catchy songs, composed by Mark Volman and Howard Kaylan (former members of the sixties pop group, The Turtles). And there is certainly nothing violent or threatening here. On the contrary, Strawberry Shortcake and her friends, Lemon Meringue, Huckleberry Pie, Butter Cookie, and the rest, are perfect little epitomes of sweetness and light.

The plot, on the other hand, is more or less nonexistent. The entire cartoon deals with the efforts of two comic villains—The Peculiar Purple Pieman of Porcupine Peak and his female counterpart, Sour Grapes (who wears a real, live boa around her neck)—to sabotage a pet show staged by Strawberry Shortcake and her pals. Nothing much happens, though girls between the ages of five and eight seem to find the Shortcake crowd so irresistible that just watching them parade around is enough. Adults will probably sympathize more with Purple Pieman and Sour Grapes, who sing a genuinely witty duet called "I'm Much Lower Than You" (in which each claims to be the more despicable human being) and whose hatred of Strawberry Shortcake's "strawberry language" (she's given to saying things like, "What a berry, berry pretty day!") seems perfectly understandable and sane.

Parents might also consider the implications of encouraging young girls to worship a cartoon character who extols cuteness, prettiness, and charm as the highest virtues, while the equivalent role-models for young boys are aggressive go-getters like He-Man and G.I. Joe.

This one-hour tape concludes with two nonanimated Strawberry Shortcake stories read by an offscreen narrator and illustrated with drawings from Strawberry Shortcake books. Following up a cartoon with a read-aloud experience is a nice idea. But by prefacing this segment with a plug for the "new Parker Brothers series" of Strawberry Shortcake books, the whole thing ends up seeming like another merchandising gimmick.

All in all, the Strawberry Shortcake cartoons are the video equivalent of those highly sugared, kiddie breakfast cereals: artificial, overly sweet, appealing to unformed tastes. They're not harmful by any means if consumed in small quantities, but you wouldn't want your child's diet to consist entirely of this stuff, since it is not very nourishing to young imaginations.

Other cartoons in this series are: *Strawberry Shortcake and the Baby Without a Name*, *Strawberry Shortcake in Big Apple City*, *Strawberry Shortcake's House-Warming Party*, and *Strawberry Shortcake Meets the Berrykins*.

STRONG KIDS, SAFE KIDS

PARAMOUNT (1984), $29.95, 42 min.
Preschool and up, ★★★★

If, like millions of other parents, you worry about protecting your children from the dual horrors of sexual abuse and abduction, you should proceed directly to the nearest video shop, get hold of a copy of this cassette, and sit down to watch it with your kids. Once you do you'll probably want your children to see it a number of times until its lessons sink in. Fortunately, *Strong Kids, Safe Kids* has been priced low enough to make it affordable. You'll be glad to own it—and deeply grateful to the people responsible for making it.

Produced with tremendous care, intelligence, and love, this entertaining program is a kind of video instructional manual aimed at both parents and children. The approach is positive, friendly, and very nonthreatening. Henry Winkler (who appears as both himself and The Fonz) makes a first-rate host, offering straightforward, sensible advice in a firm but reassuring way. He is assisted by a number of fellow TV celebrities (John Ritter, Mariette Hartley), folksinger Chris Wallace, several nationally known experts (Dr. Sol Gordon, director of the Institute for Family Research and Education, and Kee McFarlane of the Children's Institute International), plus some animated characters (including Yogi Bear, Fred Flintstone, Scooby-Doo, and Baby Smurf), all of whom help deliver and reinforce the program's messages in short segments that are simple, sensitive, and to the point.

This tape won't alarm children (on the contrary, it is designed to increase their sense of confidence and self-respect). But it will instill some healthy caution and provide them with the basic skills they need to arm themselves against various threats—not only ill-intentioned strangers but anyone who makes a sexual overture. Among other things, it teaches them exactly what a stranger *is* and the tricks used by certain grown-ups to lure children into bad situations. It helps them distinguish between different kinds of touches and reassures them that it's okay to say "No!" to the ones that make them uncomfortable. It demonstrates practical techniques for dealing with unwelcome advances ("The Big No," and a self-defense danger-yell called "The Honk"). It teaches them important rules ("Nobody is supposed to touch your private parts but you") and encourages them to tell their parents immediately about any adult who tries to force them to do something they don't want to do. Finally, to children who *have* been the victims of sexual abuse, it offers the reassuring message, "It's not your fault!"

Parents will learn a lot from this cassette, too: how to really hear what their children are telling them; how to talk openly and honestly about sexual matters without feeling ashamed or resorting to euphemisms; how to be "askable" parents—the kind that children can turn to when they need someone they can trust. In fact, one of the wonderful things about this tape is its emphasis on open communication between parents and children. Throughout the program, there are places where Henry Winkler tells viewers—grown-ups and kids—to turn off the tape and talk to each other. (Whatever you do, don't simply rent this tape and then plunk your kids down in front of the VCR to watch it alone.)

Strong Kids, Safe Kids is a must-see. Even the most enlightened and capable parents will learn valuable things from it—and for kids, it could well be a life-saver.

SUPERBOY

WARNER (1966–68), $24.98, 60 min.
Ages 6–9, ★½

SUPERMAN

WARNER (1966–68), $24.98, 60 min.
Ages 6–9, ★½

These poorly animated volumes, containing seven cartoons each, are part of Warner Home Video's *Super Powers Collection*, a series of tacky Saturday-morning cartoons reissued in shiny new packages.

(See review of *The Super Powers Collection*.)

THE SUPER POWERS COLLECTION, Four volumes (SUPERMAN, BATMAN, AQUAMAN, and SUPERBOY)

WARNER (1966–68), $24.98 each, 60 min. each
Ages 6–9, ★½

To cash in on the burgeoning kidvid market, video distributors are relying more and more on a clever (if shoddy) technique: taking moth-eaten TV cartoons, packaging them in flashy formats, and peddling them as exciting new video programs. *The Super Powers Collection*—four video cassettes containing inane, cheaply made cartoons from the late 1960s—is an example of this practice.

The cartoons on these tapes—starring four of DC Comics' most famous superheroes—are perfect specimens of that supremely tacky genre, the Saturday-morning cartoon. They contain as little animation as they can possibly get away with. Though the action is nonstop (in fact, these cartoons consist of nothing *but* action), it is extremely dreary, since the characters move with all the dynamism and grace of cardboard cut-outs. As for the artwork: It doesn't even match the level of most coloring books. In spite of the melodramatic titles attached to each episode ("The Great Kryptonite Caper," "The Onslaught of the Octamen," etc.), you won't find any plots in these cartoons—just a series of dimwitted and depressingly repetitious battles between the "costumed crimefighters" and their non-sensical foes. Batman and the Boy Wonder fight their familiar, high-camp adversaries (the Joker, the Penguin, the Riddler, etc.); Aquaman and Aqualad —accompanied by their pet walrus, Tusky—vanquish one ridiculous underwater villain after another (the Black Manta, the Fisherman, Octaman); and Superman (in both his grown-up and adolescent incarnations) uses his array of mighty powers to deal with the usual parade of mad scientists, megalomaniac crooks, and extraterrestrial villains wielding kryptonite ray guns.

These cartoons have nothing to recommend them. If you want to get hold of some good Superman cartoons for your children, stick to the splendid (though occasionally scary) Paramount shorts from the early 1940s, animated by Max Fleischer and available on videotape from various distributors, including Media Home Entertainment and Wizard Video.

SUPERTED III: THE ADVENTURES CONTINUE

WALT DISNEY HOME VIDEO (1982), $49.95, 49 min.
6 and up, ★★★

See review of *The Premiere Adventures of Superted.*

SWISS FAMILY ROBINSON

WALT DISNEY HOME VIDEO (1960), $69.95, 126 min.
7 and up, ★★★½

Kids are sure to love this lavish, entertaining adventure film, which makes life on a deserted isle seem exactly like a neverending vacation at Disney World. Based (very loosely) on the famous novel by Johann Wyss, the film tells the story of a shipwrecked family—father, mother, and three spunky sons—who turn their new wilderness home into a tropical playland. Never has life in the jungle seemed like so much wholesome family fun. After using the salvaged materials from the foundered ship to construct an elaborate three-unit tree house (complete with elevator, skylight, and indoor plumbing), the family spends the rest of its time relaxing, basking in the sun, frolicking with a whole menagerie of friendly creatures, and splashing around in the nearby waterhole (which comes complete with its own natural slide).

The only threat to this idyllic existence is a boatload of supposedly sinister buccaneers who turn out to be so comically inept that they make the Pirates of Penzance look like Hell's Angels. There's a fair amount of violence in the climactic stand-off between the Robinson family and this horde of supremely klutzy cut-throats (led by Sessue Hayakawa), but it's all handled in an exaggeratedly slapstick style. It seems far less like the life-and-death struggle it's supposed to be than an elaborate, make-believe battle between two bands of kids playing cowboys and Indians.

In fact, the entire movie possesses this quality of elaborate make-believe. It's a child's adventure fantasy brought to vivid and exuberant life by the slick cine-magicians of the Disney studio. It's packed with standard Disney touches. One of the things that initially attracted Walt to the story was the opportunity it afforded for including lots of nature photography, and I can't think of another Disney feature that contains so many exciting or comical animal sequences—shark attacks, tiger attacks, boa constrictor attacks, as well as a rollicking wild animal race in which the brothers ride around on the backs of jungle creatures (a zebra, a baby elephant, and an ostrich). In fact, this sequence sums up the essence of the movie, which is obviously intended to be the cinematic equivalent of an exhilarating amusement park ride.

Beautifully photographed and well acted by a generally strong cast (including John Mills as the father, Dorothy McGuire as the mother, and James MacArthur and Tommy Kirk as the two older brothers), *Swiss Family Robinson* is a first-rate Disney feature. Grownups may well find some of its wilder improbabilities a bit hard to swallow, but it's hard to imagine a child who won't have lots of fun watching it.

THE TALE OF THE FROG PRINCE

CBS/FOX VIDEO (1982), $39.98, 60 min.
6 and up, ★★★½

The Tale of the Frog Prince—the first show in the highly popular *Faerie Tale Theatre* series—set the style for most of the productions that followed. Written and directed by Monty Python's Eric Idle, this brash, high-spirited but essentially faithful retelling of the famous Grimm Brothers story is distinguished by stunning sets (based on the artwork of illustrator Maxfield Parrish), fine acting and direction, and an outstandingly funny performance by Robin Williams, who brings his special brand of manic charm to the role of the title character.

Williams spends most of his time inside a ridiculous-looking frog costume, and sophisticated video effects are used to make him look only inches tall. His unprepossessing appearance, however, doesn't cause him any embarrassment. Quite the contrary. Unlike the enchanted prince in the first-rate Muppet version of this fairy tale (see review of *The Frog Prince*), this bewitched young man is, as he tells anyone who is willing to listen, "fiercely proud" to be a frog. And when he wangles an invitation to the king's banquet from the vain, spoiled princess (Teri Garr), he entertains his hosts with a one-man (or, more accurately, one-frog) variety show that's the comic high point of this program. After warming up the audience with a string of corny jokes ("Sorry to emote like this. And speaking of a moat . . ."), he segues into a flipper-footed soft-shoe routine and ends with an amphibian version of Shakespeare ("Now is the winter of our frog-content . . . And yet I shall not croak").

As is the case with a number of the programs in this series, there is a certain amount of sexual innuendo in this production, though, to a certain extent, that's probably unavoidable in any faithful adaptation of "The Frog Prince." (The tale—about an enchanted frog who retrieves a princess's lost golden ball on the condition that she carry him back to her castle, befriend him, and take him into her bed—is generally interpreted as a story about a young girl's sexual awakening.) The only really jarring note—and one that might, indeed, make some parents justifiably uneasy —is Williams's remark to the princess, "You're very beautiful in your own bitchy way."

Apart from this one (rather glaring) lapse in taste, this program really is—to use the overworked cliché —fun for the whole family.

(See review of *Faerie Tale Theatre* for a description of this series as a whole.)

A TALE OF TWO CITIES

VESTRON (1978), $59.95, 72 min.
8 and up, ★★½

This animated version of the Dickens classic is part of Vestron Video's well-intentioned but rather dull *Charles Dickens Collection*. See review of *Great Expectations*.

TEENY-TINY AND THE WITCH-WOMAN AND OTHER STORIES

WESTEN WOODS/CC STUDIOS (1985),
$29.95, approx. 40 min.
6 and up, ★★★★

The title story—about a cannibalistic witch whose cottage is furnished with the bones of her small victims —is too scary for younger viewers. For children six years and older, however, this brilliantly animated collection (Volume Five in the splendid *Children's Circle* series) is one of the best video cassettes available. (See review of *The Children's Circle*.)

THE TERRYTOONS GOOD GUY HOUR

CHILDREN'S VIDEO LIBRARY (1951–67),
$39.95, 53 min.
Ages 5–8, ★½

Even at their best, Terrytoons featuring characters like Heckle and Jeckle and Mighty Mouse can't hold a candle to the classic cartoons made by the Disney studio, Warner Brothers, and MGM. On the other hand, in comparison to most of the animated junk being cranked out today, some of the old-time Terrytoons look pretty good. The two Mighty Mouse cartoons included in this animated collection, "A Cat's Tale" (1953) and "The Magic Slipper" (1948), aren't big on plot (like most Mighty Mouse shorts, they are little more than comical slug-fests between the stalwart super-rodent and some oversized foes), but they're done with far more energy and style than almost anything your children are likely to see on the average Saturday-morning cartoon show.

Unfortunately, the rest of this tape is made up of pretty mediocre stuff. There are two extremely dreary Deputy Dawg cartoons, a pair of secret-agent parodies starring a trenchcoat-wearing character called "James Hound," and a couple of knockabout adventures featuring a ridiculous team called "The Mighty Heroes," made up of five highly eccentric members—Tornado Man, Strong Man, Rope Man, Cuckoo Man, and Diaper Man (an infant superhero who clobbers bad guys with his bottle). The two Mighty Heroes cartoons are the best of this undistinguished bunch—they have a brash, zany quality that makes them fairly amusing. Still, they're pretty silly. This cassette can't really be recommended for children. (Serious animation buffs, however, might find it interesting, since the James Hound and Mighty Heroes cartoons were directed by Ralph Bakshi, who later gained fame for such animated features as *Fritz the Cat*, *Heavy Traffic*, and *The Lord of the Rings*.)

THE THREE LITTLE PIGS

CBS/FOX VIDEO (1985), $39.98, 60 min.
6 and up, ★★★★

One of the most purely delightful shows in the *Faerie Tale Theatre* series, *The Three Little Pigs* focuses on a trio of porcine brothers, Peter, Paul, and Larry. Peter is a money-hungry fellow who sits around reading books like *The Lazy Pig's Guide to Riches* and throws together a flimsy shack because straw is the cheapest building material he can find. Paul is a vain, primping playpig and party animal with a repertoire of slick pick-up lines ("Hey there, bacon bits, where have you been all my life?"); he constructs a hastily built bachelor pad out of sticks to entertain the voluptuous Tina (Valerie Perrine). The hero of the tale is the sweet-natured Larry (Billy Crystal), who builds his house of brick —not because he's the most practical pig (as in other versions) but, on the contrary, because he's the most artistic and appreciates bricks for their aesthetic qualities (they're red and symmetrical).

Jeff Goldblum gives an amusing performance as the swaggering tough guy, Buck Wolf, who terrorizes everyone but his nagging wife, Nadine. With gorgeous sets, great costumes, nonstop laughs, and some nifty effects (the scenes in which Buck blows down the straw and stick houses are beautifully done), this cassette is a treat for grown-ups and children alike.

(See review of *Faerie Tale Theatre* for a description of the series as a whole.)

THREE RICHARD SCARRY'S ANIMAL NURSERY TALES

GOLDEN BOOK VIDEO (1985), $9.95, 30 min.
Preschool–6, ★★★

Golden Books—those slender, hardcover volumes with cheery illustrations and easy-to-read texts—have been favorites of parents and small children for over forty years. More than five billion have been sold since they were introduced in the 1940s. Now, the folks at Western Publishing have entered the burgeoning kidvid field with a charming, inexpensive line of "video storybooks" based on their best-selling titles.

These brief, likable videotapes use a technique that the producers call "Picturemation," which is basically a fancy term for minimal animation. The visuals consist of the original book illustrations, which are given a bit of liveliness and movement with some rudimentary camera effects. Every now and then an eye will blink, a mouth will open and close, an arm or a leg will wag, or a character will hop up and down. Meanwhile, an offscreen storyteller provides the narration, while some actors recite the dialogue. It's a simple technique (these videos don't have enough animation to qualify as cartoons) but, because the stories themselves are so simple, the method works surprisingly well.

Three Richard Scarry Animal Nursery Tales contains a trio of adaptations from the popular children's book illustrator—"The Gingerbread Man," "Goldilocks and the Three Bears," and "The Three Little Pigs." They are all very well done, with spirited narrations and bright, appealing artwork. Younger children are sure to be charmed by them. Occasionally, some of the text will be printed on the bottom of the screen —presumably to encourage the development of the viewer's reading skills.

The danger of a tape like this is that parents might use it as a substitute for reading aloud to their children. No videotape should take the place of literature. But, as an adjunct to reading, the Golden Book Videos are a perfectly nice line of videotapes for preschool-age children.

Besides the Richard Scarry tape, there are seven Golden Book Videos available to date: *Three Favorite*

Golden Stories ("Scuffy the Tugboat," "Theodore Mouse Goes to Sea," "What Was That!"), *Three Best-Loved Golden Stories* ("Poky Little Puppy," "The Sailor Dog," "Little Toad to the Rescue"), *Three Golden Amye Rosenberg Stories* ("Tale of Peter Rabbit," "Polly's Pet," "The Little Red Hen"), *Four Masters of the Universe Stories*, *Three Sesame Street Popular Stories*, *Five Sesame Street Favorite Stories*, and *Three Looney Tunes Favorites*.

THE THREE ROBBERS AND OTHER STORIES

WESTON WOODS/CC STUDIOS (1985), $29.95, approx. 40 min.
Preschool and up, ★★★★

The Children's Circle is the best line of children's tapes available. Each outstanding volume contains four beautifully animated adaptations of award-winning children's books. This cassette (the sixth in the series) features Tomi Ungerer's *The Three Robbers*, James Flora's *Leopold the See-Through Crumbpicker*, Steven Kellogg's *The Island of Skag*, and *Fourteen Rats & a Rat Catcher* by James Cressey and Tamasin Cole. (See review of *The Children's Circle*.)

THUMBELINA

CBS/FOX VIDEO (1983), $39.98, 60 min.
6 and up, ★★★½

At the start of every *Faerie Tale Theatre* presentation, the actress Shelley Duvall, the creator and executive producer of the series, comes out to offer a brief summary of the story's message. Unfortunately, her summaries often bear little relation to the ensuing tales. *Thumbelina* is a glaring example. In describing *Thumbelina* as the story of a "plucky little girl who has strength and intelligence enough to insist on leading her own life," Duvall suggests that this version will give the traditional fairy tale a contemporary, feminist twist. In fact, the heroine of this *Thumbelina* turns out to be a completely conventional (if miniscule) damsel-in-distress, who requires a steady stream of male saviors to rescue her from the assorted pickles she finds herself in.

Apart from this inconsistency, *Thumbelina* is a very entertaining production. The heroine's adventures begin when she is carried off to a swamp to be the bride of a toad named Herman. Parents should be advised that, though Herman is a comical character (a pudgy momma's boy in a straw hat and coveralls), some children might find him scary—he looks like the overweight cousin of the Creature from the Black Lagoon. Escaping down the stream on a lily pad (with the help of a pair of fish in English barrister getups), Thumbelina makes it to shore and builds a hut of leaves and twigs where she lives contentedly until winter comes. She is saved from an icy death by a friendly fieldmouse who takes her home, becomes her guardian, and introduces her to a nearsighted, scholarly mole named Mortimer. This deeply unattractive creature instantly takes a shine to the fetching girl. In gratitude to the fieldmouse, Thumbelina agrees to become Mortimer's bride and spend the rest of her days underground. She is rescued at the last moment by a grateful swallow (whom she had earlier nursed back to health) and is carried away to a luminous fairy-tale kingdom where she meets and falls in love with the handsome Flower Prince.

Carrie Fischer is a little bland as the title character

(and Conchata Ferrell as her mother is terribly wooden) but the other performers are first-rate, particularly Burgess Meredith as the amorous antiquarian mole. With marvelous animal costumes, outstanding effects, and splendid sets (especially Herman's misty swamp, Mortimer's stuffy, cluttered burrow, and the luxuriant garden kingdom of the Flower Prince), this video fairy tale has enough genuinely magical moments to enchant children and grown-ups alike.

(See review of *Faerie Tale Theatre* for a description of this series as a whole.)

TIP TOP! WITH SUZY PRUDDEN—AGES 3–6

WARNER (1982), $39.95, 53 min.
Ages 3–6, ★★★★

TIP TOP! WITH SUZY PRUDDEN—AGES 7 AND ABOVE

WARNER (1982), $39.95, 48 min.
7 and up, ★★★★

Fitness expert Suzy Prudden turns exercise into fun on these entertaining, briskly paced workout tapes for kids. *Tip Top!* won't transform your children into junior Jane Fondas or mini–Sly Stallones. But it *will* introduce them to the pleasures of regular exercise and help them to develop sensible shape-up habits that should stand them in good stead throughout their adolescence—and later.

Although tailored for different age groups, both

cassettes follow the same format. On each one, Suzy leads a lively group of youngsters through a series of brief but energetic routines, that get progressively harder (though none is overly complicated or difficult). Ms. Prudden is a warm and cheery instructor with a talent for turning exercise into a game. Younger children stretch their arms by flapping like a butterfly, tone up their midriffs by crawling on their tummies like inchworms, and exercise their shoulders by pretending to "row, row, row the boat" gently across the floor. Working out becomes a form of play. (At times, this preschool version of *Tip Top!* seems like a *Romper Room* segment filmed at Jack LaLanne's.) Children are also discouraged from overexerting themselves. The exercises are grouped into six individual segments, and viewers are told to do only as many of these as they feel comfortable with. In addition, there are regular rest breaks throughout the program.

The second tape uses the same approach, though here the games are slightly more sophisticated (instead of pretending to be animals, the children perform movements based on sports—fencing lunges, swimming backstrokes, etc.) The exercises are also a bit more advanced.

One small problem with this tape is that a number of the routines are exceptionally brief. Some of them last less than a minute. As a result, first-time viewers will have trouble following many of the exercises. On the other hand, this isn't a tape designed for one-time viewing. It's meant to be seen—and used—on a regular basis, and once your child has watched it a few times, she or he should have no trouble following the instructions.

One of the best things about these cassettes is that they are virtually guaranteed to get your kids onto the floor and moving. When I showed this tape to some preschool children, they were on their feet and following along within minutes. It's nice to see a video cassette that turns TV watching into such an active and healthy experience.

TOM & JERRY CARTOON FESTIVAL, Vols. 1–3

MGM/UA (1944–54), $39.95 each, 60 min. each
Preschool and up, ★★★

Before they became famous (or infamous, depending on your point of view) as the pioneers and chief practitioners of low-grade, mass-produced TV animation, William Hanna and Joe Barbera were a top animation team at MGM, where, over the course of seventeen years, they turned out a remarkable cartoon series that many film buffs regard as the best in Hollywood history: *Tom & Jerry*. Devoid (more or less) of dialogue, and constructed around the same stock situation—cat chases mouse—these marvelously inventive, beautifully drawn shorts (which won seven Academy Awards in the 1940s and 1950s) are cherished by fans for the virtuosity of their visual gags and the vivid personalities of their two stars.

Of course, not everyone is a fan of Tom & Jerry cartoons. To many parents, in fact, they are synonymous with gratuitous, kiddie-show violence. It is certainly true that these cartoons rely heavily on extremely boisterous slapstick. In a single Tom & Jerry short, the hapless cat might get his face slammed with a book, his front paw smashed by a mousetrap, his scalp blown off by a shotgun, his head flattened by a hammer, and his skin punctured by hat pins (all of this—and more —happens to poor Tom in the 1944 cartoon, "Mouse Trouble," found on Volume 2). Human beings in all times and places have delighted in this sort of humor

—but if you're not one of them, or if you think this kind of comedy is unsuitable for children, then these cassettes are definitely not for you.

On the other hand, if you're looking for cartoons that have the exhilarating, often roaringly funny quality of Max Sennett slapsticks, you won't do much better than these three compilation tapes, which bring together Tom & Jerry's greatest hits (including such gems as "Hic-Cup Pup," "The Milky Waif," "Mouse in Manhattan," and Oscar-winners like "Cat Concerto" and "The Little Orphan"). Brilliantly animated and bursting with vitality, these vintage cartoons have no other purpose than to generate as many bellylaughs as possible. Grown-ups can enjoy these three cassettes as much as children, and animation buffs will regard them as a treasure trove.

Tom & Jerry cartoons may be low comedy—but they are low comedy of a very high order.

TOO SMART FOR STRANGERS

WALT DISNEY HOME VIDEO (1985), $29.95, 40 min.
Preschool and up, ★★★★

Given the terrifyingly high incidence of child abduction and sexual abuse, most parents feel an urgent need to teach their children how to protect themselves against strangers and other predatory adults. Several videotapes now on the market are designed to meet this need by imparting basic defensive skills to young children. Although *Too Smart for Strangers* doesn't cover as much ground as *Strong Kids, Safe Kids*—the first and best of this type of cassette (see review)—it is still an extremely well-done and worthwhile program.

In *Too Smart for Strangers*, the costumed characters

from the Disney Channel's "Welcome to Pooh Corner" cable-TV series deliver vital safety messages in an entertaining, nonthreatening way. Through songs, dances, and short, humorous sketches, Winnie the Pooh and his pals Piglet, Tigger, and the rest of the Pooh Corner crowd teach young viewers a number of invaluable lessons, beginning with the most basic of all—how to tell a stranger from someone who isn't. Interspersed among these sketches are brief simulations (featuring children and adults in everyday settings) of real-life situations. These live-action segments dramatize certain dangers and demonstrate the best ways of dealing with them. Children learn how to avoid unsafe places, how to recognize the tricks that might be used to lure them into danger, how to respond if a stranger comes to the door while they are home alone, and much more. Again and again, the same fundamental rule is emphasized: If you are approached or asked anything by a stranger, you should say "no," run away, and tell your parents or an adult you trust.

In addition to giving kids practical tips on self-defense against strangers, this program very sensibly tells children that danger can also come from people they know—even from people at home. In sensitive, supportive tones, it teaches young viewers that they have the right to say "No!" to *any* grown-up who tries to touch their bodies—and specifically their genitals —in a way that feels wrong to them. It also reassures children that they are not to blame in the event that an adult *does* do something bad to them.

Endorsed by a large number of professional organizations (including the National Committee for Prevention of Child Abuse, the American Academy of Family Physicians, and the National Education Association), this excellent videotape will significantly increase your children's safety skills and—in doing so—will greatly increase your own peace of mind.

THE TRANSFORMERS, VOLUME I: MORE THAN MEETS THE EYE!

FAMILY HOME ENTERTAINMENT (1985),
$24.95, 70 min.
5 and up, ★★

THE TRANSFORMERS, VOLUME II: THE ULTIMATE DOOM

FAMILY HOME ENTERTAINMENT (1985),
$24.95, 70 min.
5 and up, ★★

Transformers—little plastic robots that, when folded up, turn into different kinds of vehicles (race cars, motorcycles, tractors, and the like)—are pretty neat toys. It's easy to see why so many children love them. Following the increasingly common (and highly dubious) practice of basing cartoon shows on best-selling toys, the folks at Family Home Entertainment have now released a pair of video cassettes featuring animated versions of these versatile cyborgs.

In *The Transformers, Volume I: More Than Meets the Eye!*, we are taken to the distant world of Cybertron, a mechanized planet that has been devastated by a war between the peace-loving Autobots and the evil Decepticons. In desperate need of new energy sources, the Autobots and Decepticons fly off into space, engage in a fierce laser-gun battle (one of about fifty that take place in the course of this 70-minute tape) and crash-land on prehistoric earth. Awakening four million years later—in the present—the Decepticons (commanded by the megalomaniacal Megatron) launch a series of attacks on American oil rigs, hydroelectric dams, and rocket sites, opposed along the way by the feisty Autobots and their heroic leader, Optimus Prime. In *The Transformers, Volume II: The Ultimate Doom,* the ruthless Decepticons continue their diabolical quest for intergalactic domination.

Young fans of the Transformers are sure to be pleased by these slickly made cartoons, but before you decide to rent (or purchase) one or both of them, you should ask yourself the following questions:

1. Do you want your child to spend his or her time watching what amounts to an hour-long commercial for Transformers merchandise?

2. Do you want your child to spend his or her time watching an endless series of violent battles between two armies of giant samurai robots from outer space?

3. Do you want your child to admire and emulate a group of cartoon superheroes whose main attribute is the ability to transform themselves into a convoy of jeeps, minivans, and recreational vehicles, and who are given to exclaiming things like "Leaping lubricant!" when excited?

If the answer to any of the above is "no," then these cassettes aren't for you.

In addition to the two 70-minute video cassettes, Family Home Entertainment has released five half-hour "Transformer" episodes, which sell for $14.95 each: *Transport to Oblivion, Divide and Conquer, Fire in the Sky, S.O.S.—Dinobots!,* and *Roll for It.*

TWENTY THOUSAND LEAGUES UNDER THE SEA

WALT DISNEY HOME VIDEO (1954), $79.95, 126 min.
7 and up, ★★★★

When Walt Disney decided in the early 1950s to make a live-action version of the classic Jules Verne story, he spared no effort or expense to do the job right. The skill, care, and money lavished on this production are visible in every frame. This wonderful movie is not only the best live-action film Disney ever made—it is one of the great adventure fantasies of the screen.

James Mason shines as the misguided genius, Captain Nemo. Filled with a bitter hatred of humankind, Nemo roams the Pacific Ocean attacking warships with his atomic-powered craft, the Nautilus, a submarine shaped like a sea monster. When a French scientist, Professor Pierre Aronnax (Paul Lukas), is sent to investigate, Nemo destroys his ship and picks up the professor along with two companions, Aronnax's faint-hearted assistant, Conseil (Peter Lorre), and a swaggering harpooneer named Ned Land (Kirk Douglas). The film follows the adventures of this mismatched trio as Nemo introduces them to the wonders of his underseas world and the futuristic marvels of the Nautilus.

Twenty Thousand Leagues Under the Sea is a lavishly produced, highly imaginative, and continuously entertaining film. The Nautilus itself—built full-scale and sumptuously designed—is a wondrous creation. Another is the mechanical monster created for the film's most dramatic scene, a pitched battle between the crewmen of the Nautilus and a giant squid. This slimy, tentacled nightmare (designed by special effects wizard Robert Mattey, who, years later, was brought out of retirement to create another aquatic terror, the giant white shark of *Jaws*) is one of the scariest sea monsters ever put on screen. Younger viewers, in fact, may well find it a bit *too* scary. For older children, however —and grown-ups, too—this first-rate fantasy film is one of the best video cassettes around.

TWENTY THOUSAND LEAGUES UNDER THE SEA

PRISM (1972), $29.95, 60 min.
Ages 6–9, ★★

Viewers in the market for a juvenile, poorly animated adaptation of *Twenty Thousand Leagues Under the Sea* will be hard pressed to choose between the Hanna-Barbera production and this equally low-grade cartoon from the Rankin/Bass organization. The graphics in this two-part, made-for-TV adaptation aren't awful —they have the bold, vigorous quality of decent comic book art—but the movements of the characters are wooden and absolutely minimal. What saves this cartoon from utter hopelessness is that—like the Hanna-Barbera version—it sticks closely enough to the original story line to be interesting, even in this highly mediocre form.

Once again, we follow the adventures of Professor Arronax, his assistant (here named Conrad), and the bold harpooneer, Ned Land (who is drawn to resemble Kirk Douglas) as they explore the underseas domain of the mad Captain Nemo. There are the usual aquatic adventures—attacks by hammerhead sharks and giant squid—and a suspenseful episode in which the Nautilus is trapped in a giant block of polar ice. Though the characters seem pretty lifeless, the story itself is fast-paced and dynamic enough to keep most young children happy for an hour. The only significant way in which this cartoon differs from the other movies based on Verne's novel is in its addition of a new and totally superfluous character—a supposedly adorable porpoise named Fifi, who saves the heroes from a variety of perils and (in the single dumbest scene in this or any other version of the story) appears at one point riding merrily on the back of a giant seahorse.

If this is the only *Twenty Thousand Leagues Under the Sea* your video shop carries, go ahead and rent it. Your children will probably find it entertaining, and it might even inspire them to become interested in the book. Otherwise, stick to the Disney version.

TWENTY THOUSAND LEAGUES UNDER THE SEA

WORLDVISION (1973), $39.95, 60 min.
Ages 6–9, ★★

This cartoon version of Jules Verne's classic adventure story is about what you'd expect from Hanna-Barbera, the pioneers of low-budget, limited TV animation. It faithfully follows the original plot, but it's so visually uninteresting—stiff, flat, lifeless—that all the wonder and drama are gone.

The giant squid attack—one of the most exciting episodes in the story—is typical of everything that's wrong with this film. For his great, live-action version of Verne's novel, Walt Disney went to great expense to do the scene right. The mechanical squid his effects artists constructed is one of the screen's most memorable monsters. By contrast, this cut-rate cartoon gives us a crudely drawn mollusk with a single animated tentacle that waves back and forth in the air while the rest of the creature remains totally motionless. Watching this sequence is about as interesting as staring at a metronome. Another corner-cutting ploy here is the substitution of talk for action. Instead of thrills and adventure, we get scene after scene of people standing around discussing their predicament—a cheap way of animating a film, since nothing has to move but a couple of jaws. It's easy to see why this type of animation has been ridiculed as "illustrated radio": you can watch it with your eyes closed and not miss very much.

Twenty Thousand Leagues Under the Sea is such a terrific story that even an adaptation as dull and wooden as this one is watchable. Still, with the Disney version available on video cassette, it's hard to see why anyone would be interested in this mediocre cartoon.

THE UNDERSEA ADVENTURES OF CAPTAIN NEMO, Vol. 1

FAMILY HOME ENTERTAINMENT (1975), $29.95, 49 min.
Ages 5–9, ★★★

The packaging of this video cassette doesn't do it justice. "Join Captain Nemo and his crew in a series of daring battles and rescues," says the blurb, suggesting that the cartoons on this tape are nothing but action-oriented rip-offs of *Twenty Thousand Leagues Under the Sea*. In fact, they're nothing of the kind. On the contrary, they are skillfully made, completely nonviolent cartoons that teach interesting lessons about ocean life in the form of entertaining stories.

In spite of its title, this cassette has no connection with *Twenty Thousand Leagues*. The hero of these cartoons is not Jules Verne's mad genius, but a blond, all-American scientist named Mark Nemo. And the Nautilus is a state-of-the-art super-sub belonging to a conservationist group called the United World Organization. Each of the dozen brief episodes finds Mark and his crew—a young brother and sister named Robby and Chris—off on an important mission. There's plenty of drama here. These cartoons don't skimp on the kinds of things you expect from a nautical adventure: buried treasure, sharks, giant squid. For the most part, however, the plots are really a device for serving up interesting and educational facts.

A story about a community of Hawaiian fishermen whose oyster beds are being decimated by unknown predators turns out to be a lesson on the amazing varieties, eating habits, and regenerative abilities of starfish. In another episode, Robby becomes lost in an undersea cave while pursuing a coelacanth, which, we learn, is a "living fossil, the world's oldest unchanged fish," whose "direct ancestors go back to the Devonian Period, three million years ago." Other episodes deal with the dangers of nuclear waste disposal, the Save the Whales movement, the methods used by Polynesian natives to fish for octopus, and so on. The title of this cassette makes it sound like a typically low-grade kiddie show, but it's really more like an animated *National Geographic* special, or a cartoon version of "The Undersea World of Jacques Cousteau."

These cartoons have some minor flaws. The animation isn't anything special, though—within the obvious limitations of the budget—the producers have clearly gone to some trouble to portray the ocean world with accuracy and care. There are a few jarring details, like a Tunisian fisherman who speaks like a Texas ranch hand ("I don't want no truck with pirates"). But on the whole, this is an intelligent, well-intentioned, and worthwhile cassette.

Also available: *The Undersea Adventures of Captain Nemo*, Volumes 2 and 3 (60 minutes each).

THE VELVETEEN RABBIT

KING OF VIDEO (1983), $39.95, 60 min.
Preschool–9, ★★★

Margery Williams's touching story of a stuffed toy rabbit who is brought to life by the magic of a child's love is charmingly dramatized in this live-action musical production starring Marie Osmond in the title role. The story opens on Christmas morning, when a young boy receives the "fat and bunchy" little toy in his Christmas stocking. At first, the rabbit is consigned to a cupboard in the nursery, where a wise old rocking horse teaches him about "the magic called Real." "Real isn't how you are made," the horse tells the Velveteen Rabbit. "It's a thing that happens to you. When a child loves you for a long, long time, not just to play with, but REALLY loves you, then you become Real." The story of how the endearing little toy becomes a living rabbit, first in the boy's eyes, and then (with the help of the "Nursery Magic Fairy") in reality, is the heart of this lovely and poignant fable.

The half-hour version on this cassette is a likable and entertaining production, with pretty sets, clever special effects, several bouncy tunes by the Sherman Brothers (the well-known song-writing team, best known for their work on *Mary Poppins*), and an engaging performance by Marie Osmond, who spends most of the show dressed up in a shapeless, overstuffed bunny costume (she also appears—looking far more glamorous—in the role of the Nursery Magic Fairy). There *is* one slightly off-key element here. In some of the scenes (the ones in which the Velveteen Rabbit is being picked up, carried around, or held by the actors), the bunny is an actual stuffed toy, with the beaming, painted face of Marie Osmond on it. This is a little jarring, especially if you're used to William Nicholson's lovely, poetic illustrations of the Velveteen Rabbit, which appear in the original book. In all other respects, however, this is a well-done and faithful adaptation. It's no substitute for the book, but it makes a nice complement to it.

The remaining half-hour on this cassette is filled with three delightful episodes from the zany, animated series, *Arthur and the Square Knights of the Round Table*. These witty cartoons—which are similar, both in graphic style and comic sensibility, to the old Bullwinkle show—don't have anything in the world to do with *The Velveteen Rabbit*, but who's complaining? Any chance to see a few of these genuinely funny and imaginative shorts is welcome. (See review of *Arthur and the Square Knights of the Round Table*.)

THE VELVETEEN RABBIT

RANDOM HOUSE VIDEO (1985), $24.95, 26 min.
Preschool–9, ★★★★

Like all great children's books, Margery Williams's *The Velveteen Rabbit* is a seemingly simple tale that resonates with larger meanings. This story of a homespun toy bunny that becomes a real, living rabbit is a moving, poetic fable about love, self-sacrifice, the bittersweet pleasures of growing up, and the magical, transforming powers of the child's imagination.

Featuring a marvelous reading by Meryl Streep and scores of exquisite illustrations, this video adaptation of *The Velveteen Rabbit* does a remarkably good job of bringing Williams's classic to the screen. The technique is simple but highly effective. Streep narrates the story while the drawings are shown on the screen. There is no animation involved, but the illustrations are edited in such a skillful and fluid way that the program never for a moment seems static. On the contrary, watching it is like seeing a picturebook come magically to life.

This splendidly made version of *The Velveteen Rabbit* is one of the best children's tapes around—a cassette that captures, in all its richness, the very special poetry of this joyful, poignant tale.

VOLTRON, DEFENDER OF THE UNIVERSE: THE CASTLE OF LIONS

SONY (1985), $49.95, 83 min.
Ages 5–9, ★½

There are lots of nifty-looking spaceships in this Japanese-made cartoon. Otherwise, it has almost nothing to recommend it. It's just another trashy, crudely animated video cassette connected to a hot-selling toy.

Voltron is a giant samurai robot who has been transformed by a space witch into five individual units, each in the shape of a mechanical lion. When an evil reptilian alien named Zarkon (who looks like the Creature from the Black Lagoon in a Louis XIV costume) attempts to take over the planet Arrus, a heroic crew of exceptionally dull space explorers must travel to the Castle of Lions in order to put Voltron back together again. It takes almost the entire movie for the five explorers to find, reassemble, and reactivate Voltron, who appears for less than ten minutes at the very end of the cartoon. The rest of the time is taken up with a numbing succession of laser battles, space chases, and futuristic kung fu fights. Even the technical quality of the cartoon is poor—the whole thing has a dark, muddy cast to it.

From beginning to end, *Voltron* is a mess—a murky, mindlessly violent, and indescribably stupid program.

WALT DISNEY'S STORIES AND FABLES
Volume 1: SIMPLETON PETER, THE WELL AT THE WORLD'S END

WALT DISNEY HOME VIDEO (1981), $49.95, 50 min.
5 and up, ★★★½

These handsomely produced fairy tales, filmed on locations around the world, have the tasteful, highly polished style of *Masterpiece Theatre* presentations (they are, in fact, made in Britain). Each cassette contains two twenty-five minute stories, which are told by an offscreen narrator while costumed players silently act out the parts. Watching one of these tapes is like having a beautifully illustrated children's book read aloud to you and seeing the pictures magically come to life before your eyes.

The tales themselves are traditional favorites from around the world (each one is introduced by an animated, singing minstrel who represents the spirit of international storytelling). In "Simpleton Peter," the sweet but slow-witted title character journeys to the cottage of a spooky old hag who promises to give him wisdom if he answers three riddles. "The Well at the End of the World" tells the familiar but ever-appealing story of a mistreated heroine—a Cinderella-like character named Rosemary—who encounters a magical toad that turns out to be an enchanted prince.

Everything about this series is exceptionally well done, from the elegant soundtrack music to the stunning photography (many of the scenes are as richly colored and carefully composed as fine landscape paintings). If there *is* one flaw here it is that the pacing may, on occasion, be a bit slow and the tone a trifle too solemn. In "Simpleton Peter," for example, there are a few too many scenes of the hero walking thoughtfully through the forest (though the woods look so deep and mysterious that it's hard to complain). On the other hand, there are images here that are so perfectly realized that they are impossible to forget: Peter's interview with the white-haired sorceress in the gloom of her cottage; Rosemary bestowing a kiss on the shimmering, golden-eyed toad. All in all, this is a thoroughly distinguished series—a feast for the eyes as well as the imagination.

Here are the contents of the other volumes in this series:

Volume Two. The Soldier Who Didn't Wash is a tale about a young guard at the Czar's palace whose every wish will be granted—if he doesn't bathe for fifteen years. *The Five Loaves* is a story of friendship, the problems of sudden wealth, and exact justice.

Volume Three. In *The Forbidden Door,* a young wastrel is lured into disturbing adventures. *Cap O'Rushes* concerns a quick-tempered father who learns a lesson in love after he banishes his daughter from his home.

Volume Four. In *The Priest Know-All,* a religious imposter is exposed by a king's unusual request. *The Grief of Pi Kari* takes place in a tropical island village haunted by the spirit of a beautiful young woman.

Volume Five. The Haunted Pastures tells the story of an enchanted meadow that makes all who enter it disappear. In *Riches or Happiness,* a servant learns the distinction between wealth and satisfaction.

Volume Six. The Foolish Brother is the tale of a not-so-foolish young man who manages (albeit unwittingly) to thwart a gang of bandits. In *The Twelve Months,* a young girl accomplishes some amazing tasks, to the dismay of her stepmother and stepsister.

Volume Seven. Clever Manka is a judge's new bride who brings down some unexpected judgments of her own. *The Russian and the Tartar* are traveling companions who scheme and plot against each other.

Volume Eight. The Straw Hat, a tale of revenge, concerns three brash youths who steal a farmer's prized possession. *Moses and the Lime Kiln* shows how gossip, envy, and mistrust can ruin a friendship and even endanger an innocent life.

Volume Nine. In *Morwen of the Woodlands,* a wise monk concocts a magic spell (which backfires). *Nikorima* is the tale of a lone warrior who must protect his village.

Volume Ten. The Widow's Lazy Daughter, betrothed to a prince, must first pass some overwhelming tests devised by her future mother-in-law. *Hinemoa* is a beautiful young girl, who—separated from her true love by her irate father, a lake, and an underwater monster—plots a reunion (at great risk).

Volume Eleven. The Emperor and the Abbott concerns a clever shepherd who saves his friend, the abbott, from public embarrassment by answering three difficult riddles posed by the emperor. In *The Pedlar's Dream,* a good-natured peddler named Jack learns the value of believing in and following his dreams, which lead him to a treasure in his own back yard.

Volume Twelve. The Enchanted King is about a beautiful peasant girl who saves a handsome young king from a spell cast by a family of vain, dancing fairies. In *The Lost Ruby,* an arrogant monarch plays a cruel trick on his devoted chief minister and ends up learning a lesson about humility.

Volume Thirteen. The Surprise Gift concerns a banished young princess who finds happiness as the wife of the King of Beggars. *The Miraculous Doctor* is a hapless peasant named Peter, who finds himself burdened with an undeserved reputation as a miracleworker.

Volume Fourteen. The Woodcutter and the Devil involves a frustrated woodcutter who is rewarded when he rescues a little troll from a deep well. In *The Talking Pony,* an impoverished youth must pose as an enchanted pony in order to retrieve his savings from a greedy merchant.

Volume Fifteen. In *The Hired Help,* a hard-working pauper teaches a deceitful farmer about The Golden Rule. *Blind Beauty* concerns a handsome young man who, through hard work and patience, overcomes his poverty and wins the hand of a beautiful girl.

THE WATER BABIES

EMBASSY (1978), $29.95, 120 min.
5 and up, ★★★★

This highly entertaining feature combines live action
with an extended animated sequence. Based on Charles
Kingsley's classic children's book, it concerns a young,
mistreated chimney sweep named Tommy, whose cruel
master, Mr. Grimes (marvelously played by the late,
great James Mason), hatches a plan to pinch the silver
from the estate of Lord Harthover. Caught in the act,
the villainous Grimes tries to pin the blame on Tommy,
who escapes across the countryside and dives into an
enchanted pool.

At this point, the film switches to animation. In order
to find his way back home, Tommy must travel to the
magical, underwater kingdom of the Water Babies. He
is accompanied by three friends he meets along the
way: Jock, a jolly, ruddy-faced lobster who speaks with
a thick Scottish accent; a sweet, extremely fey seahorse
named Terrence; and the dashing swordfish-cavalier
Claude (a kind of undersea D'Artagnan). However, no
sooner does Tommy arrive at his destination than the
Water Babies are kidnapped by a monstrous, armor-
suited shark and taken off to Shark Castle in chains.
Tommy must undertake another perilous quest—first
to the home of the Kraken, Lord of the Ocean, and
then to Shark Castle (where he and his friends stage a
heroic rescue of the enslaved Water Babies)—before
he can return to the surface.

Everything about this film is exceptionally well done.
The live action sequences—which move from the slums
of Victorian London to the baronial splendors of

Harthover Hall—are skillfully acted and beautifully filmed. James Mason is particularly fine as the rascally Grimes (who, in his ratty black overcoat and moth-eaten top hat, looks like the world's most disreputable undertaker). There are a number of wonderfully catchy songs. And the animated undersea adventure—the whimsical centerpiece of the film—is continuously enchanting. That overworked (and frequently inaccurate) claim—"A film the whole family will enjoy"—really applies to this extremely enjoyable fantasy movie.

WELCOME TO POOH CORNER, Vol. 1

WALT DISNEY HOME VIDEO (1983), $49.95, 111 min.
Preschool–6, ★★★½

Gentle charm and wholesomeness are the hallmarks of *Welcome to Pooh Corner,* a collection of four half-hour segments from the cable TV program of the same name. Introduced by a kindly, avuncular Englishman —whose soothing voice and childlike enthusiasm make him an ideal storyteller—the show features actors in full-size, puppet-like costumes that do a surprisingly good job of capturing the look and personalities of Pooh, Tigger, Owl, Eeyore, Roo, and the rest of the A.A. Milne gang.

Each episode is built around a particular theme. For example, in "You Need a Friend," Pooh and his pals learn just how important friendship is. This idea is conveyed in skits and songs, and reinforced by the host, who appears intermittently to spell out the message to his audience. The show also manages to work in a few other simple lessons. A brief skit about a magical door deals with such basic concepts as in-out and open-closed. Later, when Piglet decides to make some gifts for his friends, he provides a short arts-and-crafts demonstration, showing how to make a charming little Piglet doll out of simple materials like paper cups and popsicle sticks.

The remaining episodes (on tidiness, making the most of your talents, and having fun outdoors) follow the same format and contain the same combination of sweet, low-key humor, catchy music, amiable skits, and gentle instruction.

With a running time of nearly two hours, this warm-hearted, sweetly entertaining videotape contains enough material to keep most preschoolers happily —and profitably—occupied over the course of many viewings.

WHERE THE RED FERN GROWS

VESTRON (1974), $59.95, 90 min.
8 and up, ★★

This middling boy-and-his-dog(s) movie, based on a highly regarded children's novel by Wilson Rawls, tries its best to be exciting, dramatic, stirring, and poignant. It never really manages to be any of these things (Disney's *Old Yeller* is much more emotionally involving), but it's a reasonably entertaining film that touches on such themes as love, loyalty, sacrifice, and the growth of a young boy into manhood. There are a few parts of the film, however, that might make certain viewers—parents and children alike—a little bit uneasy.

Set in the Ozark mountains during the Great Depression, the story is about a ten-year-old farm boy named

Billy, who spends all his spare time working at odd jobs until he has saved enough money to afford the thing he wants most in the world: a pair of pure-bred coon hound pups that he names Dan and Ann. The rest of the film is essentially a series of episodes involving Billy, his dogs, and coon hunting. There is a sequence in which Billy, using a raccoon pelt tied to a string, trains his pups and turns them into the best hunters in the county. There is Billy's first coon hunt, which ends triumphantly when Billy manages to chop down the mighty tree in which his prey has taken refuge. There is a sequence involving a pair of nasty neighbor boys who bet Billy that his hounds can't track down the legendary "Ghost Coon." When Ann and Dan do succeed in treeing the elusive animal, the brothers renege on their bet, and a vicious fistfight follows, with tragic consequences. Shortly thereafter, Billy and his dogs enter a statewide coon hunting championship. During the tempestuous night of the big contest, Billy proves his maturity by ordering Ann and Dan to leave three raccoons up a tree so that the dogs can search for his grandfather, who has gotten lost in the storm. The next year, Dan is killed while saving Billy from a mountain lion, and Ann pines away and dies of a broken heart. At the very end of the film, Billy discovers a red fern (the symbol, according to Indian legend, of "the strongest kind of love") growing out of the dogs' double grave.

This movie should be better than it is. The story has a built-in appeal (it's almost impossible to make a terrible film about a country boy and his courageous, beloved ol' dawg). The film features some lovely rural scenery and a number of pretty songs (written by the Osmonds and performed by Andy Williams). But it never really comes alive. Part of the problem is the acting, which, with one or two exceptions (such as James Whitmore's portrayal of the grandfather), is pretty terrible. Unfortunately, the weakest actor in the film is the boy who plays the major role. He looks the part, but his acting is extremely wooden. He has one, unvarying expression —a look of mild bewilderment—that never leaves his face. It makes no difference whether his hounds have just won the statewide coon hunting championship or been mauled by a mountain lion; he registers no feelings at all.

In fact, the only time the film manages to work up any emotion is in the hunting scenes. Billy's first coon hunt is a good example. Dan and Ann chase a raccoon, which scrambles into the branches of a huge, majestic tree. Determined not to let his quarry escape, Billy spends all night and part of the next day chopping away at the giant trunk. Finally, on the brink of exhaustion, he prays to God for a helping hand. Seconds later, the tree topples, the coon scurries out of the branches, the hounds pounce, and Billy bags his first dead animal. The whole sequence is intended to be very stirring, but I suspect that the sight of Billy destroying a beautiful, centuries-old tree in order to kill one trapped, terrified raccoon (and calling on God to assist him in the undertaking) will seem stirring only to hunting buffs. Other viewers are more likely to find this scene—and others very much like it—pretty distasteful.

WHO'S AFRAID OF THE DARK?

AVG (1985), $19.95, 30 min.
Preschool–7, ★★★

See review of *Read-Along Magic Videos*.

WHO'S AFRAID OF OPERA? Vol. 1

MGM/UA (1982), $39.95, 57 min.

7 and up, ★★★★

In the world of children's video—a world heavily populated by cutesy-pie cartoon characters, muscle-bound, mythic warriors, and robot commandos from outer space—this splendidly conceived and produced video cassette is a real standout. It is (along with its two accompanying volumes) a delightfully entertaining mini-course in music appreciation designed to make opera less forbidding to children. It might not make your kids instant buffs, but it will give them a lively sense of the rich pleasures opera affords: drama, spectacle, and, of course, some of the most stirring and exquisite music ever composed, performed by the world's greatest singers.

The setting of this program is the stage of an opera house, and the star is Joan Sutherland, the internationally famous soprano. Backed by the London Symphony Orchestra, Sutherland and a first-rate cast sing and act out the highlights from two operas: Gounod's *Faust* and Verdi's *Rigoletto*. Meanwhile, occupying the box seat just above the stage are three delightful handpuppets: an educated, bespectacled goat named Sir William, his eager nephew, Billy, and a high-spirited lion named Rudi. Before each performance begins, Sutherland comes out and tells her puppet friends what the opera is going to be about. At the start of *Faust*, for example, Rudi (seeing Joan dressed for her role as the lovely, ill-fated Marguerite) exclaims, "Joan, you're a vision! I'd sell my soul for a girl like you."

"Tonight's opera is about a man who does just that," Sutherland replies.

"Sell your soul?" asks Billy. "Who would you sell it to?"

"When Gounod composed this opera," explains Sutherland, "most people believed that God fought the devil for each man's soul."

"And you mean this guy makes a deal with the devil?" says Rudi.

"Exactly," the diva replies.

Sutherland then moves onto the stage and begins the performance. Between each aria, the three puppets comment on the action, explaining the unfolding story in intelligent, easy-to-understand terms. As a result, even young children should have no trouble following the plots of the two operas.

Moreover, they will discover just how entertaining and exciting opera can be. They will come to see that an opera isn't some intimidating, incomprehensible work of art that requires a college degree to understand, but a form of musical theater full of action, excitement, vivid emotions, and gorgeous music. Many adults will come away from this program with a better appreciation of opera, too. *Who's Afraid of Opera?* is a very special video cassette, one that parents and children can enjoy—and learn from—together.

There are two more volumes in this first-rate series, both of which are hosted by Beverly Sills. Volume Two introduces viewers to Verdi's *La Traviata* and Donizetti's *Daughter of the Regiment*. Volume Three features highlights from Rossini's *Barber of Seville* and Donizetti's *Lucia di Lammermoor*.

WILLY WONKA AND THE CHOCOLATE FACTORY

WARNER (1971), $59.95, 100 min.
Ages 6–9, ★★½

Roald Dahl's popular children's book, *Charlie and the Chocolate Factory,* is the basis for this mediocre musical-fantasy film. The movie tries hard to be bright and magical, but it just manages to seem overblown. Moreover, parts of it are extremely unsettling.

The hero is a very engaging young boy named Charlie Bucket, who lives in a cramped and squalid room with his overworked mother and his four grandparents, a decrepit quartet that have been bedridden together (in the same bed) for the past twenty years. Soon after the story opens, Willy Wonka—the world's greatest and most mysterious candy maker—announces that, hidden among the countless billions of Wonka Bars scattered across the earth, are five golden tickets. The lucky finders will win a lifetime supply of chocolate, plus a guided tour of his legendary candy factory. The entire first half of the film concerns the outbreak of Wonkamania that sweeps the world as the result of this announcement. There are some amusing moments here (a wife unwilling to ransom her kidnapped husband because the price—her box of Wonka Bars—is too high, a psychiatrist so desperate to find one of the golden tickets that he looks for clues to their whereabouts in his patients' dreams), but most children will undoubtedly find this section of the film pretty slow going.

Things pick up in the second half of the film, in which the enigmatic Wonka conducts the five winners (including Charlie) on a magical mystery tour of his enchanted realm. Wonka's factory is a true wonderland, complete with chocolate waterfalls, wild rides, and marvelous contraptions (not to mention Wonka's army of orange-skinned Oompa-Loompas, weird-looking dwarves who serve as his workforce).

Unfortunately, what begins as a journey through an amusement park funhouse quickly deteriorates into a voyage through hell, as each of the contestants is doled out a bit of Wonka-style poetic justice. A piggish young boy named Augustus, who can't stop gobbling and guzzling sweets, falls into a chocolate river and is sucked up into the machinery. An inveterate gum-chewer named Violet pops a stick of experimental gum into her mouth and turns into a human blueberry. A television addict named Mike Teavee is miniaturized by a contraption called Wonkavision. Even Charlie and his Grandpa Joe almost come to a bad end after sipping some of Wonka's "Fizzy Lifting Water," which causes them to float up a chute toward the blades of a giant exhaust fan. The scariest scene of all, however, is a bizarre boat journey, which has the quality of a particularly bad LSD trip, complete with the most nightmarish visions: a giant centipede crawling over the mouth of a sleeping man, a chicken having its head chopped off, an insect-devouring lizard. While all these images are flashing on the screen, Wonka intones a spooky little poem in a voice that breaks with barely suppressed hysteria: "There's no earthly way of knowing/ Which direction we are going/ Not a speck of light is showing/ Are the fires of hell aglowing?/ Is the grisly reaper mowing?" Exactly what this scene is doing in a kiddie movie is anybody's guess.

This film does have some virtues. Peter Ostrum is very appealing as young Charlie, and so is Jack Albertson as Grandpa Joe. Best of all is Gene Wilder, who makes Wonka seem like a genuinely larger-than-life, uncanny figure—a being from the world of legend and myth. Though the music (by Leslie Bricusse and Anthony Newley) is, for the most part, entirely forgettable, there are a couple of nice songs, including "Candy Man" (which was a big hit for Sammy Davis, Jr. in the early 1970s). And the sets are genuinely imaginative.

Some children find this film very entertaining. Others, however, find it so unpleasant—and even terrifying—that they simply can't watch it.

THE WIND IN THE WILLOWS

WALT DISNEY HOME VIDEO (1949), $49.95, 47 min.
Ages 5–8, ★★★½

Released in 1949 as part of a feature called *The Adventures of Ichabod and Mr. Toad*, this boisterous, brilliantly animated adaptation of Kenneth Grahame's classic children's book takes a number of liberties with its source. Characters are added, important episodes are altered or eliminated entirely. The most obvious change, however, has to do with the mood of the cartoon. Grahame's book is pervaded with the rich, golden atmosphere of a lazy summer afternoon. By contrast, the Disney cartoon is a rollicking, fast-moving comedy. It's a lot of fun, but it doesn't quite capture the essence of the book.

What it *does* capture, to perfection, is the gloriously crazed personality of its madcap main character, Mr. Toad. This childish, utterly spoiled, wild-eyed individual has a passion for living that, while intensely appealing, is totally out of control. The cartoon deals with the consequences of Toad's sudden, insane desire for a motorcar, a craving that ultimately lands him in prison for auto theft. Making a daring escape, Toad enlists the help of friends, Ratty, Mole, and Badger. In a wonderfully choreographed, climactic battle, this foursome manages to reclaim Toad's home from an occupying army of villainous weasels.

This freewheeling adaptation is bursting with energy, invention, and humor. It lacks the warmth and sweetness of many other Disney cartoons, and its breakneck pacing can leave you a little breathless. But it's a very enjoyable cartoon.

To fill out the cassette, the Disney people have added two vintage shorts, selected, apparently, because they deal with motor vehicles and therefore fit in with Toad's obsession. In "Motor Mania" (1950), Goofy appears as a Jekyll-Hyde character, a meek, mild pedestrian who is transformed into a homicidal speed demon as soon as he gets behind the wheel of his car. In "Trailer Horn" (1950), Donald Duck's peaceful wilderness vacation is wrecked when his trailer is invaded by his two tiny tormentors, Chip 'n' Dale.

THE WIND IN THE WILLOWS

CHILDREN'S VIDEO LIBRARY (1983), $79.95, 97 min.
Ages 5–8, ★★★

This animated feature, produced by Rankin-Bass, is much blander than the Disney version. Small children, however, may well find its gentle charm more appealing than the raucous comedy of the Disney cartoon. The animation, though uninspired, is colorful and quite pretty. The action is punctuated with a number of lively, Broadway-style tunes (there is also a lovely theme song performed by Judy Collins). And though the characters are not especially vivid, they have sweetly appealing personalities, with voice characterizations provided by Roddy McDowell (as Ratty), José Ferrer (as Badger), Eddie Bracken (as Mole), and—most amusing of all—Charles Nelson Reilly in the key role of Toad.

The movie sticks very closely to the original story line. At the center of the action is the wildly impulsive and irresponsible Toad, whose life consists of a series of extremely short-lived enthusiasms. When we first meet him, he is a boating fiend, tearing around the river on his racing yacht, the S.S. Toad. This hobby is soon replaced by a passion for traveling the open road in a gypsy caravan, an infatuation that comes to a crashing end when Toad's wagon collides with a glittering motor-car. The reckless and none-too-stable Toad is instantly infatuated with this shiny contraption and turns into a motoring maniac, zooming around the country and piling up so many cars that his friends, Ratty, Mole, and Badger, are convinced that he will soon be either dead or bankrupt. They try to talk him out of his obsession, but to no avail, and it isn't long before Toad finds himself in prison for car theft. Disguised as a washerwoman, he manages to escape and makes his way back to his ancestral home, Toad Hall, where he and his friends engage in a climactic battle with the army of weasels and stoats who have occupied the place in his absence.

A few of the episodes do an especially good job of capturing the spirit of Grahame's classic. The scene in which Toad tearfully repents of his "misguided conduct" (and then instantly changes his mind) is a comic high point. And there is an enchanting moment when Mole, wandering through the moonlit forest in search of his friend Ratty, catches a glimpse of the nature spirit, Pan—"the Piper at the Gates of Dawn."

This isn't a terrific movie by any means, but it's a perfectly nice one that young viewers in particular will enjoy.

THE WIND IN THE WILLOWS

THORN/EMI (1984), $29.95, 78 min.
5 and up, ★★★★

Of the three available adaptations of Kenneth Grahame's novel, this British-made program is not only the most faithful, but also the most beautifully produced. Unlike the Disney and Rankin-Bass versions, which are both cartoons, this one uses puppet animation to bring the classic children's story to life. Created by Brian Cosgrove and Mark Hall—the same people responsible for the exquisitely animated versions of "The Pied Piper" and "Cinderella" (also available on video cassette)—this lovely film is far and away the best *Wind in the Willows* that we have or are likely to get. In fact, it's one of the very best film adaptations of *any* children's classic, and an altogether lovely family film.

Whereas the Disney and Rankin-Bass cartoons both focus mainly on the incorrigible Toad, this version (like the book) pays at least as much attention to the genuinely heartwarming friendship between Mole and Ratty. All the characters are beautifully sculpted and move with subtle, expressive, and entirely convincing gestures. With voices provided by a cast of distinguished English actors (including Michael Hordern, Ian Carmichael, and Beryl Reid), the characters seem real enough to be alive. This film also does a wonderful job of reproducing the book's atmosphere—not only the Edwardian period in which the story takes place but, even more important, the timeless, golden world of lazy afternoons, carefree adventures, close friends, and the soul-satisfying splendors of nature. The miniature sets are marvels of craftsmanship. Every detail, from the grassy banks of Ratty's beloved river to the baronial splendors of Toad's ancestral hall, are perfectly rendered. Scripted by Rosemary Anne Sisson—one of the creators of *Upstairs, Downstairs*—this program is a real gem. For children unfamiliar with the enchantments of *The Wind in the Willows*, it will serve as a charming introduction. Those who already know and love Grahame's book will be equally captivated by this delightful cassette.

Note to Parents: A book edition of *The Wind in the Willows*, containing all of the original text and illustrated with stills from this film, is available from Methuen publishers.

WINDS OF CHANGE

RCA/COLUMBIA (1979), $39.95, 90 minutes.
7 and up, ★★

This cartoon retelling of Ovid's *Metamorphoses*, narrated by Peter Ustinov and set to a disco score, is about as mixed-up as it sounds. The main problem with this movie is that there is a built-in contradiction between its style, which is clearly meant to appeal to small children, and its content, which is, for the most part, much too intense and sophisticated for young viewers. The filmmakers do their best to resolve this problem, but without success. The result is a very strange brew.

The movie consists of five episodes based on classical Greek mythology. There is the story of Perseus and his slaying of the snake-haired monster, Medusa; the tale of the hunter Actaeon, who spies on the goddess Diana, is transformed into a stag, and is torn to pieces by his own hounds; a story involving Hermes and a jealous girl named Agraulus, who is turned to stone by the god; the myth of Orpheus and his descent into the underworld in search of his wife, Eurydice; and the tale of Phaeton and his catastrophic ride on his father's sun-chariot.

To make this particular material accessible to kids, the filmmakers invent a cute, big-eared character named Wonderworker, who plays the role of the hero —Perseus, Actaeon, Hermes, etc.—in each of the stories. In addition, the stories are narrated (by Ustinov) in slangy, everyday language. Theoretically, it's a nice idea to retell the Greek myths in a style that will make them seem interesting and understandable to today's children. But in practice, this film ends up reducing these marvelous tales to a trivial, schoolyard level. It's disconcerting to hear Diana's sacred fountain described as a "great piece of plumbing." It's also a little bizarre to have Greek myths set to a disco beat (the first episode has a catchy theme song called, "Where Are You Going, Perseus?")

More seriously, there are elements of violence, horror, and—yes—sex here that seem wholly inappropriate for the film's apparent audience. Medusa is depicted as a green-skinned horror with clawed feet, fur-covered legs, red-nippled breasts, bat wings, lizard tail, fangs, and (of course) a headful of writhing serpents. Of course, she's *supposed* to be a nightmare. The problem might simply be that there is no way to be faithful to this story while making it suitable for small children. The same is true of the myth of Actaeon: after committing his blasphemous act of voyeurism (Diana, incidentally, is shown fully nude) he is changed into an extremely cute-looking cartoon deer. Unfortunately, the story dictates that this adorable little critter has to be ripped to shreds by a pack of ravening dogs. This film tactfully cuts away from the actual killing, but the results are still very upsetting (it's a little like watching "Bambi Meets Cujo").

In short, this film is an interesting and even admira-

317

ble failure, which ends up being too sophisticated for young viewers and too puerile for mature ones.

WINSOME WITCH

WORLDVISION (1965), $39.95, 51 min.
Ages 5–9, ★★½

For a Saturday-morning cartoon show cranked out by the Hanna-Barbera animation mill, *Winsome Witch* is a cut above average. Its heroine, "Winny," is a dumpy middle-aged lady who looks more like a jolly washerwoman than a witch. A dropout from the Fairy Godmother School, she zooms around the city streets (her business card reads, "Have Broom, Will Travel") looking for work and performing a variety of magical deeds, most of them for noble causes.

There are eight cartoons on this cassette. About half are farcical versions of traditional fairy tales. In "Prince Pup" (in which the character of Winny is first introduced) the freelance witch is hired by the Evil Queen to get rid of Snow White, portrayed here as an overworked housemaid who is fed up with doing chores for a bunch of little men (when Winny knocks on the door to Snow White's cottage, the girl mutters, "Who can that be? With my luck, it'll probably be another dwarf"). There are also amusing retellings of "Little Red Riding Hood," "Hansel and Gretel," and "Cinderella." The other episodes are a mixed bag of gently humorous adventures in which Winny becomes a star pitcher for a sandlot baseball team, outsmarts a couple of Russian spies (who do great voice imitations of Peter Lorre and Boris Badenov), takes a job as a cleaning woman in a classroom, and (in one of the funniest cartoons in the collection) finds herself baby-sitting for a pair of demonic twin brothers named Ringo and Clyde.

In most respects, *Winsome Witch* is a purely conventional Saturday-morning cartoon show, with limited, low-budget animation and stories that are, at best, mildly imaginative. Still, there really is something winsome about it. The humor is unforced and, at times, genuinely amusing, the graphics have a simple charm, and Winny herself is a very engaging creation.

THE WIZARD OF OZ

MGM/UA (1939), $59.95, 101 min.
5 and up, ★★★★

Fantasy films are pure escape—the celluloid equivalent of a magic carpet ride. Their job is to carry us away from the everyday world to a wonderland of enchantment and adventure. In the history of Hollywood only a handful of films have managed to perform that feat as well as this 1939 classic. *The Wizard of Oz* is not only one of the best children's movies ever made—it's one of the greatest movies in any genre. Any home video library that's missing a copy of this musical-fantasy masterpiece is seriously incomplete.

The Wizard of Oz is a child's daydream brought to full and glorious life. The story itself—about a heroic quest through a strange, enchanted realm—has a deep and perennial appeal (it is, in fact, the underlying plot of virtually all myths and fairy tales). The cast (Ray Bolger as the Scarecrow, Jack Haley as the Tin Woodman, Bert Lahr as the Cowardly Lion, and, of course, Judy Garland as Dorothy) is flawless. The costumes, special effects, and, in particular, the sets (the entire movie was shot indoors on MGM's sound stages) are spectacular—Hollywood movie magic at its greatest. It has unforgettable songs ("Somewhere Over the Rainbow," "Follow the Yellow Brick Road," "Ding Dong, the Witch is Dead"), laughs, thrills, dancing Munchkins—in short, just about everything.

Some parents are afraid to show this film to their children because of the character of the Wicked Witch of the West, and there's no doubt that Margaret Hamilton, with her warty nose, pointy hat, and vicious cackle, is one of the scariest incarnations of pure evil ever captured on film. Still, the terrors here (which include the witch's army of flying monkeys and the climactic scene in which Dorothy melts the villainess by dousing her with a bucket of water) are no more extreme than those contained in many fairy tales. If your child gets easily upset by the notion of witches, you might want to wait a bit before showing him or her this movie. But no child should be deprived of its deep and enduring pleasures.

THE WIZARD OF OZ

PARAMOUNT (1983), $16.95, 78 min.
Ages 5–9, ★★★

Although this cartoon version of L. Frank Baum's classic is inferior in every way to the great MGM classic, it's not without its charms. The animation (done in Japan) is limited, but the artwork is polished and the fantasy settings are colorful and lush. There are some snappy songs (by Sammy Cahn), good voice characterizations by Aileen Quinn (of *Annie* fame) as Dorothy and Lorne Greene as the Wizard, and interesting, offbeat designs for the Scarecrow, Tin Woodman, and Cowardly Lion. Fans of Baum's book will also appreciate how closely this film sticks to the original story line. In fact, it's a much more faithful (if far less magical) adaptation than the famous 1939 film.

Many of Baum's charming absurdities, absent from the Judy Garland film, are included in this cartoon. For example, the Scarecrow, who has no trouble opening his mouth to speak, tells Dorothy that he can't eat because his lips are only painted on. And although the Tin Woodman has no heart, he cries so bitterly when he accidentally steps on a beetle that his jaws begin to rust. Some of the most dramatic moments from the book can also be found here, such as the encounter between the heroes and the monstrous Kalidahs (horrific beasts with the bodies of bears and heads of tigers), and the Tin Woodman's fierce battle with the Wicked Witch's legion of magical wolves. As in the original Baum story, the Wizard appears to each of the four questers in a different form: as a giant head to Dorothy, a beautiful winged lady to the Scarecrow, a fire-breathing rhinoceros to the Tin Woodman, and a great ball of fire to the Lion. Some of these images may well be unsettling to younger viewers. Even scarier is the Wicked Witch—a purple-skinned hag with stringy white hair, a hooked nose, and a single eye.

If you rent (or buy) this cartoon in the belief that you are getting the 1939 *Wizard of Oz*, you'll be sorely disappointed. But if you're interested in a second version of the story to show children who have already seen the Judy Garland classic umpteen times, then this faithful (if workmanlike) version of Baum's wonderful novel is worth a look.

THE YEARLING

MGM/UA (1946), $24.95, 128 min.

8 and up, ★★★★

Marjorie Kinnan Rawlings' 1939 Pulitzer Prize-winning novel about a family of Florida settlers in the late nineteenth century is the basis of this beautifully made, deeply moving family film. Gregory Peck and Jane Wyman star as Penny and Ora Baxter, a pair of hard-working pioneers who have carved out a small, barely self-sustaining farm in the lush Southern wilderness. Peck, radiating his usual mixture of strength and sensitivity, makes Ezra into an intensely appealing figure, a tough but tender individual who faces the hardships of frontier life with quiet heroism and unshakable decency. Wyman's Ora, on the other hand, is a more complex and far less lovable character—a good but ungiving woman, whose heart has been hardened by the rigors of her life and especially by the early deaths of all but one of her children.

That last surviving youngster, Jody, stands at the center of the story. A dreamy, lonesome twelve-year-old with a rawboned frame and the face of a cherub, Jody yearns for a pet to keep him company. One day, Penny is bitten by a rattlesnake and shoots a doe in order to use its heart and liver as a poultice. After his father recovers, Jody adopts the slain deer's orphaned fawn. The middle section of the film depicts the deep, idyllic love between the farm boy and the fawn (named Flag because his tail is like a "little white merry flag"). Trouble arises, however, when Flag grows into a yearling and begins to graze on the family's precious crops.

Faced with the threat of starvation, Penny orders his son to shoot the deer, and in a genuinely heartbreaking climax (that is much too intense for younger viewers) Jody is forced to kill his pet.

Though the movie seems a little sugar-coated at times (the Baxters' farm is a technicolor paradise that wouldn't seem out of place in Disney World), it avoids sentimentality by refusing to deny the pain and hardships that life inevitably entails. Jody progresses from childhood to maturity by learning the lesson his father sums up at the end: "Every man wants life to be a fine thing, and easy. And it *is* fine, powerful fine, but it ain't easy."

This film version of *The Yearling* is a true family classic—a powerful, beautifully photographed movie, full of drama, humor, tenderness, and wisdom.

YOGI'S FIRST CHRISTMAS

WORLDVISION (1980), $49.95, 99 min.
Ages 5–9, ★★½

In this cheery, reasonably entertaining cartoon feature, a bunch of familiar Hanna-Barbera characters—Yogi Bear and his little buddy Boo Boo, Huckleberry Hound, Augie Doggie, Doggie Daddy, and Snagglepuss—get together for some wintertime fun at Jellystone Lodge. The story involves the lodge's owner, Mrs. Throckmorton, who is going to sell the place to land developers unless she enjoys herself during Christmas Carnival week. Meanwhile, a nasty old mountain man named Herman the Hermit, who lives in a cave above the lodge and hates Christmas, is determined to sabotage everyone's fun. It is left to Yogi and his friends to see that Herman is thwarted and Mrs. Throckmorton has such a good time that she will decide to preserve the lodge after all.

Needless to say, this meager plot is nothing more than a way of stringing together a series of mildly comic episodes involving Yogi and his pals. There's nothing particularly imaginative about this cartoon. For the most part, it's a typical Hanna-Barbera production, with bargain-basement animation and a spate of threadbare sight gags (Yogi slipping on ice skates, Yogi slipping on skis, Yogi losing control of his snow plow, etc.). And the story line—about a Grinch-like killjoy who learns the true meaning of Christmas—is completely unoriginal.

Still, *Yogi's First Christmas* ends up being a surprisingly amiable cartoon. This is partly because of its tuneful, toe-tapping musical numbers, and partly because of the easy-going charm of its animated cast. Yogi, Augie, Snagglepuss, and the rest are the best of all the Hanna-Barbera characters. Even when they are not doing anything particularly funny (which is most of the time in this cartoon), their personalities—and voices—are extremely engaging. This cartoon won't enrich your children, but it *will* provide them with 90 minutes' worth of very likable entertainment.

YOU CAN DO IT

MGM/UA (1984), $29.95, 60 min.
Ages 5–8, ★★★

Shari Lewis (looking no older than she did twenty-five years ago, when she hosted her own Saturday-morning kiddie TV show) is the star of this breezy, hour-long tape that teaches young children all kinds of charming projects and magic tricks. The setting is Shari's house, where a birthday party is in progress. There are lots of perky songs and sweetly amusing comedy bits involving Shari and her hand puppets, Hush Puppy, Charlie Horse, and the genuinely adorable Lamb Chop. Most of the tape, however, consists of Shari's do-it-yourself demonstrations.

Children watching this tape will learn how to make several kinds of puppets out of everyday objects —paper, handkerchiefs, even apples. One of Shari's most charming creations—a blinking face puppet called Winky—requires nothing but a felt-tip pen and the child's own right hand. Shari, also an accomplished magician, teaches young viewers how to perform some simple feats of prestidigitation (or presto-refrigeration, as Hush Puppy calls it): card tricks, number tricks, mind-reading tricks. Two of her niftiest feats are slicing a banana while it's still inside the peel and turning two pieces of string into one. This cassette also stresses the pleasures and importance of imaginative play. When Lamb Chop complains because she doesn't have a battery-operated mechanical toy, Shari shows her how to make a menagerie of shadow creatures and an origami sailboat.

Shari Lewis is a wonderful children's-show host: warm, witty, bubbling with enthusiasm and energy. She's also a terrific ventriloquist, and her three lovable puppets seem completely alive. There are only two things wrong with this tape. While Shari shows home viewers how to perform some easy but impressive magic tricks, she demonstrates a handful of stunts (changing water into punch, tearing a newspaper to shreds and then restoring it, and a few others) without explaining how they're done. Some small viewers might feel cheated. More seriously, a number of her tricks and projects are too sophisticated for her audience. The banana trick, for example, requires the use of a long needle, carefully inserted into and rotated around a banana. At the very least, this is a bit of magic that requires the close supervision of an adult. Similarly, her paper-folding projects are extremely complicated for little kids, demanding a kind of dexterity (as well as an ability to follow fairly intricate directions) that many younger children are unlikely to possess. Apart from these shortcomings, however, this is a very worthwhile video cassette—enjoyable, entertaining, and instructive.

ZIGGY'S GIFT

CHILDREN'S VIDEO LIBRARY (1982), $19.95, 30 min.
5 and up, ★★★½

Parents who object to the slam-bang action of Tom & Jerry–type cartoons or the prefabricated cutesiness of Strawberry Shortcake and the Care Bears should find this animated story—a half-hour Christmas cartoon starring the popular comic strip character, Ziggy—a thoroughgoing delight. It is, in every respect, a lovely little film: charmingly animated, full of gentle humor, and with a simple message of love and kindness that (instead of being tacked onto the end in the crudely moralistic manner of He-Man cartoons) shines through every moment of the story, and most especially through the beguiling character of its roly-poly leading man.

Ziggy is not much to look at, and he can't even brush his teeth without squeezing the contents of the tube all over his pajamas. He is life's patsy: When he sticks out his tongue during a snow flurry, he manages to catch the only foul-tasting flake ever to fall from the sky. But his misfortunes never sour him. He is a good and generous little soul who moves through life with the inner serenity of a born saint.

Answering a want ad for street corner Santas, Ziggy sets out across the city with a collection kettle and a bell. The only problem is that, although he doesn't know it, the "charitable organization" employing him is really a racket run by a fast-talking con artist. As a result, sweet, innocent Ziggy ends up being sought by the police. At the same time, he is pursued by a skulking pickpocket who is trying to get his hands on Ziggy's kettle, which turns out to have the magic power to produce its own money (though only for charitable purposes). Ziggy, however, remains cheerfully unaware of his problems as he travels through the streets dispensing kindness: tying a scarf around a shivering kitty, buying a crateload of terrified Christmas turkeys just to set them free, taking the very coat off his back to cover up a freezing derelict. For all his funny looks and worldly incompetence, he clearly embodies the true spirit of Christmas.

Because *Ziggy's Gift* is so full of delightful little touches and subtle bits of comedy, your children will get more from it if you watch it along with them—an experience you won't regret, since this is a cartoon that grown-ups will find genuinely enjoyable (in fact, much of its humor will probably go over the heads of younger children). Incidentally, this cartoon first saw life as an Emmy-winning TV special, and every ten minutes or so the action fades to black. One five-year-old viewer, watching it for the first time on tape and curious about these periodic blackouts, wanted to know if anything had been cut out. The answer is, yes: the commercials.

SUBJECT CATEGORY INDEX

Friz Freleng's Looney Looney Looney Bugs Bunny
   Movie
The Further Adventures of Superted
Hurray for Betty Boop
Inspector Gadget
It's Flashbeagle, Charlie Brown/She's a Good Skate,
   Charlie Brown
It's Magic, Charlie Brown/Charlie Brown's All Stars
It's Your First Kiss, Charlie Brown/Someday You'll Find
   Her, Charlie Brown
Little Lulu
The Little Prince: Next Stop, Planet Earth
The Looney Tunes Video Show
Nelvanamation
The New Three Stooges
On Vacation with Mickey Mouse and Friends
Popeye—Travelin' On About Travel
The Premiere Adventures of Superted
Puss 'n Boots Travels Around the World
Race for Your Life, Charlie Brown
Richie Rich
Snoopy Come Home
Superboy
Superman
Superted III: The Adventures Continue
The Terrytoons Good Guy Hour
Tom & Jerry Cartoon Festival
Winsome Witch

EDUCATIONAL
Animal Quiz
Bill Cosby's PicturePages
Free to Be . . . You and Me
Imagine That! Great Moments in History
The New Zoo Revue
Read-Aloud Magic Videos
Romper Room and Friends: Go to the Zoo

Romper Room and Friends: Numbers, Letters, and Words
Romper Room and Friends: Movement and Rhythm
Strong Kids, Safe Kids
Too Smart for Strangers
Welcome to Pooh Corner
Who's Afraid of Opera?

EXERCISE
ABC Funfit
Mousercise
Tip Top! with Suzy Prudden

FRONTIER ADVENTURE
Davy Crockett, King of the Wild Frontier
Davy Crockett on the Mississippi
The Leatherstocking Tales

FAIRY TALE, MYTH AND LEGEND
The Adventures of Sinbad the Sailor
Aladdin and His Wonderful Lamp
Beauty and the Beast
The Boy Who Left Home to Find Out About the Shivers
Cinderella
The Dancing Princesses
The Emperor's New Clothes
The Frog Prince
Fun and Fancy Free (includes "Mickey and the Beanstalk")
Goldilocks and the Three Bears
Hansel and Gretel
Jack and the Beanstalk
Jason and the Argonauts
The Little Mermaid
Little Red Riding Hood
The Nightingale
The Pied Piper/Cinderella

331

The Pied Piper of Hamelin
Pinocchio
The Princess and the Pea
The Princess Who Had Never Laughed
Puss in Boots
Rapunzel
Rip Van Winkle
Robin Hood
Rumpelstiltskin
Sleeping Beauty
The Snow Queen
Snow White and the Seven Dwarfs
The Tale of the Frog Prince
The Three Little Pigs
Thumbelina
Walt Disney's Stories and Fables
The Winds of Change

HOLIDAY SPECIALS
The Bear Who Slept Through Christmas
The Berenstain Bears' Comic Valentine
The Berenstain Bears' Easter Surprise
The Berenstain Bears Meet Big Paw
The Box of Delights
A Christmas Carol
The Easter Bunny Is Coming to Town
The Little Rascals Christmas Special
Yogi's First Christmas
Ziggy's Gift

HOW-TO
*Draw and Color Your Very Own Cartoonys Right Along
    with Uncle Fred*
Jon Gnagy Learn to Draw
Romper Room and Friends: Playful Projects
You Can Do It

PUPPET COMEDY
Children's Songs and Stories with the Muppets
Country Music with the Muppets
Gonzo Presents Muppet Weird Stuff
Gumby's Incredible Journey
The Kermit and Piggy Story
Kooky Classics
The Muppet Revue
Muppet Treasures
Pinocchio's Storybook Adventures
Pogo for President
Rock Music with the Muppets

SCIENCE FICTION AND FANTASY
The Absent-Minded Professor
The Adventures of Captain Future
The Adventures of Ultraman
Blackstar
The Brothers Lionheart
Captain Scarlet vs. the Mysterons
The Comic Book Kids
Dunderklumpen
The Fantastic Adventures of Unico
The Hobbit
Journey to the Center of the Earth
The Last Unicorn
The Magic of Dr. Snuggles
Mighty Joe Young
The NeverEnding Story
Nutcracker Fantasy
Puff the Magic Dragon
Pinocchio in Outer Space
Romie-0 and Julie-8
Space Angel
Space Ghost and Dino Boy
Spaceketeers
Spectreman

Twenty Thousand Leagues Under the Sea
The Undersea Adventures of Captain Nemo

STORYBOOK
The Adventures of Buster the Bear
The Adventures of Huckleberry Finn
The Adventures of Reddy the Fox
Alice in Wonderland
Around the World in 80 Days
Babar
The Beast of Monsieur Racine and Other Stories
Black Beauty
Chatterer the Squirrel
The Children's Circle
Curious George
David Copperfield
Doctor De Soto and Other Stories
Dr. Seuss—The Cat in the Hat/Dr. Seuss on the Loose
Dr. Seuss—The Lorax/The Hoober-Bloob Highway
Dr. Seuss Festival
Dorothy in the Land of Oz
Fables of the Green Forest
The Foolish Frog and Other Stories
Great Expectations
Heidi
Heidi's Song
Jacob Two-Two Meets the Hooded Fang
Johnny Woodchuck's Adventures
Journey Back to Oz
The Lion, the Witch, and the Wardrobe
Little Women
The Many Adventures of Winnie the Pooh
Mary Poppins
Nicholas Nickleby
The Old Curiosity Shop
Oliver Twist
Peter Cottontail's Adventures
Pickwick Papers

Pippi Longstocking
Sammy Bluejay
The Secret of NIMH
Sherlock Holmes and the Sign of the Four
Smile for Auntie and Other Stories
The Snowman
Storybook Classics
Swiss Family Robinson
A Tale of Two Cities
Teeny-Tiny and the Witch Woman and Other Scary Stories
Three Richard Scarry Animal Nursery Tales
The Three Robbers and Other Stories
The Velveteen Rabbit
The Water Babies
Willy Wonka and the Chocolate Factory
The Wind in the Willows
The Wizard of Oz
The Yearling

TIE-IN
The Care Bears in the Land Without Feeling
The Care Bears Movie
The Charmkins
G.I. Joe: A Real American Hero
He-Man and the Masters of the Universe
My Little Pony
Poochie
Rainbow Brite in "Peril in the Pits"
Strawberry Shortcake—Pets on Parade
The Transformers
Voltron, Defender of the Universe

CLOSED CAPTIONED INDEX

Following is an alphabetical list of children's videos currently available with closed captions. Captioning of all programs is provided by NCI, the National Captioning Institute, Falls Church, Virginia.

Great Expectations
Hansel and Gretel (Faerie Tale Theatre)
He-Man and the Masters of the Universe, Vols.
   7–11
Jack and the Beanstalk (Faerie Tale Theatre)
Journey to the Center of the Earth
The Kermit and Piggy Story
The Little Mermaid (Faerie Tale Theatre)
Little Red Riding Hood (Faerie Tale Theatre)
The Muppet Revue
Muppet Treasures
The NeverEnding Story
Nicholas Nickleby
The Nightingale (Faerie Tale Theatre)
The Old Curiosity Shop
Oliver Twist
The Pickwick Papers
The Pied Piper of Hamelin (Faerie Tale Theatre)
Pinocchio (Disney)
Pinocchio (Faerie Tale Theatre)
The Princess and the Pea (Faerie Tale Theatre)
The Princess Who Had Never Laughed (Faerie
   Tale Theatre)
Puss in Boots (Faerie Tale Theatre)
Rapunzel (Faerie Tale Theatre)
Rip Van Winkle (Faerie Tale Theatre)
Robin Hood
Rock Music With the Muppets
Romper Room and Friends: Go to the Zoo
*Romper Room and Friends: Numbers, Letters, and
   Words*
Romper Room and Friends: Movement and Rhythm
Romper Room and Friends: Playful Projects
Rumpelstiltskin (Faerie Tale Theatre)
Sleeping Beauty (Faerie Tale Theatre)
Snoopy, Come Home
The Snow Queen (Faerie Tale Theatre)